Irreversible

Irreversible

Taylor Mason

Copyright © 2019 by Taylor Mason.

Library of Congress Control Number:	2018915084
ISBN: Hardcover	978-1-9845-6966-0
Softcover	978-1-9845-6965-3
eBook	978-1-9845-6964-6

All rights reserved. No part of this book may be reproduced or transmitted in any form or by any means, electronic or mechanical, including photocopying, recording, or by any information storage and retrieval system, without permission in writing from the copyright owner.

The views expressed in this work are solely those of the author and do not necessarily reflect the views of the publisher, and the publisher hereby disclaims any responsibility for them.

Any people depicted in stock imagery provided by Getty Images are models, and such images are being used for illustrative purposes only. Certain stock imagery © Getty Images.

Print information available on the last page.

Rev. date: 01/11/2019

To order additional copies of this book, contact:
Xlibris
1-888-795-4274
www.Xlibris.com
Orders@Xlibris.com
779420

Contents

Introduction ix

Chapter 1	Whatever It Takes 1
Chapter 2	Ventriloquism 9
Chapter 3	Sock It to Me 23
Chapter 4	Sumo 34
Chapter 5	The Quality of Laughter 48
Chapter 6	Non Sequitur 54
Chapter 7	Frat Boy 73
Chapter 8	The Theory of Relatives 90
Chapter 9	The Second City 103
Chapter 10	Moonlighting 112
Chapter 11	Trainspotting 120
Chapter 12	Zanies Comedy Club 133
Chapter 13	Not Afraid to Fail 151
Chapter 14	New York City 174
Chapter 15	Catch a Rising Star 193
Chapter 16	Back to College 211
Chapter 17	A Life of Crime 224
Chapter 18	The Dance 244
Chapter 19	Romeo 255
Chapter 20	The Gym 264
Chapter 21	Moorestown 268
Chapter 22	On Tour 279
Chapter 23	Get a Gig, Get There, Get Paid 283
Chapter 24	A Bronx Tale 303
Chapter 25	Mickey Mouse Operation 319
Chapter 26	Synergy 327
Chapter 27	False Ending 338

For Marsia, Hank and Ev

Introduction

I Am Jim Bouton

I was fourteen years old when *Ball Four*, Jim Bouton's seminal tell-all was published. It had everything a bored teenager in the monotonous suburbia of 1970 could want—scandal, sex, and deviance. Bouton was a professional baseball player who loved his job, gave the best years of his life to it, finally realized his career was almost over, and wanted to try to get back into the game. *Ball Four* is the book he wrote about it.

I distinctly remember the first line: "I'm 30 years old and I have these dreams."

An immature teenager in the Midwest, I had nothing in common with Bouton, but I understood right away. His dreams were about making a comeback, beating the odds, becoming a star in "the show" one more time. His pitching arm was gone—wasted, destroyed from throwing too hard and too much as a young player. Now he wanted, more than anything, to fight his way back. He was so desperate that he turned to a pitcher's last resort.

He taught himself to throw a curious pitch called "the knuckleball."

The knuckleball is a baseball oddity, the kind of rarity that *talented* players scoff at. A peculiar pitch that has to be conceded if not accepted, it is unlike any other pitch because neither the pitcher—nor the catcher tasked with grabbing the ball—has any idea what will happen. A good knuckleball actually dances in the air, similar to a butterfly, making it almost impossible to hit. Or catch.

It can be effective, however, because it gets hitters out.

How does this apply to me? A knuckleball pitcher is to baseball what a ventriloquist is to comedy—a novelty. And like a proficient knuckleball pitcher, a good ventriloquist can be more than competent. A great ventriloquist can make audiences laugh. Hard. Sometimes harder than the best stand-up comics.

Also specific to me, I have no idea what is going to happen. In fact I have no idea how what *has* happened really did actually happen!

I am a ventriloquist. I've been working with and voicing puppets for more than fifty years. I've made a living as a "vent" for almost that long. Add the fact that I use a piano and try to appeal to a broad base of reference, and you have the whole premise.

The Comedy Knuckleball

Don't get the wrong idea. I love all forms of comedy. I can be a stand-up. I've done some acting. I have written a couple of books, a bunch of songs, countless song parodies, and a lot of jokes. Just like my literary inspiration, Mr. Bouton, "I have these dreams."

Here's the difference. I'm five decades (*decades*!) into my chosen field. I've already had and tried and given *one last chance* to a countless number of "comebacks." I still audition a few times a year, hoping for major, career-enhancing, overnight-success event I can juxtapose with my modest accomplishments.

I can hear you thinking, *This man is delusional.*

No kidding I'm delusional. I'm a professional ventriloquist! That makes the word "delusional" redundant.

I am Walter Mitty-ing my way through life, fantasizing about my "big break." My imagination is hyperactive. I don't have daydreams; I have one long daydream that never ends, on a loop, constantly updating according to the zeitgeist, where I'm always in the company of the impossible-not-to-like showbiz celebrities that dot the entertainment landscape. Here I am explaining the intricacies of ventriloquism to Ellen DeGeneres! There I am with one of my puppets, the one named Romeo, doing "Carpool Karaoke" with James Corden! Wait! I can hardly believe it! I'm on *The Tonight Show* exchanging witty, applause-inducing banter with Jimmy Fallon:

Jimmy: "Well, tell us about yourself, Taylor."

Me: "Ah, Jimmy, you know how it is—a little song, a coupla jokes, a little dance."

Jimmy: *interrupting.* "Wait. (*Takes a beat, looks at the audience mischievously.*) Did you say *dance*?"

(Audience applause and laughter.)

Me: "Well, I've been known to cut a rug or two."

Jimmy: "You're talking about dance moves, right? Not the other kind of rug?" (*Points to my hair*)

(Audience applause and laughter.)

Me: *tussling my own hair to show it's real.* "Ha ha ha. Well, yeah. As you know, I got to the fourth round of *Dancing With the Has-Beens* ... I mean *stars*! *Dancing with the Stars* I meant!"

(Huge whoops and hollers and laughs from the audience. Oh my gosh, they love me!)

Jimmy: "Oh. I was hoping we could recreate some of that magic tonight."

Me: "Right now? You wanna dance right now?"

(Cheers and applause)

Jimmy: "Yeah. Hit it boys!"

(*The Tonight Show* band, Questlove and the gang, begin playing Barry Manilow's "At the Copacabana" as Jimmy Fallon and I take to the dance floor and do a few turns. The crowd goes crazy. Questlove is laughing and gives me a thumbs-up. And they cut to commercial.)

Then—OMG!—I cannot believe this, but I have a bit part in a new Kevin Hart movie. And check it out. I just got cast to do a voice-over in the next Disney animated spectacular! Whoa! I gotta pinch myself! Did I really just get asked to host the Emmy Awards?

Got it? Nobody daydreams better.

This book—I will not use the term "memoir"—is a "recollection" of what I did with my life. Some of the stories might not be exact because I'm depending on my memory. It was pretty good at one time. But like Jim Bouton's arm, it's gone. So my modus operandi and my rationalization for everything is, "That's how I remember it!" I've used real names of real people when appropriate, and in cases where someone's name might sound accusatory, incriminating, or just plain mean, I didn't use real names. I'm sure there will be discrepancies, particularly with family members and close friends. To you, I ask forgiveness after the fact.

It's nonfiction, but let's be honest—I fantasize for a living. I make up jokes and stories. My coworkers are made out of foam. I exaggerate for effect. I emphasize the little things. I extemporize. I use metaphor and hyperbole to make a point.

I bring inanimate objects and creatures to life, giving them more zest and energy and personality than some *living* souls, and I get paid to do it.

So if I wrote something here that doesn't jibe with how it supposedly happened in actuality? Think of it as a knuckleball that got away from me. A pitch that zagged when it shoulda zigged. A careening, dancing, butterflying knuckleball that just never looked right, coming from a pitcher who, when you study him for a moment, doesn't look right either.

Yet here I am, going into my windup.

As a follow-up to my poor memory, it should be noted that I live by this adage: "If I don't remember it, then it never happened." This allows me to sleep with all the solace of a Ti-betan Buddhist monastic, while alleviating all guilt and misgivings. Just FYI.

Chapter One
Whatever It Takes

As long as there is injustice, whenever a Targathian baby cries out, wherever a distress signal sounds among the stars, we'll be there. This fine ship, this fine crew. Never give up ... and never surrender!
—Jason Nesmith (Tim Allen) in *Galaxy Quest*
(Based on Winston Churchill's speech "Never Give In, Never, Never, Never,"
Given during WWII, 1941

They're not laughing.

I've been on stage for a minute and a half.

Ninety seconds.

Ninety seconds is three, four, maybe five jokes and at least one big booming laugh. Ninety seconds is the time it takes a casting agent to decide yay or nay based upon your look or your attitude or your "vibe." In ninety seconds, a booker or an agent can size up an act and make a preliminary (often valid) assessment.

And ninety seconds is the time it takes for all of them—casting people, directors, bookers, agents, and this audience in front of me to decide: "Funny / Not funny."

So I can feel a little desperation creeping into my voice, the same fear of humiliation that grabs you after you've been ranting about air travel or sports or politics at dinner in some nice restaurant when you realize the person sitting across from you—a date, someone from the office, your spouse—is staring at you with an oh-my-God-he/she's-insane look on his or her face.

That and I'm fighting the urge to speed up.

Talking faster used to be my overreaction to the panic I felt when I thought I was losing an audience. It took a long time to overcome that habit; it's the kind of thing you can only learn by doing—knowledge that can only come from experience. In my world, that's "stage time."

It's a gray area I'm too familiar with, a part of my performance—usually near the beginning—where I have to "win" the audience. It's a constant part of the night-after-night forty-year world tour I started in sometime in the late 1970s.

This performance, where I had yet to win over the audience, was one of my first big-money corporate bookings. There will be many more to come after this initial affair in Boston, at the Marriott Copley Square, and I'm frustrated that things have started so slowly.

When I say they weren't laughing I mean *nobody* was laughing—not the petite, blond, overly-excited-but-personable meeting planner sitting in the back of the room, now staring at me with fear of job loss written across her face; not the uber friendly vice president who squeezed my hand *hard* in that macho mano a mano you-will-know-me-by-my-powerful-grip way a certain breed of man uses when meeting another man; not the busty brunette in the outrageous red dress sitting right up front, a woman who was giggling at everything her bald, pink-faced, tuxedoed husband said to her before I walked to the microphone; not any of the salesmen in sharp suits with their wives and girlfriends; not the servers and busboys still (loudly) collecting dishes and silverware; not the executives or the female staffers or even the Marriott catering manager who had given me a happy, "Good luck!" when we met and who now leaned against one of the side doors, arms crossed, looking bored.

The packed house in the Nantucket Ballroom on the second floor of this businessman's hotel in Boston was eerily silent.

It was 1992. I was then (and I am now) a working comedian—a noncelebrity entertainer in a world of celebrity, a happy bottom-feeder. Or as one of my long since discarded promo packages once put it, "Your affordable comedy alternative." This night I was the "affordable alternative" to what my client really wanted for their conference. But after learning the fees big-time comedy stars earn, they chose the next best thing, which was also a little more than they wanted to spend, so they kept looking at videotapes until they finally picked me. They might have loved my act and said, "We have to get this guy!" Maybe someone had seen me on TV or in a club before and vouched for me. Or, more probably, they just got tired of looking at the stacks of videos sent by agents trying to get one of their clients a good-paying corporate gig and put the job in the hands of a meeting planner. So I got the job, and there I was.

"Tonight we celebrate our elite insurance sales force that has formed the backbone of Alliance Insurance for fifty-six years!" read the pamphlet on the fine Marriott china at every one of the five hundred seats in the room. They'd had dinner. They'd had dessert (baked Alaska). They'd had drinks and given awards. They had even honored a fellow salesman who had died five years before with a fifteen-minute video and eulogy. That guy, who wasn't even alive, got a standing ovation.

Then they introduced me.

My job was to make them laugh for forty-five minutes to an hour. "Go longer if they're with you!" The overzealous vice president winked.

Looks like I'm gonna stick to forty-five minutes, Mr. VP, I thought to myself after telling a couple of feelers. Feelers are jokes I like to call "tells." A tell lets me know the mind-set, the demographic, and the general vibe of the folks I'm working for. What people laugh at gives you valuable information when you're working a crowd.

This group laughed at nothing.

They were tough—type A supercompetitive workaholics who "set the paradigm" and got the trips to Hawaii for "doing a gazillion point five in revenue this year!"

I'm being cynical. Stop.

Truth was, some of the men and women in front of me ere probably pretty funny themselves. There was a chance at least a couple of them could walk on stage right now, open with a zinger, and then do twenty solid minutes of stand-up comedy without callbacks or stock lines. They were smart, they were successful, and they were the kind of people who prided themselves on being hard to please. "Last year we had a magician, and, well, let's say he was out of his pay range," the little meeting planner, Cheri, had told me.

"They saw your VHS tape and just loved it!" I couldn't tell if she was flirting with me or if she was just defining the term "bubbly."

The company she worked for was based in Connecticut, and I got the feeling this might be her first big trip representing her bosses who had gotten me hired and put this shindig together.

DEFINITION: stock line. Stock lines are universal, very general clichéd jokes used by showbiz people and especially comics. These are frowned upon by most people in the business because anyone can use them. Example: "A policeman pulled me over today. He asked if I knew why. I said, "*Because my car smells like a donut.*" This is not just a stock line; it's a stock *premise*—that the police eat lots of donuts. I don't even know if it's true that police eat more donuts than the rest of humanity, but it's been said and joked about so much that it's taken for granted. It's a surefire laugh, but it's not very original. The more stock lines you use in your act, the more you define yourself as a comedy "hack."

DEFINITION: callback. A callback is a joke that sort of piggybacks on a joke or reference made earlier in a performance. Magicians use callbacks frequently, where something went wrong or was lost early in a given

performance but "appears" as part of another illusion or effect later in the show. Comedians use the technique as well, referencing something that happened or alluding to a previous joke at a later time in their presentation.

But that all happened before my set started, before my VP buddy David introduced me as "Mason Taylor," and before I told my first joke ("I know you wanted someone famous, but I'm someone you can afford"). And it got no response at all. Now, up here in the lights, the flop sweat starting on my forehead, I was thinking that the $1,500 (plus expenses!) I was getting paid—what would have passed as a fortune for my wife Marsia and me just a couple of months before—might be out of my league.

I had been earning money as a comedian for more than a decade. I had a wife and a three-year-old and a newborn at home. I had been through the comedy wars. I had gone through some bad nights (many more to come). And I had reached the point where putting myself in no-win positions wasn't unusual or unexpected. Besides, I had done the really nasty stuff already—the tough one-nighters in New Jersey and on the south side of Chicago, the roadhouse joints in the middle of the country, the angry South Boston shows in dying discos, and the surfer bars in California, all featuring the late-night craziness of young people, attitudes, and booze. Stand-up comics used to call these "hell gigs" for a reason. You were playing to wild crowds of beer-guzzling people intent on playing with you, interrupting you, and teasing you just to get you off your game. If you can get through gigs like that with your sanity intact, you're gonna be okay.

Those awful shows in saloons on weeknights in little bars paid $100 to $250 a night. With this corporate show, I'd moved up in the world, with a first-class ticket back to LA in the morning, a suite here at the Marriott, and my $1,500 already in pocket. They were expecting a return on investment.

Okay. So maybe they'd earned that. Most people want to laugh. They really do. The job was, and always will be, to find what is going to work this night.

I employed a trick I learned on those battlefields of live performance where many of us learned to survive. Sometimes you just had to power through your set and act as if you were better, bigger, stronger, and funnier than you really are.

I take a long beat. My mouth had gone dry, another telltale sign that things are about to go code red, so I gulped a swig of water from the glass on the piano next to me. I blasted a smile, hoping it came across as something friendly and confident, not overwhelmed and scared.

One of the basic rules of comedy, like most businesses, is *know your audience*. I had studied them from the back of the room before I went on and defined them as, "been there, seen it, done it before." They'd dealt with every kind of wannabe act performing at awards nights, industry conventions, and conferences like this one. They didn't care if I stood here and humiliated myself for an hour. They'd just as soon laugh and have a great time. It was up to me.

"Ummm ... ladies and gentlemen, I don't want to start a panic or alarm anyone." I paused for a beat that stopped everything.

I hit the punch line: "But that was my best joke."

It was the first laugh of the night. It wasn't the kind where people are bent over double, hitting the table, looking at each other and pointing and shaking their heads, and letting loose. That would come. This was the icebreaker, now almost three minutes into my set, an eternity in comedy time.

But that was why I was getting the bigger paycheck.

It is why, to this day, I'm just a little ahead of the curve and still on this lifetime tour. Somehow, some way, I am going to make it work. I'm probably not the best at anything there ever was. But I never had to be.

I only had to be the best there ever was for the rest of this one night.

I did a solid fifty minutes for the group, and when I finished there was a genuine enthusiastic round of applause.

Cheri the planner was ecstatic. "That was great!" She squeezed my hand. "We'll definitely be using you again!" She hurried off, hobnobbing and accepting accolades from her client. I packed up my gear.

I would never hear from Cheri, the Marriott Copley Square, or the insurance agency again. There were thousands of nights like this to come, for corporations and businesses, in casinos and clubs and theaters and hotel ballrooms. I don't see that as negative or positive. It's my job.

I love it.

That was then. This is the future. But it's not even close to what we were promised. Yes, the self-driving cars, the drones, the robots, and the picture phones are here. But none of that is quite what was predicted. Besides, I thought the future was me starring in sitcoms and motion pictures! Frankly it feels wrong. I want the second or third or fourth "extra life" you get in video games.

FROM TAYLOR MASON'S PERSONAL DIARY.

Chapter Two
Ventriloquism

*A ventriloquist won America's Got Talent.
Proving America doesn't have any.*
—Bill Maher

Years ago, a major showbiz player, Rory Rosegarten (TV, movies, Broadway, Manager/Producer for Ray Romano), told me that "ventriloquism"—just the word—does not have a "hip" feel to it. It was disheartening to hear, but he was right. There is nothing hip about the word. Say it out loud: *Ventriloquism.* Too many syllables for one thing. Even the nickname, "vent," doesn't work. At best, vent sounds like the rectangle-shaped thing over a grill at some diner, blowing dust strings that hang off the grates. At worst, vent sounds like an unwanted rant from some political pundit on a news channel. Then there's the "Q," always awkward when used in any word unless you're playing Scrabble. Finally the kicker. It's an "ism," which Ferris Bueller pretty much defined. And I agree with him: I don't believe in "isms." But if you can use one to your advantage …

> I will admit that I do hope that someday there is an "ism" attached to my name. I'm talking about something so clever, so unique, so individually mine it will be forever known as a "masonism."

Say the word "ventriloquist" in public, and you're liable to be cursed, threatened, and maybe sentenced ten to fifteen years for even thinking about it. Tell someone that you *are* indeed a ventriloquist, and you are met with a pause so pregnant it causes men to give birth.

In our current world, where deviance is celebrated and the profane is exalted, "ventriloquism" is a four-letter word.

And I don't care.

Ventriloquism is old—as old as the Old Testament in a hotel Bible. It's been around since the beginning of time; hence the antiquated feel. It was practiced by Pythia at the Oracle of Delphi around the eighth century BC. It became legit as an entertainment vehicle sometime during the Middle Ages.

DEFINITION: Samuel I, 28:3–25. Saul calls on the witch of Endor (aka a "medium") to contact Samuel from his grave and ask what are the chances of victory in a battle with the Philistines. Samuel—via the witch—predicts annihilation, which proves true in the end. The loose analogy is that the Witch of Endor was a ventriloquist, summoning a "voice" from the grave, and people "heard" the deceased (Samuel).

The word itself conjures up visions of ugly, scary, woodenheaded puppets with slot-jaw mouths. It connotes horror movies where puppets "come to life" and kill real people who are hopeless to do anything because they didn't believe (until it was too late) that the puppet was "alive."

The ventriloquist him or herself doesn't fare much better in modern-day media. He or she is often associated with weird psychosis or personality disorders, as perhaps a psychotic whose personalities come out through his or her little "partner." Or maybe all ventriloquists are just pure evil. At the very least, they have manipulative issues and need much therapy, right?

I am a ventriloquist. I write that without pause. No misgivings. No irony. You're thinking, "But, Taylor, you seem so normal."

> It's important to remember that ventriloquism was born a couple of thousand years ago, before there was sound reproduction and amplification—no microphones, no speakers, no electronics. The ability to use, manipulate, and craft audio and create oral "voices" allowed a person to trick others into thinking they "heard" something that wasn't there.

It's not an obsolete art form, but every newspaper reporter and media "journalist" who ever interviewed me began their report with something like, "Ventriloquism is a dying art."

Wrong.

Ventriloquism isn't dying. It's more popular than ever.

I could, however, make a strong case that journalism is dead.

Still, I understand the misgivings. Ventriloquism doesn't scale in a world of facial recognition and high-definition video.

At its core, ventriloquism is a fantasy come to life. It's a connection to another dimension, a castle at the end of a rainbow where—literally—everything you envision is in play! The elves at the North Pole exist. Your childhood "imaginary friend" is not only real, but also sitting next to you. And—miracle of miracles—you're having a dialogue! It's a crazy fairy tale from the furthest corner of your imagination brought to life in your living room. And as a ventriloquist you share this experience, this enchantment, and this *inspiration* with others.

I know it's always been a little odd. I prefer the term "eccentric." But I'll accept "unconventional."

Forget ventriloquism's association with "black magic" and the occult. Ignore the fact it's reviled by most stand-up comics, talk show hosts, and the terminally hip entertainment media. Forget the movies, the books, the TV shows about creepy ventriloquists and ugly puppets and X-rated jokes.

> If you are an adult, and you're *scared* of puppets, please look around. There is a lot of stuff in this world to be scared of. There are people, events, and situations where we should truly be frightened. Puppets are not one of those things. So stop.

DEFINITION: hack. **A hack in the world of comedy is an act who steals other people's jokes, is dependent on props or music in live performances, or uses lots of dated and "generic' (see the definition of "stock lines") material. Ventriloquists are considered hacks for a mix of all these but mostly because they fall into the props/music categories. Note: I don't care.**

Maybe you haven't noticed. The top-grossing comedy act in the world during the early 2000s (Jeff Dunham) was a ventriloquist. As of this writing one of the top Las Vegas acts (Terry Fator) is a ventriloquist. Not to mention that *America's Got Talent* has chosen a vent as its champion three times, while having numerous other ventriloquists wow the judges and the audience on many shows. Every cruise line has a full-time ventriloquist who works its main stage. There are more ventriloquists, full-time, part-time, and amateur, than ever before in history. It's a growth industry!

DEFINITION: ventriloquism. The word "ventriloquism" comes from the Latin "ventro," which means "belly" and "qui" which means "speaker." More directly, ventriloquism is "speaking from the belly." Ventriloquism can loosely be defined as the art of making vocal sounds come from a place other than the speaker—usually a "dummy." (So it stands to reason that, like an opera singer, the bigger the body, the better the ventriloquist, right? Because you're

"speaking from the belly." Not true. I base that on personal experience.)

Ventriloquism is human beings interacting with beings from an alternate universe, where animals and creatures and puppets and sprites all have personalities and characteristics and faults—just like us—which is the stuff of legend. It's integral in literature and science fiction and movies. It is theater, and just like theater, it includes all the components that make up any production—writing, acting, story arc, and three-dimensional characters. It also contains two elements that are very fundamental to show business—comedy and music.

For the generations who grew up on *Dungeons & Dragons*, video and role-playing fantasy games, not to mention otherworldly movies and books, ventriloquism isn't a stretch as an entertainment.

> There is no such thing as "throwing your voice." Ventriloquism is really just the *illusion* that a voice is coming from inside a box or under a rock or behind a wall. It requires a variety of skills to pull that off, which include acting; vocal and breathing control; and the ability to mimic sound and then use it, manipulate it, and present it accordingly. It requires much preparation. In short, it's a talent that requires the same kinds of things that make successful musicians, actors, comedians, athletes, business people, and on and on and on.

I think of ventriloquism as defying the laws of nature. "You can make it sound like there's a person inside the refrigerator? But that's impossible!"

Not impossible. It's a superpower. I have conquered physics! Let's all be thankful I have chosen to use my superpower for good.

In Victorian England, the author Henry Cockton wrote a best-selling novel called *Valentine Vox the Ventriloquist: His Life and Adventures*. The author, not a ventriloquist himself, taps into the misconceptions of ventriloquism, including the idea that it's possible to "throw" one's voice. The story line revolves around a crime-fighting vigilante who rights wrongs and captures criminals by using ventriloquism. It's a bit far-fetched. Vox "throws his voice" in theaters, crowded marketplaces, and empty rooms, making it sound as if there are people where there re none, creating comical situations, and doing what is humanly impossible. But during the 1840s when it was published, ventriloquism had become part of the culture and was commonplace in beer halls and theaters. It was misunderstood and strange and otherworldly. There were no microphones at the time, no speakers, no headphones—no electronic amplification of sound. To manipulate the human voice, creating the illusion it came from behind a door or inside a box, was cutting-edge show business.

I've used a parlor trick similar to the fictional Mr. Vox on occasion. Best example: I'm with friends in a hotel hallway. We are walking to separate rooms on the same floor, and as my friends pass in front of my room, I open the door and say, "See you guys later."

I take advantage of the unexpected and perform. As my friends continue walking, I "throw" my voice into the empty room and make it sound as if there is someone there (female) waiting for me, who says, "Hi, Taylor!"

My friends hear this—stunned that a woman is in my room—and they stop in the middle of the hall. They crane their necks, looking past me into the room, while I keep up the illusion by pretending to dialogue as I walk in the room: "How did you get in here?"

The voice responds, "I stole your key."

I look back to my friends and invite them in, which exposes the fraud.

I don't do it often.

That's ventriloquism boiled down to its essential ingredients—surprise, misdirection, and a performance.

Learning ventriloquism is just like learning any skill or craft—riding a bike, dribbling a basketball, playing an instrument. To become a ventriloquist, you learn the basics, you improve, you create your own style, and you perfect your execution to the point where you can get paid.

The three essentials:
1. Perfect technique (lip control and manipulation)
2. A clever, interesting, unique puppet/figure/partner
3. Great content as a comedian/singer/performer

If you can do one of those, you will get bookings at some level. If you can accomplish two of those, you will be paid as a professional, and you'll manage a career. But if you can nail down all three? You'll be able to perform your act across all media, on stages around the world, and you'll make a very good living.

> I've seen a lot of beauty pageant contestants who use ventriloquism as their "talent," and I always thought a good line for them might be, "I am blessed because I did not have to overcome a debilitating injury or affliction or life-threatening illness. *But*—I *have* overcome my ventriloquism!" Hopefully the audience gets the self-deprecation, and then the contestant performs a killer vent act and earns the crown.

> Ventriloquists, by the way, do not care for the word "dummy." To some, it's an insult. The preferred, politically correct, and accepted terms are "figure" or "character." You can use "partner" or "sidekick" as well. Personally, I like "muse" or "codependent," and I'll even accept "inner child."

> When I'm driving in the HOV lanes on major city expressways, I use the word "passenger" to describe my puppet/partner Romeo in the seat next to me while I drive with my left hand, using my right to ever so slightly move his head, just in case a police officer looks in the passenger-side window. In that case, I'll have Romeo turn his head toward mine, as if we're in conversation. Don't tell anyone.

Perhaps the best-known ventriloquist dummy (until Jeff Dunham changed the rotation of the earth with his partners "Walter" and "Peanut") was Charlie McCarthy, a spectacular accomplishment in wood carving and craftsmanship, whose features were smooth and carefully burnished.

You can make your puppet out of anything—something as simple as a sock can work. Or you can spend $10,000 and get something state of the art. I go with the old simplest-is-best approach. Besides, the puppet can be a work of art. But if you don't have the technique or the material? Don't quit the day job.

The difficult sounds the ventriloquist has to reproduce are the letters *B, F, M, P, V, W* and *Y*. All except Y require the human lips to touch—try making the sound "B" without moving your lips, for example. Every ventriloquist has his or her own technique, substituting other sounds to replace the Bs and Fs and so on. The Y, although it does not require a meeting of your lips to sound it out, still means lip movement. Spend six months perfecting the replacement for those sounds, creating something similar to the real thing, and you're going to wow people. Take another month to learn how to move your "dummy" and bring it to life and—*welcome to showbiz*!

DEFINITION: ventriloquism. The tongue is quicker than the ear, and I'm talking faster than you can listen!

> The way I make the "Y" sound is a simple cheat: I put "ooh" and "eye" together and say them quickly—"ooh-eye." Try it without moving your lips. See? You're on your way to putting me out of work!

Well you're ready except for one more thing.

By far the most important ingredient—more important than lip control, manipulation of the character, or the quality of the puppet—is the material being presented by the ventriloquist. Because if the content is excellent, everything else is probably going to work no matter what.

So if the ventriloquist is an incredibly talented singer and can make that inanimate object on their hand hit those high F sharps and carry a tune? That's pretty impressive.

Ditto for comedy. If a ventriloquist's act is blow-the-ceiling-off-the-room funny, other essentials like the puppet and the technique aren't as important.

> There are three ways to get content for a ventriloquist act. Material can be written, rehearsed, and performed; material can be purchased and performed (that goes for jokes, routines, music, and songs); or the material can be stolen from other performers.

I enjoy ventriloquism for many reasons. I think of myself as the head writer, producer, director, and talent for my little business. Puppets are really actors playing roles that are part of the narrative. The great thing about *these* actors is their eagerness to do the lines the way I wrote them. Plus, they're always on time. No personal issues with families and drugs, no dissension, no complaints about pay or billing, and they don't have egos. *They do exactly what I tell them to, when I tell them to, and they never complain*!

Since I see the puppets as actors, I delve into character traits for each of the characters I use in performance. This creates an organic reality for me when I'm in front of an audience. I need to "buy" the reality of my partners so the audience will feel that dynamic and buy into it as well.

> Content is everything. Old jokes, bad jokes, stupid jokes, and predictable routines have people covering their ears and running for the exits in a recreation of the running of the bulls in Pamplona, Spain. Great material makes everything work.

There are some idiosyncrasies that cannot be hidden. The odd facial expression the "vent" has while the figure is talking is rarely "natural." I smile or contort my face with lips slightly parted in a way that looks as if I'm about to open my mouth and say something, or maybe I was just caught midsentence before being interrupted. It looks as if 'm doing something. But no matter how "good" my technique, it just doesn't feel "natural."

I worry about it every time I work.

When ventriloquism is done badly in a public setting, it sets the art form back two decades.

When it's done well, it's a crowd-pleaser and a genuine celebration of human creativity and talent.

Bill and Patricia

My predilection for ventriloquism is in my DNA—literally. Patricia and Bill Mason ("Mom and Dad") grew up during the Great Depression. Born in the 1920s, they lived much of their childhoods during a desperate time in American history, where many, many families were penniless. That means I come from a generation of American culture that heard, daily, "You didn't grow up in the Great Depression! You don't know what hardship is!" It's undoubtedly true. And it was repeated so often that, by the time I became a teenager, I decided the Great Depression apparently existed to make children like myself feel guilty for not having lived through it.

Eventually, I started responding, "No, I didn't grow up in your Great Depression. But I had to endure eighth grade, and that scarred me for life. So we're even!"

Both of my parents came from Illinois—my dad from a farming community ninety minutes southwest of Chicago called Grand Ridge and my mom from a tiny southern Illinois town called Palestine.

The common denominator for my folks was—like for most Americans at that time—the radio. My dad's family had a big radio console in the living room. My mother would go down the street to a neighbor's house to listen along with other children and parents in someone else's home. People would gather around the big speakers and listen to voices from far away, from a place where there was plenty of food and work and excitement. There was hope. There was money. There was *life*. The favorite show for my folks? *The Chase and Sanborn Hour*, a prime-time radio program starring the iconic ventriloquist Edgar Bergen and his sidekick "dummy," Charlie McCarthy.

A ventriloquist on the radio. *What*!? Isn't the whole point of ventriloquism based on the visual act, whereby the audience *sees* the ventriloquist's technique—not moving his or her lips as the puppet talks—and appreciates the skill and talent of said performer?

Obviously not.

The show was simple, easy to understand, and hilarious. Radio was "theater of the mind" that made you forget you were broke and living in a dead-end place surrounded by a bunch of other broke people who didn't have any hope and weren't going to get anywhere. I never got the whole ventriloquist-on-the-radio thing, but I always got the humor. When I listen to Bergen/McCarthy stuff today, they sound like a solid comedy team.

At its core, ventriloquism represents fantasy, escape, fun, and laughter. So as a consequence, shouldn't the biggest-name comedian from the 1930s be a ventriloquist? Someone who takes your imagination and lets you escape reality for a while? And I don't think it's surprising that ventriloquists like Jeff Dunham and Terry Fator became superstar-popular during the Great Recession of 2007 to 2015 here in the United States of America.

Edgar Bergen had started on the vaudeville circuit and had parlayed his ventriloquist act—he was *funny*—into a starring role on radio, where he became an international superstar. He made movies. There were magazine articles featuring him with his "partners" Charlie, Effie (an older woman), and Mortimer (a lovable goof). There were lunch boxes and plates and toys and buttons and hats and posters all bearing Bergen's image with his buddy Charlie—the beginning of corporate sponsored tie-ins—so every item imaginable featured a picture or reproduction of the ventriloquist team. Edgar Bergen was, by any standard you can apply, a superstar.

And to Bill and Patricia Mason, Edgar Bergen was the epitome of showbiz.

My mother's family had come to Illinois from Massachusetts. A distant relative was a published author. Or maybe a professional musician/songwriter? Whatever, the family was Puritan, strong-willed, and educated. Her mother, my grandmother, was a teacher. Her dad worked in the mill. *He was grinding flour in a mill!* It's like saying, "He was a milkman," or, "He owned a video rental store."

He played trombone and was instrumental in teaching me to love the Chicago Cubs. Mom had an uncle with some money who paid for her education at the University of Illinois. She wanted to write copy for radio programs.

Bill Mason was raised by his hardworking mom and his farmer father, a "horse trader," another term (like "miller") that's long retired but had a certain connotation in rural Illinois. They raised horses and corn. They sold Oldsmobiles. They made ends meet, and my father yearned to get away from the hardscrabble life and enjoy the fruits of his dream—radio.

There are no ironies. My parents met at a radio station in Decatur, Illinois—WSOY, named for "the Soybean Capital of the World." That was sometime in the late '40s, when television was in its trial stages and radio was still the link to living rooms across America. All the broadcasts were still done live. My mother was a "Kelly Girl," singing live commercials for Kelly's Potato Chips and doing secretarial work in the office. How my folks got together for a first date is no mystery—radio and small towns and the Depression. They fell in love and got married. She convinced him to go to college at the University of Illinois, where they attended football games and fraternity parties and, years later, alumni functions. They loved the showbiz productions there, especially the musicals put on by the theater department. The college scene was important for them. A Big Ten University experience was validation they were "getting out."

Bill Mason became a farm news broadcaster, first on the radio and later on television. "Farm broadcaster" is another one of those positions that doesn't exist except for a very, very few rural radio stations scattered across the United States. He was a frustrated actor, performing in community theater and singing along to show tunes in the car.

> Both my mom's and dad's family members had lots of jobs that no longer exist. One example was my dad's career as a "farm news broadcaster". My uncles were "pinsetters" at a bowling alley. I had an aunt who was a switchboard operator. Thank goodness I'm a comedian, a job that will never be replaced ... right?

Their vows lasted until my father's passing in 1998. They were a living throwback, their marriage a testament to the old-school way of doing things. They only had one argument that I remember, and it lasted all forty-seven years they were together as the joke goes.

Their stories, from rural Depression-era childhoods; their agriculture roots; the University of Illinois; their love of laughter and music; and their desire to escape to a better life produced me.

Chapter Three
Sock It to Me

Sock it to me, baby!
—Mitch Ryder and The Detroit Wheels

Puppet I

> The phrase "sock it to me" was used in many rock and R & B songs during the 1960s, including Aretha Franklin's version of "Respect." It was lifted by various commercial enterprises and entertainers, especially by the TV / comedy/ variety show, *Rowan and Martin's Laugh-In*, which co-opted and turned it into an ironic cliché, overusing it to the point of absurdity. I watched that show many nights with my Aunt Ardie.

Sometime in the 1960s, while the British Invasion and Motown and James Brown were taking over the radio, as the civil rights movement was escalating and a cultural revolution was exploding, I woke up one morning and went to the clothes chest in the suburban bedroom I shared with my brothers. Inside were my socks, carefully rolled and grouped by my mother. The way she folded and twisted each pair meant the opening was on top of the sock/ball and gave each a kind of smile. So when I pulled open the drawer, a bunch of soft, round, happy creatures were grinning up at me.

This day, instead of putting the socks on my foot, I pulled one sock on over my hand, the way that the TV ventriloquist Shari Lewis did on her show with her puppets Lamb Chop and Charley Horse. I pulled the sock tight over my fingers, forming a "mouth" between my thumb and forefinger, and when I opened my hand ... *whoa*.

The puppet opened its mouth.

I voiced it. "Hello, Taylor!"

It was the 1960s—Black Panthers and Flower People, riots and peace signs, the Monkees and Charles Manson. The world was changing. I was completely unaware. For me, the biggest change on the planet, the biggest revolution in the world, had just taken place in my bedroom with a sock on my hand.

A short time later, visiting my grandmother where she worked as a seamstress at the JC Penney in Ottawa, Illinois, I shared my sock story. My grandmother looked at the sock and said, "It needs a pair of eyes and hair." So she sewed some yellow yarn on its head, sewed two black pieces of felt below the yarn for eyes, and handed it back to me.

"Now try it."

Show business! I performed—who knows what I did—for her and the other grandmother types there in the back of the department store.

They laughed. They encouraged me. It didn't seem weird or wrong or "out of place."

It seemed like a natural thing to do. I make the puppet talk. The people laugh. What's wrong with that?

Shari Lewis is an American ventriloquist and showbiz icon who I watched on her original network TV show *The Shari Lewis Show* in the early 1960s. She made a major showbiz comeback in the '90s with another children's TV program, *Lambchop's Play-Along!* featuring her wonderful characters, Lamb Chop,

> Hush Puppy, and Charley Horse. Her puppets were really just socks with accessories like hair and eyes, but Shari brought them to life. Ms. Lewis passed away in 1998. She was a ventriloquist, a singer, a live performer, and TV star. She came to see me in the mid-1990s while we both worked in Branson, Missouri. She was elegant, talented, decent, and kind. She wrote a lot of books. She is worth researching

Mrs. Randall

There was a big old piano in the house where I grew up in Clarendon Hills, a sleepy suburb of Chicago. My mother was a decent sight reader and would sometimes sit and play show tunes for my brothers and me. She painted the outer casing white, with a sort of greenish tint, so it looked a little like cotton candy in the shape of a baby grand. It sat there by the living room window on the periphery of my life, kind of waiting for me as I went to school, played Little League, and delivered papers—all the stuff suburban boys did.

On a shelf over my bed was a green plastic AM/FM radio. I think my dad put it there so my brothers and I could turn it on and listen to him do the farm news on WGN radio.

Or we could listen to Top 40 on WLS and WCFL.

Top 40 won.

My brother Locke became an avid fan of pop and rock music overnight. That radio was on *a lot*. The first songs I remember are Beatles tunes, Simon and Garfunkel doing "Mrs. Robinson," a band called the Lemon Pipers singing "Green Tambourine," and a novelty piece about an insane person called "They're Coming to Take Me Away." This crazy song, featuring just a voice spoken over a drum and tambourine, had the following lyrics:

They're coming to take me away, ha ha!
They're coming to take me away hee hee!

To the funny farm where life is beautiful all the time!

I remember running around the public pool in Clarendon Hills, leading all the other kids my age as we sang along to this song playing through the loudspeaker. We'd run up to moms and shout, "They're coming to take me away ha ha!" The women laughed. My friends laughed. Star for a day!

My brothers and I loved the radio. We experimented a lot, listening to everything *except* my father and WGN (which seemed old-fashioned and skewing toward an older demo; it was). So we heard the "underground" music on FM.

Eventually I stumbled on WVON, a station all the way at the end of the AM dial, and the voice coming through the tiny speaker was different than all the other voices on all the other stations. His name was Pervis. He did his own commercials— "Come on down to JP's used car lot on the south side, and we'll set you up." More different than his voice was the music he played. It was stuff you would never hear on AM radio—the blues, Stax Records, Willie Dixon and Muddy Waters, and John Lee Hooker.

> The name "JP" would later be part of my job, as I named a woodenheaded ventriloquist figure for the radio commercial I heard on WVON from Pervis.

By the time I was eleven or twelve years old, I had this fantasy about pop culture and music and show business. All the big stars—the Fab Four, Aretha Franklin, Bill Cosby, Johnny Carson, and all the other celebrities I could think of— got together in New York every Saturday night at a big show. Everyone played their songs or told their jokes and had more fun than anybody has a right to. Show business seemed exotic and exciting. How could I break in?

After listening to the hits of WLS one afternoon, I went down to the piano and tried to pick out "Gotta Get a Message to You," a Bee Gees song that was part of the rotation on WLS four times every *hour*. My mother was thrilled that someone else was touching the keys, so the next day we went to meet a piano teacher, Mrs. Randall.

Revolution II

Mrs. Randall lived in a house that looked like one of the lawn gnomes in her garden might live there. Walking in her front door was like walking through a portal from the real world into a movie set, like Dorothy waking up in Oz, like going from black-and-white to color. It was a fantasyland. Her living room, filled with knickknacks and tiny glass unicorns and figurines sparkling and reflecting sunlight, was friendly and warm. Her upright piano was in perfect condition, sounding like an orchestra from some fantastic place where it was always you-can-do-anything day. I'd never been in such a warm, fun, positive environment or heard a piano sound anything like hers; nor have I since.

The piano, like ventriloquism, was not part of most children's day-to-day world in suburban Chicago, with school and Little League and swimming lessons and birthday parties with friends. That was normal. Routine. Expected.

But the piano? The ventriloquist puppet? That was escape. More fantasy. A joy. It was sometimes lonely, but I was happy. I practiced solo. I performed for myself. It was *mine*.

Sometime in that first year of piano lessons, I learned "The Bumble Boogie."

"I picked this just for you," Mrs. Randall said before handing me the sheet music. It looked imposing, all those eighth notes and sixteenth notes and complicated right-hand runs. Mrs. Randall told me it was "my piece," so we worked on it for a few months before I played it at a recital in front of all her students and their moms (dads didn't go to piano recitals).

The response, the appreciative applause, and the compliments I got after my big finish (which I made up myself, and Mrs. Randall allowed it; I played just the left hand for two measures and then hit one plaintive high C with my right forefinger and "let ring" for another four beats) were empowering. It made my mother proud. It made my teacher smile. I was doing stuff my friends in the neighborhood and at school didn't even know about.

Years later, I caught up with one of my childhood buddies, Doug Ingraham. We had spent days and weeks and years of our youth together in Clarendon Hills, playing ball and riding bikes and being kids. Now, years later, he had taken up guitar. We were in our thirties and sat down at someone's house, me on piano and him on guitar, and banged out a couple of tunes. "Why didn't we do this when we were kids?" he asked.

I couldn't bring myself to tell him that I was embarrassed. I couldn't tell him that, when we were children, the music and, in turn, the ventriloquism and performance and the practice, all that was mine. I was selfish. It was years before I started "sharing" all those years of practice.

My loss.

A Christmas Carol

My first casting in any kind of production, my first theatrical stage appearance, was in sixth grade at Walker School in Clarendon Hills, Illinois. I auditioned for the lead role in the Christmas play, age eleven, and I *got it*.

Maybe Mrs. Fleming—teacher/director—cast me in the role because I was loud.

I played Scrooge in A *Christmas Carol*.

I was brilliant.

Never mind that, after weeks of rehearsals and preparation, I completely forgot the Ghost of Christmas Present and skipped right to the Ghost of Christmas Future (my favorite part of the play). The boy playing the role of Present was standing in the wings, maybe ten feet from me, but I failed to notice him waving and jumping up and down and trying to get my attention. I was *focused*. I was *in the moment*. I was an *actor*. It was sixth grade, and nobody seemed to care that I left out a key segment in the play, because everyone—friends, teachers, parents—was congratulating me. The parents in particular seemed to be very appreciative of my work.

I'm guessing that was because most of them were ready to go home.

No matter. My folks were very proud. And I, at age eleven, had a career path.

"Showbiz is my life!"

Puppet II

It was 1967—the Summer of Love. The Beatles released *Sgt. Pepper's Lonely Hearts Club Band*. The United States sent half a million soldiers into Vietnam, and the city of Detroit went up in riots.

Keeping with the times, my father gave me a plastic-headed, pull-string Danny O'Day puppet.

It was a cheap remake of the great ventriloquist Jimmy Nelson's woodenheaded partner, although I'm sure my dad wasn't aware of that. It was a novelty, something he might have received from an associate at WGN where he was working at the time. Maybe he paid twenty dollars for it. Whatever, he brought it home and gave it to me.

It was next to impossible to manipulate. The molded head had the slot-jaw mouth that all ventriloquist "dummies" have, but the operation was impossible. There was a tiny string coming out of a hole in the back of the neck. The body was a thickly padded sock covered with a poorly made checkered suit.

No matter. I practiced with it. I made a connection. It was *mine*. And *bonus*, it was more advanced than the socks. Add the fact that I was interested in an "art form" that my dad had loved since he was a kid listening to the radio? Hey, it's father-son bonding time!

He had a brilliant idea: "Let's rebuild the puppet!"

Maybe that was his plan all along. We completely dismantled the body, cut off the bottom of the neck so we could see the mechanics of the pull-string mouth, and rebuilt the puppet starting with the head.

He made a wooden base for the neck, with a dowel that acted as a control stick, which I could grab with four fingers. We lengthened the string coming from the small hole in the neck, and put a metal ring at the end of that, which was perfect because it made opening and closing the puppet mouth very easy by pulling with my thumb.

For the body, we made a wooden base in the shape of a rectangle, with four wooden braces glued into place, looking like a tiny upside down table. We built the "shoulders" in a similar shape to the base, with a hole in the middle of the piece, sanded down to replicate kind of a mortar and pestle, the puppet's neck fitting in the hole. This allowed the puppet some personality; it could move its head back and forth (think someone shaking their head no), nod, or make all sorts of humanlike movements by turning the joystick. We attached the shoulders to the four wooden braces, put terry cloth around all the wooden parts to alleviate splinters, and made legs using cloth and rags, which I sewed up and stapled to the body.

We bought toddler's clothes—shirt, pants, a sports coat, and shoes—at a department store and *boom*! I was an official ventriloquist. My dad named it "Ted." Ted was for Ted Kennedy, which my pops thought was a brilliant sociopolitical statement. ("The puppet is named for Teddy Kennedy! Har har har.")

> Jimmy Nelson is one of three (the other two being Shari Lewis and Paul Winchell) who formed the "holy trinity of ventriloquism" on television in the 1950s and 1960s. Nelson was most famous for his Nestle's Quick chocolate milk commercial which ran for *ten years* on TV, featuring his dog puppet, Farfel.

> Nelson would sing, "N-E-S-T-L-E-S, Nestle's makes the very best." And the dog would sing in a low voice, "Chocolate," followed by the clap of the wooden mouth snapping shut on the last syllable. To this day, when children are focus-grouped and watch different television ads for "memorability," Nelson's always ranks number one.

Consider: I was an actor, I was a rockin' pianist, and now I had my ventriloquist partner! Could life possibly get any better?

Fun would turn to tragedy, as a short time later, I was headed to seventh grade—junior high, middle school—where the real world smacks you like a bug on the windshield of life. You don't go to junior high school to learn history or math or English. Every one of us knows that seventh and eighth grade exist for your education in societal evolution.

It's where they (don't ask me to define them because I can't, but I know who they are) identify exactly where you stand in the binary structure of life.

Cool/Dumb.

One of us / Not one of us.

In/Out.

Getting on the bus for my first day at Hinsdale Junior High School, books in one arm and my partner "Ted" in the other, guess what group I was in?

> Life, in many ways, is Legos, those little snap-together plastic modules that are a wonderful learning toy. Legos are binary—a way of composing, creating, or building as a result of two parts. It's like computing, where it's 1 or 0. In real terms, they're fun to play with or extremely painful to step on—fun or pain. Like life?

So. Bus ride, first day of school, seventh grade. I'm sitting in the last row by the emergency exit door, having been specially invited there by three eighth graders—Keith, Greg, and Dean. They've avidly encouraged me to perform a show with my little partner, "Ted."

I've been practicing, and I have a short set that's been waiting for the exact moment, the perfect time, the zenith at which I share my skill with the world.

I went for it.

I stood up between the seats at the back of the bus, in front of the exit door, and began the act I'd been preparing for months.

It was a disaster.

I didn't even get to the first punch line (which was, "If I was your mother, I'd take the poison!" Feel free to write your own setup).

What followed was a great introduction to humiliation, embarrassment, and fear—the three-headed hydra of showbiz.

Some of us never get over that.

Keith, Greg, and Dean didn't just heckle me; they mocked me. They shouted me down. They imitated me. They're doubled over in laughter, and they had the entire bus laughing at me—not because I was doing a funny act.

They were laughing *at* me.

I felt stupid, out of it, and ignorant.

The experience had such an effect on me that I didn't bring Ted out in public (except to show off for my youngest brother, Tony) for six years. I kept my ventriloquist "skill" hidden.

why johnny can't read — (the video)

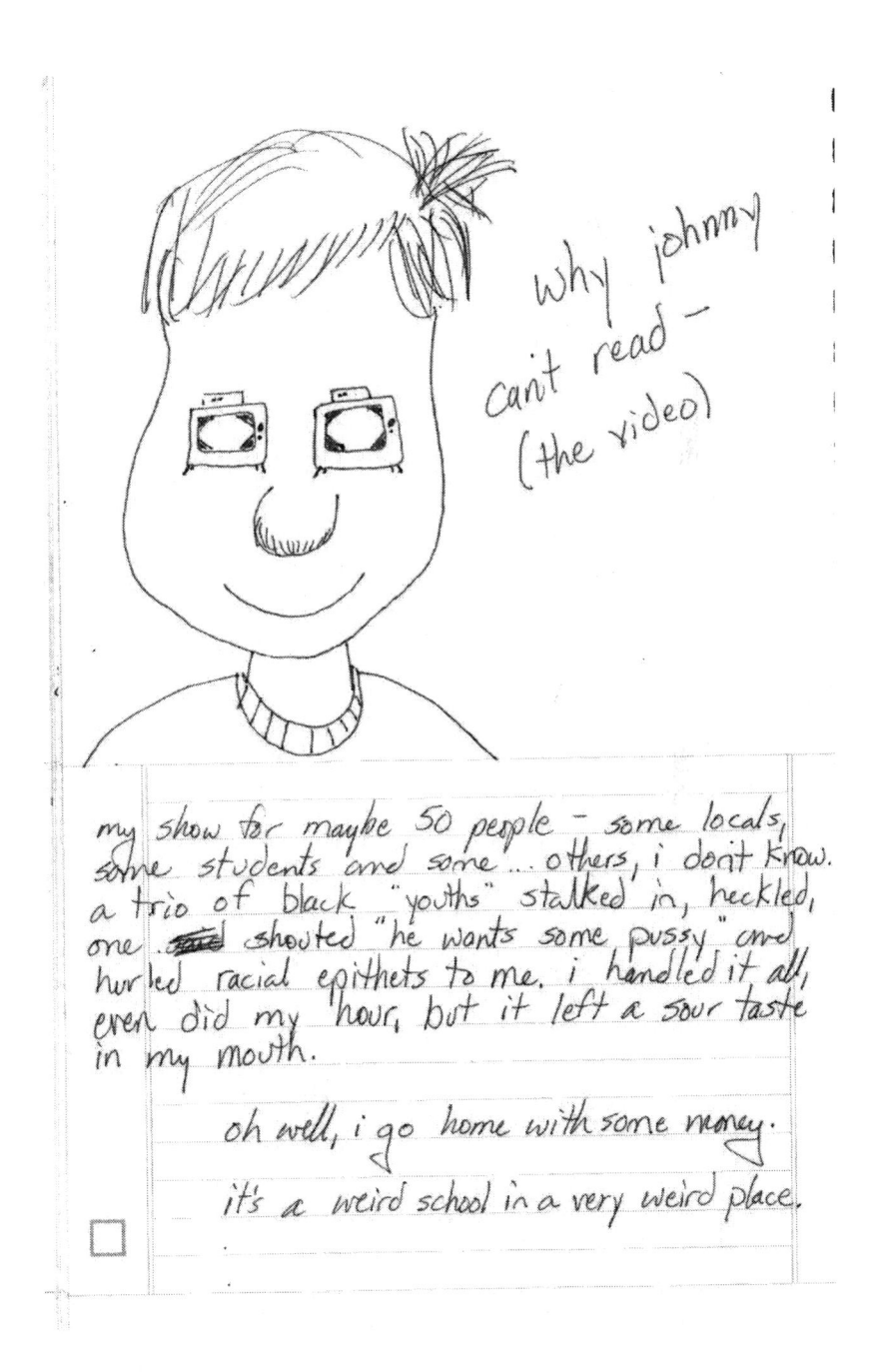

my show for maybe 50 people — some locals, some students and some... others, i don't know. a trio of black "youths" stalked in, heckled, one shouted "he wants some pussy" and hurled racial epithets to me. i handled it all, even did my hour, but it left a sour taste in my mouth.

oh well, i go home with some money.

it's a weird school in a very weird place.

FROM TAYLOR MASON'S PERSONAL DIARY.

Chapter Four
Sumo

The last night of a sumo wrestling tournament is called the pleasure of a thousand autumns.
—Japanese playwright Zeami Motokiyo

Sometime in the early 1990s, the brilliant puppet builder and artist Mary Ann Taylor built me a life-sized sumo wrestler puppet. I sent her a cartoonish drawing of what I wanted. I explained the concept and asked if she could build it. I wanted something big and unforgettable and realistic. She made it to specification and it was *huge*. Literally *huge*. Hugely *huge*!

It was exactly what I wanted.

And it didn't work.

I had this *giant* puppet that had been built with painstaking perfection by a premier puppet maker but no premise for a routine.

I didn't have an act for it.

Great.

I would throw Sumo in at the end of my performances, almost apologetically, hoping something would miraculously happen, waiting on a lightning bolt of creative spontaneity that never came. I did it everywhere, and nothing happened. Audiences weren't impressed. I didn't introduce him correctly. I didn't set it up. I just kinda threw it out there. I was doing Mary Ann—the person who created it—and all those audiences a disservice by pretending it was part of my set. I finally reached the point where it was time for Sumo to be thrown into the dust heap of all my other long-forgotten puppets and jokes and unfunny material when I took the puppet to Governor's Comedy Club on Long Island for one last attempt at funny.

Most distressing, Sumo was so big he required his own, hard-to-find travel case, which drew unwanted and suspicious attention from the airlines.

"What's in there?"

I had wrapped the puppet in a bedsheet and then covered him with two big black taped-together plastic garbage bags and put him in a giant canvas bag. If it sounds laborious, it was.

Airline ticket agents and skycaps would eye the giant package, which looked conspicuously like a body bag, wondering what, how, and why this humongous *thing* had been dropped in front of them. They all had the same reaction when they picked it up, because it really didn't weigh much. I had to explain the reasons it was so light.

Because it is a big puppet.

Because I am a ventriloquist.

Because I spent a lot of money, and I'm taking this with me everywhere I go until I find some jokes.

All this earned me sympathetic looks—as in, *Poor man, he doesn't even know he's gone over the edge. Maybe his ventriloquism is a desperate cry for help. So sad. I hope he never flies with us again.*

When I got to a venue or performance space, things got really weird. Mary Ann's genius was her concept for Sumo's girth. Instead of filling the stomach and torso with foam or filler (which would have added prohibitive weight), she left it empty, just a cavern of empty space in the middle of the puppet. To fill it required a beach ball—the biggest, roundest beach ball available. It required a ball that had to be special ordered—one that, in all its latex glory, weighed more than the puppet itself!

DEFINITION: mawashi. A mawashi is the belt or loincloth that a sumo wrestler wears in training or competition. There are different styles and divisions and levels of mawashi, but my Sumo only had one.

To fully expand Sumo to his stage-ready size, I would position the puppet facedown on a table or bench. Mary Ann had left a slot in his lower back, just below where the "mawashi" tied. I'd bend down over his back, his legs splayed on either side of mine, and pull the slot open. I would push the deflated beach ball into the body, being careful to leave the inflation valve sticking out. Then I'd put my head down, right on the puppet; take the valve into my mouth; and blow it up. It took twelve to fifteen minutes of hypoxia-inducing inhaling and exhaling, expanding Sumo's body until the beach ball was completely inflated.

I think you get the visual. It was one of those things I had to do *alone*. On the few occasions people had seen the procedure, they had been emotionally damaged for life.

That this puppet finally became part of my act was a fluke.

It was a Friday night, and I did the first of two sets at Governor's, which went fine except for the five-minute lull caused by the unfunny Sumo character. Disgusted with myself, I threw the giant wrestler in a closet behind the stage between shows and went to meet some friends in the lobby as the late-night second-show crowd filtered in.

One of the people with the group, sitting at a small table by a brick wall sharing drinks and showbiz conversation, was a secretary from my management company at the time. She was definitively Long Island, smoking a cigarette, nursing a beer, and speaking up every once in a while to voice a loud opinion—the way certain Long Island girls do. Just before showtime, everyone got up and went into the show room.

Except for her.

She wanted to discuss my act.

She had a suggestion. She wanted to help. She had an idea.

I paused. Uh-oh. And before I could say, "Umm ... I gotta go. I just remembered I left my car in the parking lot," she stated the obvious: "Sumo is not funny."

Thanks.

"Why even do it if it doesn't work?" she asked pointedly. Not angrily. Just honestly. Plaintively. The way certain Long Island girls will ask you because it's as much a part of her personality as breathing.

I wanted to tell her, "I paid someone a ton of money to make it for me, and I don't just give up on something because it doesn't work."

But before I got a word out of my mouth, she said, "I think it would be *much* funnier if you brought someone out of the audience—like a woman—and had her operate the sumo wrestler. Maybe you could try to do the voice when she moves the mouth."

Jump cut!

> Cue the lighting director for the Movie In My Head. The room goes blackout, immediately followed by a pinpoint spotlight that illuminates the shock and utter understanding on my face. An angelic choir does the "aah" voice for a full beat. I look up into an overhead camera. The room slowly lights up and does a slow spin around me, while I—stationary as the room turns—look into the lens and mouth the words, *Thank you.*

Cut! The lights came back up. I was no longer standing. I was sitting across the table from the secretary, who took a last drag on her cig, stuffed it into the ashtray, and said, "I gotta go."

I mumbled something like, "Uh ... thanks. I'll try your idea ... maybe this show."

But she didn't hear me because she was out the front door into the night.

She was a secretary, a part-time employee who moved on in her life without knowing what an impact she had made on mine.

I would never see her again.

But the idea—her suggestion—was valid. Why not do some audience participation? Why not put the puppet into someone else's hands? Why not? Why not? *Why freaking not?*

I was bouncing off the walls with anticipation out in the lobby as the other comics did their sets. Was the audience good? Bad? Attentive? Responsive? I didn't know. I didn't care. All I could think about was getting Sumo up on stage, grabbing a "volunteer," and trying out this new routine.

I had it all mapped out: I would bring the unknowing audience person up. I'd sit her on a stool. I wouldn't show her the puppet until after I explained what I was going to do. She'd have to agree (what choice would she have?), and then I'd get the big puppet. I'd put it on her lap and teach her how to make the mouth move. And then, whenever she opened and closed the mouth, I'd fit words in, kind of like lip-synching. How could it miss?

And it went, for once, according to plan. It went better than I could have possibly hoped for.

I didn't wait. I was introduced, and right away, I asked for a volunteer. Why put Sumo at the end of the act? Let's *do this*! Was it going to work or not? The girl I brought up was very cute, wearing jeans (instead of a skirt, which was important as I would soon learn, because a skirt was awkward for this particular routine) and a loose T-shirt, so there is freedom of movement in her arms. I explained what was going to happen. I got the puppet …

And here, for the first time, came an explosion of I-can't-believe-it laughter and applause. I put Sumo on her lap. The audience was laughing hysterically. I taught the girl how to put her hand into the head so she could control it, and she did so, laughing at the absurdity of the situation.

She opened his mouth right away and I—using ventriloquism—lip-synced without moving my lips. I improvised and put words in Sumo's mouth.

He screamed, "Help!" I

The comedy club crowd exploded. The room filled with the big, bawdy, booming laughs that every comedy act searches for—the ones that define you in the eyes of an audience as "very funny" and will get you booked. A lot.

From that night came more than a decade of laughter and applause. Sumo was a routine that I had to close my set with because nothing could follow it. It was that great.

Sumo was my finale for many years.

> *The Movie in My Head*—I have been aware, at least since college and probably before, that I am starring in my own movie. Long before handheld devices allowed you to selfie / record video of oneself, I've been living a major motion picture. It stars me. Yes, it's all in my head, what my parents would slough off saying, "What an imagination!" Most of it is stock footage and B-roll, mundane stuff that will be discarded or dumped. I'm acutely aware of it at the least opportune times, when I really should be concentrating and focused on the task at hand. What's worse, I sometimes watch the video feed of myself doing something *as I'm doing it*. Some call that an "out-of-body" experience. That's not really what I have. I don't know who's directing, but it's annoying and thrilling at the same time. It's recording as I write this. I can't turn it off.

Years later we were living in New Jersey. The kids were in good schools. Marsia was a substitute teaching, home when the kids came home, working when/if she wanted to. Life, especially for an unknown comedian without any celebrity, was pretty good. We owned a home. We took family vacations. Marsia had a large local network of friends, many of whom dated back to her childhood, and I went to bed each night feeling at least thankful for what we'd made for ourselves.

It was the end of summer, and I was looking forward to whatever the fall might bring. There was some stability in my work between the colleges, the clubs, the casinos, and the corporate gigs. I was getting auditions, and I felt as if something was going to pop. I was optimistic as ever, and all I had to do was keep working hard.

I was at the post office in Moorestown, talking with the counter people there, who I'd come to know as friends since I was there so much. I was joking with the clerks, John and Ida, just enjoying a late-summer day. And an hour up the turnpike, two planes flew into the World Trade Center.

I was booked to play a college in Boston on September 12, 2001. I called my college booking agent, Joey Edmonds, the morning of the twelfth, when the entire nation was in shock, when nobody knew what to do or how to act or what to say.

What do we do about the gig? They want to cancel, right? Why would anyone want to do a show after what just happened?

But the college wanted to honor the contract. They wanted the show. The activities director said, "We all need to laugh," and, "The kids really deserve to know we can go on with our lives," and, "Doing this show is important!"

Well, okay, lady. But I wasn't so sure this was the time to do a puppets and comedy show.

She was adamant. She was definite. She wanted the show.

Marsia gave me the you-cannot-be-serious look when I told her I was driving to Boston to perform. She shook her head and said, "Fine."

But what choice did I have? The show must go on and all that. I packed up the puppets, including Sumo. I drove the six-hour trek to the college and found the room I'd be playing.

It was a small campus just to the west of Beantown, a liberal arts school that looked the part as you rolled in. The walls of red brick buildings were covered in ivy and kids walked around with backpacks and books alongside trees and lawns. Only there was an obvious pall over the place as I found the union building and went downstairs into the student activities area. I found the director. I asked one more time, "Are you sure you want to do this?" She was. So I got my props and did a sound check and wait for showtime.

It was, without any doubt, the most depressing night I would ever work. The students who attended, to their credit, tried to give me some support. But it was pointless. We all knew the truth—thousands of people had died. Heroic emergency support personnel and firemen and women, policemen and women, bystanders, and concerned citizens were doing everything they could. The illusion of "safety" had been shattered. There was no overcoming the sadness and the fear and the unknown that hung over all our heads.

I did my hour on stage. Sumo got some laughs, but nothing like what I had come to expect. I sheepishly accepted a check. I loaded my puppets into the back of my minivan, Sumo half sticking out of his big bag, and headed back for New Jersey.

There was little traffic. I drove alone for long stretches down I-95 thru Connecticut, listening to the news and feeling lost.

When I got to New York State, coming off the Merritt Parkway, I decided to drive to Manhattan. The radio was filled with updates and stories about people helping down in the financial district, "ground zero" as it was already being called. And there were constant advisories that nobody was allowed in the area now. But I thought, *What the heck? I'm gonna see what I can do.*

There was no traffic on the roads but more and more police presence the closer I got to New York City. I took the Cross Bronx Expressway—alone except for occasional squad car—to the Hudson Parkway and turned south toward the city. As I approached the tollbooth just north of the George Washington Bridge, I came to a slow crawl. There were police and armed military personnel waiting. I stopped and rolled down my window just before the tollgate.

"You cannot go into the city, if that's what you're thinking," said an armed policeman, his eyes darting all over the front seat.

I nodded.

Police with flashlights were peering through the windows on both sides of my minivan. I noticed a couple more police appear out of the darkness. And I then was surrounded.

There was a moment of discussion and then, "Sir, step out of the car."

I wasn't going to disagree. I wasn't scared. Everything was suspicious. I understood. I got out of the van. Police opened all the doors, and one of them lifted the back gate to the minivan.

"Sarge, we got a body!"

One of them had seen Sumo, my giant puppet, half-wrapped in the sheet and big travel bag—it probably looked like a military body bag. It probably looked pretty suspicious on September 12, the day after 9/11. I tried to shout, "I can explain!" But it was too late. Somebody yanked the giant puppet out.

A man in military-grade fatigues with a gun stood there holding my puppet. *"What the hell is this?"*

The soldier held Sumo—fully inflated—above his head with one hand. I walked over, carefully took the puppet from him, and explained everything—what I did, why I had Sumo, and that I had done the show in Boston. I showed them my check and the other puppets. There was some discussion.

Then someone said, "Wait here."

I heard a radio call, the distinctive staticky sound of voices on loud intercoms like you might see in war movies. I could make out the words, "And you gotta get down here *now.*"

I was standing behind my minivan, dim lights from the tollbooth making it just possible to see from out of the bushes above the steep grade and from behind the railing on the river side of the road, more armed people materializing from the darkness.

Soon I was standing in the middle of fifteen or twenty police officers or soldiers, holding Sumo, and feeling very self-conscious. There was a long moment of silence.

"Sir, you said you're a ventriloquist. Can you show us how this works?"

Surrounded by armed personnel, wondering if there was a mathematical formula that could explain how so much weirdness could be packed into one day, that is what I did. I got one of the police officers to hold the puppet. I explained what I was going to do—that I was going to voice Sumo when the officer opened and closed the mouth. And I performed.

And they all laughed.

They were an audience.

They *wanted* to be an audience.

The biggest city in the country was facing the greatest crisis on the planet. The population was gripped by fear and a future nobody could see. These officers were at the front edge of that. I think they welcomed the break.

After a ten-minute performance, I packed Sumo and everything up, closed the doors to the minivan, took the GW across to New Jersey, and drove home.

Sumo—the whole package: size, look, mawashi—lent itself to funny. Once I had the concept ... uh ... once I had been *given* the concept by a secretary who probably doesn't even remember me, everything fell into place. Sumo was a showstopper. The act absolutely worked. One reason*: It validated a ventriloquism act because it was drop-dead hysterical.*

Late '90s: I was headlining the Tropicana Casino in Las Vegas, a room called the Comedy Stop. It was a great room to play. All the acts got along, the house was always full, and the chance to play Vegas was icing on the cake. It was a Monday-through-Sunday run, two shows a night, so you became friends with the other people on the show, resulting in a certain camaraderie that rubbed off on everyone.

You got to know each other very well during a week-long gig, and practical jokes started flying as you got toward the end of the week, for the Friday, Saturday, and Sunday shows. The always funny Mary Ellen Hooper and comedy lifer (also very funny) Richie Minervini were the two comics who went on before me this particular week, and on Saturday night, they secretly put a rolled-up towel in the Sumo's mawashi. I didn't discover the prank until I had brought a woman up from the audience, introduced Sumo and sat him on her lap.

That was when saw this big bulge in his garment. It was hilariously absurd and impossible to ignore. I laughed so hard I never really got to the routine. I just stood there looking at it, and then looking at the poor woman holding this gigantic puppet with the … bulge … and reacting to the audience reacting to it and then laughing at the joke they had played on me.

It *still* makes me laugh.

I had played Deja Vu in Columbia, Missouri, once a year for years but had not played the room for more than a decade when I got booked there again. The club had moved, upgraded, remodeled itself, and it was nice. Restaurant and dancing on the first floor, bar and show room on the second—very cool. The sets were fun, and I was asked to go back a year later.

It was 2013. The audience had stayed basically the same from decades before—college students from the University of Missouri and locals from the central Missouri area. It was a drunkfest. There were frat parties and mother's weekend parties sitting with farmers and laborers from the little towns that dot the area. The comics on the show were, for the most part, very good. I was impressed.

The second show on Friday, which always lends itself to trouble no matter where you are, was threat level ten scary. Career-ending scary. Hilariously, unbelievably scary.

I got to the club late. The first show was for a corporate group in Columbia, a roomful of professionals who were having a sales conference at the bar. Not a problem. I threw on my usual uniform—slacks, shirt and tie, proper attitude.

As soon as that first show was done, I raced into the back stairway to the show room to change into my college show clothes. I had left jeans, a shirt, and sneaks there. But when I looked, all I found was the shirt and shoes. Left the jeans in the car? I ran down the stairs, and there, at the bottom of the steps, was a pair of jeans, crumpled and pushed in the corner.

I was running late. I didn't even bother to put on underwear, just pulled the jeans on. Even without underwear, they felt tight—painted-on tight. *Have I gained that much weight?*

I raced back to the show room, no time to put Sumo in place, so I left him in the black plastic liner and got ready to perform.

By the time I got on stage, I had calmed down. I eased into the jokes, doing some music and stand-up. By the thirty-minute mark, the set was going well. I went into my big finish by bringing a woman on stage, took Sumo out of the black plastic bag, got the woman to sit on a stool, and helped her hold the giant figure on her lap. I brought two more people up to work with other puppets. The routine had expanded into a little puppet singing troop, with me directing and inserting my voice as the volunteers moved their puppets' mouths. It was kind of a how-fast-can-you-lip-synch? contest.

I knelt down on one leg with my back to the audience to face my volunteers/puppeteers and direct the song that had become the staple for the Sumo routine—"Row, Row, Row Your Boat."

And that's when my jeans ripped.

Split. *Wide open.*

The jeans sheared from the knee to the crotch on my right leg, the one I was propped on, ripping apart and hanging off my leg. We were in the middle of the song, and the audience was laughing and taking pictures and recording video of the puppets and the volunteers, so nobody noticed that the ventriloquist was, uh, not wearing underwear.

I was fully exposed.

As the routine went on, the volunteers trying vainly to operate puppets as I voiced them, I grabbed Sumo's black liner / garbage bag from the floor and covered myself.

The Movie In My Head was running, doing a fast-forward to someone discovering the ventriloquist who was flashing the audience, and I tried to stay in the moment—doing my act, making the puppets talk, and getting the laughs.

That's how I finished the bit. When the song ended, I stood up, covering my right pant leg and ... myself ... with the black liner and had the volunteers / puppet operators leave the stage. I closed my set by telling some jokes and holding a black garbage liner that covered my right leg and whatever else could have been seen.

I've thought about that night for years. There were some iPhones recording everything that night, and with modern technology I am so *lucky* that someone hadn't noticed what had happened and taken video/pix of me.

That night could have been the end of a career:
"Ventriloquist Exposes Self to Audience"
"Ventriloquist Throws More Than His Voice to the Crowd!"
"Look at This Ventriloquist's Puppet!"

It turned out that one of the waitresses had done the same thing—left her jeans in the stairwell at the back of the room. She had found mine by mistake and put them on. Who else would put their jeans in the stairwell? She spent the night thinking, "I must be losing weight! These are huge now!"

I bought her a new pair.

I dropped Sumo from my act within a year of this incident in Missouri. There were many reasons. The biggest and most obvious was travel. Baggage restrictions with the airlines had become prohibitive. Even when I did manage to pack the puppet in an acceptable case, the cost and the occasional "missed connection" aside, the puppet was so big that sometimes audience members would have trouble sitting with it on their lap (particularly if they'd had a few drinks); Sumo required weekly upkeep. But mostly I decided that, in the socially and politically charged world of "gotcha" video, an Asian puppet being operated by a Caucasian man might be grounds for a lawsuit. Or a CNN expose. Or an indefensible charge of politically incorrect racism.

Why take the chance? I retired Sumo. Fans still request the big guy all these years later.

Chapter Five
The Quality of Laughter

Like the crackling of thorns under the pot, so is the laughter of fools. This, too, is meaningless.
—Ecclesiastes 7:6

Al Franken and Tom Davis were a comedy duo from Minneapolis who had worked with the *Saturday Night Live* crew from the show's inception. Davis was well known and respected for his writing and performances on *SNL*, while Franken went on to become kind of *SNL*'s own "professor emeritus" with tenure. (Not to mention he became Senator Al Franken, which I never would have guessed when we met. But with the advantage of hindsight and perspective, it makes sense). The two had a quirky, subtle, neotheatre approach to their work, and my having been a part of the comedy / Second City / theater-and-club world myself, I was attracted to their style and looked forward to working with them.

I was still kind of a showbiz newbie, getting my act together, when they came to play Zanies Comedy Club where I was the house emcee in 1984.

The guys sold all available tickets to five Zanies shows, due in part to some wonderful press locally, but mostly for the name recognition they had earned as writers and cast members of the "Not Ready For Prime Time Players" with *SNL*.

With that kind of résumé, expectations were high. It became clear very early in their first set on Friday night that they had not been working in front of live comedy club audiences for a while.

As TV writers, actors, and creative types, they didn't spend much time playing saloons. Bottom line? Franken and Davis were integral parts of a hit television program. Their skills, indomitable and rare as they were, did not allow for much stage time in comedy clubs. They had *careers*. So being thrust into a joint like Zanies, where they'd have to work with an "overachieving" (hate that word) emcee (me), who was trying desperately to be funny and clever and hoping to be accepted among his peers, you might say there was some competition.

And if this was some kind of contest? Well, I was winning this one.

People often told me after shows, "You were the best one." Every comic, magician, juggler, ventriloquist, music act, and any other performer you can think of has heard that same phrase. "Out of all the acts, you were the best."

My response was always, "Well, it's not really a competition."

Still, you want to do your best, and you always want to succeed. It's not so much trying to *show up* another act. It's more about showing off—as in showing off your effort and your ethic.

By the time Franken and Davis came to town, I had done a few hundred performances and thought of Zanies as "my" room. I knew the ins and outs of the place. I could read the audience as they came in the front door and sat down. I understood the sound system, where the best seats in the house were, and how to play to whoever was sitting in the way back. I had worked with some big-time acts—Leno, Seinfeld, Richard Lewis. Most of the Franken and Davis ticket-buying crowd was much like me—college educated, maybe grad school, with jobs, some success, and ambition. The audience had a certain frame of reference in politics, music, topical issues, and art.

So? Between my music, the puppets, and the comedy, I was having a blast as the emcee and opening act for the famous Franken and Davis Comedy Duo. If there was such a thing as "my crowd," this was it. My first show, Friday night at 8:00 p.m., could not have gone better. I opened with a twenty-five-minute set, packing into that time frame about forty minutes of jokes and songs and performance pieces. My entire act, to be honest, condensed into twenty-five minutes. There was great energy in the room. The vibe was electric. I gave the guys a rousing intro and walked off stage.

They had an hour and five minutes to kill.

They didn't make it to forty and walked off.

Ricky Uchwatt, club owner and booker, was not happy. Ricky was a businessman. And unhappy ticket buyers meant bad word of mouth, which affected future audiences. Complaints like, "We paid for this? I coulda seen a movie!" can affect ticket sales for a month. Or more. Rick had shelled out top dollar for an oh-so-hip, oh-so-happening, oh-so-hot headliner, and they hadn't done their job. Bert Haas, the club manager, was laughing. "They did thirty-nine minutes! I could do that just using stock lines!"

I was standing with them in the darkness in the back of Zanies by the bar, thinking their "close" was a joke—that they'd walk off stage and then turn around and go back on to uproarious laughter and applause. ("Oh! Wait! We get it! You tricked us! We thought you were done, but you're back! Hahahahahahaha.")

Nope. They walked off. They strode past the three of us in the back of the room as if they had just rewritten the laws of live entertainment, heads held high—which was probably what I would have done, too.

The room was applauding, a tepid "golf clap" that felt more jeer than appreciation. Bert was laughing and said, "They're gonna put us outta business."

Rick grabbed my arm. "Go up there and do twenty minutes."

I couldn't believe it.

No way.

It was an insult for the unknown emcee to "follow" the "headliner" by doing a longish set after he'd done his show. Plus I had blown almost all my material (forty minutes worth) in my first little set before F and D. I told Ricky, "I don't have that much material."

Ricky gave me his platinum stare of anger, as if I'd called him a curse word or insulted his wife. He pursed his lips. He shouted, loudly enough for half the audience to hear, "Go up there and do twenty minutes!"

I looked at Bert. Stone face. "Twenty minutes."

So I did it. I walked back on stage, I stood in front of an audience that was wondering when the joke would happen, and I pulled out a sock. It was a routine I did at the time, taking one of the socks my grandmother and I had made and turning it into all sorts of Chicago-type characters. I was so nervous my hand was shaking.

It was shaking enough that the puppet was shaking—so much so the audience could *see* my hand shaking in the sock. "Umm ... sorry," I stammered. "This puppet has Tourette syndrome."

Not politically correct.

Thank God they laughed—probably because it was such an uncomfortable moment. And I stayed up there and did another nineteen minutes. What I did, I have no idea.

By the second show that weekend, Ricky had me doing forty-five minutes—fifteen in front of and thirty after Franken and Davis.

The next night, Rick laid down the law. I would do forty-five minutes for the rest of the shows.

"But the headliners aren't even doing forty-five minutes!" I whined. "They'll hate me!"

Ricky put his hand on my shoulder and squeezed. "I don't give a sh——t if they get a gun and shoot you," he said through gritted teeth. "They're killing me. I'm cutting them back to thirty-five minutes. Give me fifteen up front, bring them up, and then go up and do another thirty."

So that's what I did. And, as expected, my new comedy "buddies" Al Franken and Tom Davis weren't happy. After the first show Saturday night, sitting upstairs in the "green room," they gave me their opinions. They were sitting with a couple of women. There were some comics hanging out just to catch on to the vibe of real success, hoping some viability might fall off and touch them, and push them over the top and into the stratosphere of name recognition and high visibility.

Me? I was just hoping to make a couple of friends in the business.

Ignorance is not always bliss.

Davis looked right at me and said, "Props are not comedy. What we do is more pure to the form. What you do is a comedy crutch."

Franken was looking at his partner, nodding and smiling. Then he turned his attention to me: "I think we get a higher-quality laugh."

Higher-quality laugh.

Higher-quality laugh. It's tattooed on my frontal lobe. I didn't know what to say in the moment. I didn't make a snide remark. I didn't act as if he'd slapped me across the face. I let it hang in the air like e-cigarette vapor. Then someone changed the subject, and I left the room.

Sometimes life is just like getting on the bus for the first time in seventh grade.

I don't know what kind of laughs I get and I don't care. I do know this. For a weekend, I was better than two people who were at the top of the comedy heap—two people who are, to this day, considered some of the best of their time.

I suppose you can count me as one of those people who—when told, "You can't; you'll never; you're not"—make it our life's mission to show. "I can, I will, and I am!" True, there is something to be said for the old can-do mentality.

There is also something to be said for accepting reality and acknowledging one's weaknesses.

Sometimes I use the words "comedy crutch" to describe what I do—as in, "This is not a puppet! *It's a crutch!*" Comics and insiders always laugh.

Mr. Davis passed away in 2012 after battling cancer, but his legacy and the *quality* (yeah, I used the word) is renowned. Davis is held in great respect by people in the business, particularly as a television comedy writer.

And Al? I hope I get to work with Mr. Franken again one day. Probably won't happen, but I remain envious and appreciative of the singular career he had in television. His long-running success at *Saturday Night Live* is unparalleled. He was part of some of the best comedy scenes and sketches ever written and performed—television or otherwise—and that's pretty impressive.

He just didn't think I get a "quality laugh."

Chapter Six
Non Sequitur

Those who survived the San Francisco earthquake said, "Thank God, I'm still alive." But, of course, those who died, their lives will never be the same again.
—Barbara Boxer (D), Senator from California

Definition: non sequitur. A non sequitur is a conclusion or statement that does not logically follow from the previous argument or statement.

If a person's life is a statement of some sort, a definitive declaration that sums up who and what we are, then I would say I'm a living non sequitur.

I am a ventriloquist. I play piano. I am not athletic.

And here's the non sequitur part: I played college football.

Not just college football. Division I, big boy, Big Ten college football.

Okay, let's be honest. I *tried* to play college football—for the University of Illinois. I've had a lot of time to think about why I did it, and I still don't have a good reason. Then again, does there have to be a reason a person takes on an impossible task, puts oneself in a no-win situation and spends five years in the street brawl known as "defensive line play" with men twice his size?

To give you a complete understanding of the weird relationship between the game of football and myself, we have to go back in time, while remembering that I'm given to fantasy and miracles and major head trips.

My football "career" started at Hinsdale Central High School in fall 1970. I was maybe a just-a-little-better-than-average athlete, *maybe*. But my father's enthusiasm and support elevated my ambition to a catchphrase—"reality be damned." His cheerleading and spirit were intoxicating. His mantra—"you can do anything you want to if you put your mind to it"—was something I took to heart, even though, let's be real, there are *limitations*. Physical, mental, real limitations. You can dunk a basketball or you can't. You are a musical prodigy or you're not.

You are a hostile, mobile, intense competitor who can play "3 technique" and chase quarterbacks sideline to sideline, or you're me.

Since I was (am) given to castles in the air anyway, those words become a rallying point. "Yeah! I can do anything I want to!"

So I went out for high school freshman football.

At age fourteen, I was only gifted in my daydreams.

But my father's unflappable support made me think that I, a pudgy, piano-playing, puppet-loving, scared-of-the-bullies dweeb could play—and succeed—at football. And there I was, first day of practice, coaches yelling at me with some sixty other freshmen in oversize pads and uniforms in the humid Midwest heat of August.

Two experiences made a difference.

The week before my first real competitive football game, on the field for a Friday night practice, I was thoroughly engrossed in the stretching regimen, getting my "muscles" ready for some athleticism. I heard the head coach, Gary Sulaski, a very decent man, shout, "Mason!" I looked up.

There was my mother standing on the practice field, looking horrifically out of place, her hair in a scarf, both hands holding a purse in front of her waist, a long yellow dress and short-heeled shoes. She was smiling. He was too.

He shouted again, "Mason!"

I began to walk toward them.

"You have a piano lesson?"

True. I had piano lessons on Fridays at 5:00 p.m. The last three weeks of summer my teacher, Mrs. Randall, had been on vacation. Now she was back, and it was lesson time. I hadn't touched the grand piano in our living room in a month. I hadn't thought about the piano or lessons or anything but football for the past two weeks. I took off my helmet, looked around at teammates and coaches, total panic setting in—the kind of panic you feel when a terrible, very personal, very *secret* secret is about to be exposed.

I held up my helmet in a defiant pose of strength: I am jock now. Me not go to piano. Me play football.

My mother was a very passive woman, about five inches shorter than I was, and would not touch me for anything other than uncomfortable hugs for our entire lifetime. But this day, maybe emboldened by the machismo of the football field, she reached up and *grabbed my earlobe.* And led me off the practice field.

It would be years before I took piano lessons again.

I started out the season on the A team, but I wasn't playing. I whined. I complained. I moaned. I wasn't complaining to the coaches or teammates of course, but to my father, who knew absolutely *nothing* about the game other than who to cheer for and what a touchdown was. Yet his advice was the best football coaching advice anyone could ever get. "Why don't you tell the coach that you'd rather play on the B team instead of sitting on the bench on the A team?"

So that's what I did. And I played all the time.

The biggest moment of my freshman year came halfway through the schedule and not even during a game. The sophomore coaches decided to give their players a little boost of confidence. It was decided the Hinsdale Central freshmen would scrimmage those sophomores on a Wednesday afternoon in October. I was nervous about it all day—the big kids on the sophomore team were more experienced, cockier, and bigger. And of course, there was Keith.

Remember Keith? He was part of the trifecta of terror on the junior high school bus, who had everyone making fun of my attempt at ventriloquism. Now he was not only bigger, he was also on the sophomore team.

During the first couple of weeks of practice, I had learned that football pads are somewhat protective and absorb some of the physical contact. No matter how hard someone ran into me, it didn't really hurt. Cool. Not only was the cumbersome gear a personal shield, it also gave me a sense of power; safe in helmet and shoulder pads, I was my own kinda plump Death Star.

More importantly, I was bigger and stronger in my mind. "They can't hurt me, but I can attack them!" This led to a life-changing discovery: High school football players do not like getting hit, really hard, particularly in the head—especially if I used my face mask and drove it into theirs. This "technique" made me something the coaches called "a hitter." (Later I would learn college players don't like getting speared in the head either. But they're real *athletes*, and they will hit you back, harder, with some sincerity. I'm not even going to bring up the obvious—head injuries and brain damage—that might lead someone to become, among other things, a professional ventriloquist.)

> This is in no way meant to disparage or demean football players suffering from severe concussions and CTE (chronic traumatic encephalopathy). Big-time football has a problem, and I'm hoping the game adapts. I'm lucky I survived. I was doing what I was coached to do, what I believed was "safe." Years later, I would teach one of my children to do the same thing—which, in retrospect, was dumb.

The coaches decided they wanted to see who in the freshmen and sophomore classes were "players." A test.

I was playing offense, and Coach Sulaski, with whom I had earned credibility after I'd asked to be demoted from the A to the B squad, had me playing offensive guard. "I've never had a player ask to be put down on the B team," he told me.

During the scrimmage, a play was called where I was to "pull" and block the defensive end. We broke out of the huddle. And there, standing in position and looking like a big oaf, was Keith.

The taunting and bullying from the back of the bus, with his pals Greg and Dean, had left one of those deep wounds that don't ever heal—an always fresh scar, a scab that breaks with just the hint of memory. The three of them hadn't forgotten either, and in the hallways at Hinsdale Central, they'd hurl insults and laughter. This was nothing like the misery I had gone through on the junior high bus, but they were still there, pushing a painful memory like a sore tooth. Hey, it's part of daily life as a high school freshman for a lot of people.

How we handle these situations is what defines us.

Here, on a practice football field, I had autonomy. I was safe in my gear. And where (God forbid!) I would never hit someone or insult a person on the school bus, now I had a reason. Plus, I had everything on my side—pads, coaches, my assignment. And looking at Keith, comically cumbersome in his awkward stance and ill-fitting equipment, I wasn't looking at the big thug on the bus. He looked like a cartoon.

I mean he looked like a target.

It was that defining kind of moment that includes every theatrical device you can think of—dramatic character arc, foreshadowing, a crisis that must be resolved, and *payback*.

Mega-adrenalin coursed through my body. I felt as if I'd been shocked with a defibrillator. There was nothing scary about Keith any more. He looked exactly like a revenge fantasy. It was hard to maintain a sense of calm to go along with my anticipation as I lined up and waited for the inevitable. I knew exactly what was going to happen. So when the ball was snapped, I exploded into a wind sprint toward my mark, who did what he had been coached to do—three steps across the line of scrimmage, turn and look into the offensive backfield. I had played the same position myself on the B team for a while, so I knew where he was going, what he was supposed to do, and how he was going to do it. Keith didn't recognize me until the last second. Our eyes met. Recognition: Taylor Mason from the back of the bus, the loser, the kid he'd been verbally abusing for years.

His eyes got huge.

I dug my right foot into the ground about two yards away from his face mask; gathered my arms and hands in fists at my waist; and threw my entire body into the block, driving my nosepiece into the crook of Keith's neck, the exact point where his helmet met his shoulder pads, right under his chin. It was a perfect fit, as if his helmet was a magnet, and my body was steel. And he went down in a heap, limp and soft, like a big stuffed toy you win at the fair. I jumped up and went back to the huddle, mission accomplished. I felt like a tough guy, like an athlete, like a winner. Like I belonged. My coaches were shouting encouragement to my teammates. Nobody said anything about what I had done, other than a general, team-wide, "Good job, boys! Keep it up!"

The sophomore staff wasn't happy. One of the coaches screamed at Keith, who struggled to his feet and tried to get his bearings. "That kid just laid you out! What are you doing? Get off the field! I'm gonna get someone who wants to play football!"

I was in the huddle, hands on my knees, smiling behind my face mask. I watched big Keith shuffle off the field of play and morph into the anonymous pack of nonplayers on the sideline.

Keith quit football that week. He and his buddies never bothered me again.

By the time I was a sophomore, I was a starter. I played "both ways" (offense and defense) and had a blast. Our family moved when I was a junior, from Clarendon Hills and Hinsdale Central High to Ottawa, Illinois. I got to play a lot there, too, for a program that had a rich history of winning championships and big games.

Until I got there.

I was on a couple of perfectly average teams at Ottawa High, teams that lost as often as we won. But who cares? My coaches, Mr. Steinbach, Mr. Murphy, and Mr. Myers, all were supportive. We only had fifteen players on the team. We were outmanned and outsized by every team we played. We lost games to the best teams by lopsided scores, but we beat teams, too. The best part? I played every play, every game.

One teammate, Donny Sutherland, went on to play ball at Augustana College in Illinois. Another, Bob McNamara, was recruited by some major schools, including the University of Illinois and Northwestern University. He accepted an athletic scholarship and played at Vanderbilt University in Nashville, Tennessee. He was a really good player who had a solid college career. I have always envied him, his work ethic, and his commitment.

Me? I was too small, too slow, too weak, and too goofy. I was not recruited by any school.

John Pont, the head coach at Northwestern University, came to Ottawa High School and spoke at our football banquet. During his speech, he described what football at a major university was like. He talked about the stadiums, the players, and the games that were televised. I was transfixed. It sounded fun and dramatic and exciting and like something I had to do!

I went up to him before he left. "Coach Pont? I played here at Ottawa. I'd like to play in college."

He gave me the look I am now used to—*poor guy*—and told me to apply to the school. He'd see what he could do.

I applied to the University of Illinois and Northwestern. Mr. Pont, for reasons I will never understand, called our house and tried to convince me to come to Northwestern. He wrote me a personal letter.

I was accepted by both schools and chose my parent's alma mater—the U of I.

In August 1974, my mother, father, and both brothers took me to Champaign and the sprawling Illinois campus in my dad's big Oldsmobile Toronado. I had a room at the Alpha Gamma Rho Fraternity House, the fraternity of my father, where I would spend a highly controversial first year. As it was mid-August, there was nobody around, so the house was depressingly dark and empty. Fortunately, it was close to Memorial Stadium, where I'd practice with the team. Most of the "brothers" of AGR were not due on campus for a couple of weeks, so I shared the three-story building with maybe two other people, sleeping on a cot on the top floor with no air-conditioning and a fan.

After my mother helped me with the unpacking—all I had were clothes, school supplies, and anxiety, everything organized and ready for my first day of school as if I was a first grader—my family got back in the car. I stood at the front door of the fraternity house. My father shouted, "I envy you, Taylor! You're going to have a wonderful time here!"

They drove away, and I went to my room where I sat and stared at the ceiling. I never went to sleep. The following morning started an intense five-year study of Division I college football. I learned everything about it—the good, the bad, and the many in between nuances of the game.

I was a "walk-on." That meant I had not been offered a scholarship. So when I walked into the bowels of the giant seventy thousand-seat stadium, nobody involved with the football program knew who I was. Nobody cared.

A walk-on is exactly that—a player who is not recruited, is not necessarily wanted, but "walks on" the field with the real players and can be used in certain situations—say as a breathing body players can practice tackling. Or blocking. The walk-on is something that stands there and allows itself to be body slammed by hulking offensive linemen who are seventy-five pounds heavier, four inches taller, and twice as fast.

> walk-on. The college football walk-on is the ventriloquist of the sports world. Ever notice they call the practice bags in football "tackling dummies"? That's not irony. That's not coincidence. That's fact. Football. Dummy. Ventriloquism. Walk-on. It all fits.

By the time my chunky little body got there, the Fighting Illini football program had fallen on hard times. After winning Big Ten Conference championships and going to the Rose Bowl in the 1940s and '50s (while my parents were in school), there had been illegal recruiting and money problems (called "The Slush Fund Scandal"), lean years where the team was a punching bag for everyone else in the Big Ten, if not the entire country, and a long drought of never even sniffing respectability. The best in-state players, from Chicago and its glitzy suburbs, not to mention the St. Louis area, went to other Midwest powerhouse programs—Notre Dame, Michigan, Ohio State, Michigan State, or Purdue. When I got to the first day of practice, the team's biggest star was the placekicker, Danny Beaver.

What did I care? I was a complete unknown.

Somehow I managed to play in games. I earned varsity letters. I am certain that I got more out of Big Ten football than just about any player in the history of the league.

It wasn't easy.

I hope you're not impressed. Our teams were bad. Especially bad. Undeniably, frighteningly, pathetically bad. The Fighting Illini won a total—*total*—of sixteen games during the five (yes, five; I'll explain later) years I wore a bright orange helmet with the word "Illini" stenciled on it.

Irreversible

DEFINITION: Illini. Illini is the name of a confederation of Native American Indian tribes who lived from Lake Michigan west to the Mississippi River in what is now Wisconsin, Iowa, Illinois, Missouri, and Arkansas. The tribes included the Cahokia, Kaskaskia, and Peoria Indians (all names of towns in the state of Illinois today). The mascot for the University of Illinois while I was in school was an Indian chief called Chief Illiniwek, based on the history and culture of these tribes. The chief was banned in 2007, lost to the advances of time and civilization—just like most of the tribes that made up the Illini Confederation.

We didn't just lose. We lost by one-sided, grotesque, impossible-to-tabulate scores. When I graduated, the local sports writers had given up trying to describe just how sad the school's football program really was.

"Illinois lost so convincingly today that school officials want to change the team's name from ILL-INI to ILL-EGITIMATE."

"After losing 52–3 this afternoon, many Fighting Illini players are questioning their right to exist."

"The 48–10 drubbing that the University of Illinois suffered today has political leaders in the state capitol of Springfield debating whether or not to send the school to Indiana."

It was horrendous.

Even more telling, there is a good possibility that I was one of the worst players on one of the worst teams in collegiate football history.

Those first few days of practice as a freshman walk-on were disheartening. Frankly, the coaches had to weed out the quitters. Separate the men from the boys. Find the real "players" and expose the "pretenders." There were costs involved with keeping people around who worked really supposed to be there.

The two-a-day practices in microwave-like August heat were an early indication of just how painful things would get, physically and emotionally, for my entire career. Coaches cajoled and complimented their favorite guys, the ones who had earned starting jobs already, men who would make or break the team. The "stars" were apparent, not so much by their action on the field but by the way the coaches talked to them, referred to them, and endorsed them with a kind of adulation that made me envious and angry.

In my half decade there, I would never be one of those players. I was the last of ninety-five people on the depth chart, even after outlasting more talented, heavily recruited, "can't-miss" kids, who left school when they realized the effort it required to get on the field. It took until the end of my "career" to acknowledge that I was not close to being a "guy."

My second ever week of practice was the first real eye-opener.

I would walk through the just built intramural sports complex (It was air-conditioned! *Hallelujah*!) to get to the stadium for practice. The first time I went through the gym, feeling self-conscious and out of place, a group of guys was playing a pick-up game of hoops. I stood to watch. A humongous human, standing six foot five and weighing at least 275 pounds stood holding a basketball, which looked like a small cantaloupe in his gigantic right palm. He was being coaxed on by a group of men standing around the free throw line at the far end of the court. He raised one hand in the air—a hand that looked to be the size of my chest—bounced the ball three times into the hardwood floor, which shook with each impact; and then grabbed the ball as it rose from the floor after the third dribble. He took two powerful steps to the basket and reverse-dunked, a resounding *event* that must have caused a wave of aftershocks and reverberations throughout central Illinois. People all over the gym stopped and applauded.

He shouted, "If it feels good!"

And a joyful group surrounding him, laughing and patting him on the back, shouted, "Say Hollywood!"

Well, our basketball team is gonna win some games, I thought to myself.

I got to the stadium early. I was nervous. Scared. Intimidated. Everyone was big. Everyone had the swagger and the body of a "jock." I was given ill-fitting shoulder pads and thigh pads. I walked out onto the field, and the real coaching started.

Not for me, of course—I was a "scrub," a member of the "scout team." I wasn't being coached. I was being used.

For my first drill ever, I was handed a large, puffy, inflatable pillow with a handle on one side. A coach told me to stand and, "Use your body and this pad to hit whatever comes at you!" That was easy enough. It was obvious who would be coming at me—a group of large, sweaty men who were fast and strong and who stood in a line about thirty feet away. They looked like otherworldly beings with a purpose.

They looked like real football players.

And they looked angry. The first one up was someone I recognized immediately, even with his pads and headgear.

It was the basketball player from the gym. His name was Revie Sorey. He would go on to block for the Chicago Bears in the NFL. He would pave the way on gridirons all over the country for Hall of Famer Walter Payton. And in a manner of moments, he would send me sprawling to the turf on a forgettable day that happened decades ago.

Revie Sorey came sprinting at me like a raging bull, lowering his face mask to the level of my head, and slamming into me the way a locomotive might run into a stack of kindling. It must have looked like a cartoon. I was Wile E. Coyote being flattened by a large Acme safe. Revie didn't even know I was there. I was, literally, a human blocking *dummy*.

Miracle of miracles, I retained consciousness. The offensive line coach (John Nelson, a short, rotund, but very loud little man) shouted something encouraging to Sorey. Some assistant coach called me "Martin"—as in, "Get up, Martin! This is football! If you want to play, you better get used to being hit." Then he laughed.

He laughed *at* me.

"You're not gonna last the day!" he screamed.

The drill was endless. I was run over forty or fifty times. Maybe more. I was sobbing uncontrollably, hoping other players and coaches couldn't see the tears mixed in with the sweat under my helmet. I wasn't in pain. I was being humiliated, embarrassed, and demeaned. It was soul crushing.

Back at the fraternity that night, I stared at the ceiling, alone on the top floor, sweating in the heat and reviewing my situation. "What is the point?"

I made a plan.

The next morning at practice, half the walk-ons had quit. By the end of that week, all but three or four of the walk-ons had walked off.

> When I finished my freshman season, there were only a couple of walk-ons left on the team, total. The others left or earned a scholarship.

I stayed.

There are very few who stayed, went to every practice, did all the drills, suited up, and played in games but were never given athletic scholarships while on the team for our entire college experience.

In my case, that is exactly how it should have been.

And once again Coach Nelson lined me up for the same stupid "blocking drill."

But things had changed.

I had changed.

This time I held the bag close to my body, exposing my helmet. And as that future NFL All-Pro offensive lineman lowered his shoulder to block me, I launched myself into him, taking my face mask and trying to drive it through his head. I was "protected" by my helmet, of course, and the resulting collision—helmet to helmet—gave me a six-hour headache.

But.

Instead of being run over by my new pal Revie, I jettisoned my entire body, face-first, into his. I knocked him off balance, and we both fell in a heap—me because I was too small to hold my ground, Sorey only because he was so surprised.

Still. I knocked Revie Sorey down.

The coaching staff went ballistic. "*Martin*! What the hell are you doing? I didn't tell you to defend yourself!" D-Line Coach John Nelson was a bowling ball of a man, my size as a matter of fact, so we saw eye to eye as I stood, shakily, to face him. He was enraged, the spittle (was he doing that on purpose?) spraying out of his mouth and onto my face, mixing with my sweat. "If you don't want to be coached, get off the field!" He tried to shove me out of the way so he could walk past.

That didn't work. I was done being a "dummy." His shove had no effect, and he was forced to stop in front of me. His face was red. I could see a vein bulging out of his neck. And now he was poking a finger into my chest—which I could barely feel through my shoulder pads. I wasn't nervous. I wasn't crying now. I stood there and let him scream at me. He was shouting something about "respect" and "players" and "cheap shots." I couldn't hear because my ears were ringing after the collision with the Sherman Tank named Sorey.

An assistant coach grabbed my arm and dragged me to the sideline. Someone replaced me. "Are you crazy? You can't do that," said the assistant. "You might get one of the starters hurt."

A month later, in the first freshman football game of the season, I was the starting defensive tackle for the Fighting Illini squad against the University of Indiana. I don't remember the score or much about the game, other than I had earned a small amount of self-respect.

Make no mistake, this was Division I, so I practiced with players who went on to stardom in the National Football League. Scott Studwell, whose name manifestly made him a pro football linebacker with the Minnesota Vikings, was a teammate. The aforementioned Mr. Sorey had an incredible pro career. Bruce Thornton, a classmate who only saw intermittent action with the Illini, went on to play for the Dallas Cowboys (which should tell you something about our coaching staff). Brad Childress was an assistant who went on to be a very successful quarterback coach and NFL head coach, while Jack Squirek scored a touchdown for the Raiders in a Super Bowl.

Other guys went on to successful careers after college football. As of this writing Jim Kogut is a high-profile defense attorney in Chicago. Keith Burlingame is a very successful international businessman. Randy Taylor runs a football recruiting operation, placing high school players in college.

The training room, where players got their ankles taped and their injuries healed, became my performance area. I spent the thirty minutes before practice and afterward making the trainers—Skip Pickering and Rod Cardinal, two very decent people who put up with a lot of losing—laugh. They were a good audience, happy to have someone entertaining them while attending to the sprained ankles, dislocated shoulders, and broken bones that come with full-contact sport.

Sometime in late autumn 1977, the Ohio State University football squad came to Champaign on a cool Saturday afternoon to face the Fighting Illini at Memorial Stadium (now Zuppke Field). I was in the end zone with my teammates, doing warm-ups and calisthenics as we prepared to get bulldozed by the Buckeyes. I was doing jumping jacks, awkward because I was wearing full pads and a helmet, when I noticed the stands behind me—part of the stadium "horseshoe" and the bleachers—were jammed with people sporting cherry red jackets and sweaters and pennants. Illinois had stuck the formidable OSU traveling fan base with the worst of seventy thousand seats in our stadium. Ha, ha, Ohio State. Maybe you'll win the game, but you'll have to use binoculars to see anything!

As I started stretching my legs, bending down to touch my toes from a standing position, the fans around me began cheering. At first I thought they were jeering me as I contorted my pudgy nonfootball body. I looked up. And there *he* was—walking straight for me and then veering off to stand in front of the faithful up in the bleachers.

They weren't jeering. They were cheering. They were euphoric—because the man walking past me was Woody Hayes.

Woody Hayes—the legendary, fiery, flamboyant football coach who made Columbus, Ohio, a destination for blue chip athletes, major television sports broadcasts, and Big Ten Championship trophies. Woody Freaking Hayes—and he was standing ten feet from me.

If you think I was in awe, it's nothing compared to Buckeye Nation, who were beside themselves with orgasmic joy and religious fervor. Woody waved. Woody laughed. Woody led them—maybe fifteen thousand fanatics—in the OSU alma mater. They had taken over our stadium! They were singing their song louder than our fans could in our own home! It was surreal.

Hayes finished the song. They went crazy. He turned. I was staring directly at him. He was small—maybe my size or an inch shorter. He got a quizzical look on his face. Eye contact. I detected disgust. He spit out these words: "*You're* a Big Ten football player?" He gave a little cackle.

He walked away.

I immediately went down on one knee and said a prayer. "Dear, God, please, please, please don't let me in this game."

It worked. I didn't play. We lost by five touchdowns.

Fast-forward to late fall, 1978. My career was fast coming to an end. The Fighting Illini had traveled to Columbus, Ohio, and we were playing Ohio State on their home field. We were getting shellacked—so much so that I got in the game. Hey, when you're down by thirty-five, there is nothing to lose.

I read a play from my noseguard position as it unfolded—a handoff to a running back—and I chased him out of bounds on the OSU sideline. There, clipboard in hand, wearing his signature windbreaker and a baseball cap with an "O" on it, was Coach Hayes. Once again he was ten feet away. I made my move.

"Yeah!" I shouted. "I am a Big Ten football player! I just pushed your boy outta bounds!"

I turned to run back into our huddle, and I could hear him shouting at me. I don't know the words, but they weren't, "Good job, kid!" He was angry. He was livid. And he was especially mad because I said something to him in his house, on his sideline, in *his* game.

It was over. We lost by a lot. I was shaking hands with players from the other team, and I just wanted to get to the locker room before I ran into Woody for a third time when an Easter Island of a defensive lineman from Ohio State named Byron Cato came over to me. "What did you say to Coach?" he asked me. "He's crazy mad!"

I got out of town with no further damage to my ego, and a month or so went by. I was watching college football, the Gator Bowl, in our TV room in Ottawa, Illinois. Ohio State was playing Clemson, and it was a close game. That is, it was a close game until a Clemson defender picked off an errant Buckeye pass and was returning it down the sideline for a backbreaking TD that would seal the deal and a loss for Ohio State.

And as I stared, openmouthed, at the little TV screen available in late-'70s America, Coach Hayes jumped off the sideline and *tackled the Clemson player*! It was epic and historic and way, way off the grid of acceptability.

Coach Hayes was obviously at the end of a distinguished career. He had championships and a legacy and notoriety. He was, and is, the definition of "bigger than life." But he had gone off the rails by the close of '78. And I, Taylor Mason, walk-on and laughable "Big Ten football player," will gladly take credit for pushing him over the edge.

The first time I actually got on the field was a home game against Michigan State. We were losing big (see the pattern?). I was thrown into the game, and my buddy Keith Burlingame gave me a hand slap as I jogged into the huddle. He had a big smile, as if we were winning. The MSU Spartans center shook his head when he saw me lining up, the customary response to me being on the field of play. Within a play or two, a running back for their team took a pitch out and began to run down the sideline—right in front of my bench, heading for the end zone.

It was time for a performance—maybe not the football kind, but a performance just the same!

"Come back here, punk!" I shouted as the much, much faster player began to put some distance between us. "What're ya scared? You better be!" If there was video, you would see our players—my teammates!—like orange-uniformed dominoes doubling over in laughter as I trotted down the sideline screaming, "You better run!"

We lost, 59–19.

My father came into the locker room after the game. He hugged me. "You did it!" he shouted. "You're a Big Ten football player!"

I tried to calm him down. Most of the team was trying to get showered and dressed and forget about the whipping we had just absorbed. But Bill Mason's son had played for the Illini, on the same field as Dick Butkus and Red Grange and all the heroes yet to come. For him, it might as well have been a Rose Bowl Championship.

He wasn't the only one acting as if something historic had taken place. There was a small band of men, excommunicated to a lonely section in the upper deck of the old stadium, partying in defiance of the score and the losing and whatever sports decorum might have dictated. They were cheering and shouting and celebrating when I ran on the field.

This was a group of men who had taken me in after I was kicked out of a fraternity. I had been rejected, told not to come back because I didn't follow the protocol and rules and the appropriate decorum of modern fraternity life.

But this group, banished to the furthest regions of a huge stadium, was having a party just because I had run on the field. They were my friends, my supporters, and my first real audience. They had my back. They were members of a fraternity called Sigma Chi, and they knew I had beaten the odds.

Chapter Seven
Frat Boy

I got something better than school, but don't tell anybody.
—John Legend / Kanye West from the album *College Dropout*

My father had been a fraternity man while in school at the University of Illinois. He was a member of Alpha Gamma Rho (AGR), populated by young men studying agriculture, and he desperately wanted me to follow in his footsteps. I was happy to do so because I had no idea what was going on. What is college? What is a fraternity? What am I doing? It was the fall of 1974. ABBA sang "Waterloo" on Top 40 radio and Richard Nixon resigned as president of the United States—his own personal Waterloo.

I walked into my father's Alpha Gamma Rho fraternity house to meet mine.

Things did not start out well with my new "brothers" and got progressively worse as the weeks flew by.

I was overwhelmed by the class work, the varsity football practices, the size of the sprawling campus, and the sheer amount of *cool things to do*. It was the middle of the 1970s, and Champaign, Illinois, was a playground of activity that had nothing to do with mundanities like getting enough sleep or applying oneself to what was expected by some fraternity. There were free concerts by fledgling rock bands, poetry readings at the student union, and outdoor preachers on the quad berating students for their "profane lifestyles in the eyes of our Lord!" Not to mention pinball machines and funky stores that sold hipper-than-thou clothing and records and underground literature. Plus, there was a spectacular environment where the leaves turned one day from green to gold and red and then, a month later, disappeared altogether—leaving bare branches silhouetted against steel-gray skies, where cold late-autumn wind lent romance and drama to a walk from Altgeldt Hall to the football stadium. Who had time to follow the rules?

And AGR had rules. I didn't conform. I didn't learn everyone's middle name. I didn't study enough. I wasn't there for important meetings and events (I had football practice). And I didn't take things seriously (studying as a great example). They yelled, and they cursed, and they threatened. One night, I came home from football practice to find a "body" hanging from a tree in front of the house. It was my shirt and pants stuffed, along with a sign that read, "Mason."

I was not a favored member.

They kicked me out of my father's fraternity at the end of the year. The embarrassment! The disgrace! My own personal Greek tragedy. It broke my dad's heart and grew the chip on my shoulder into the Rock of Gibraltar. They said I was not "AGR material." I didn't fit.

They were right.

I moved to a small red brick building the following fall, a nondescript three-story unit called the Armory House. It was far removed from popular Greek life, in another dimension that existed on the periphery, light-years from fraternity row and dormitory life and the expensive apartments that surrounded the bustling campus.

There were less than a hundred men and women living in the twenty-five or so rooms on three levels. My roommate, Stuart, was smart and articulate, a future attorney I'd meet again at a show decades later in St. Louis. There were a couple of engineering students from Saudi Arabia, as well as a mix of Asian Americans and two gay couples who lived clandestinely down the hall. I took a room there only because I had been rejected by a frat, which my new neighbors interpreted as a badge of honor: "Greek life is for the establishment. You're independent now!"

My closest friends were three women who would take me dancing at a local club where a favorite local band, "Starcastle," would play medleys of Rolling Stones and Beatles songs. Three girls and me. I was a couple of years younger, I didn't try to pick them up, and I always went along with whatever their plans were. Plus, I made them laugh.

> Starcastle was fronted by vocalist Terry Luttrell, a local celeb in Champaign. He had been the lead singer for REO Speedwagon, a band that went on to become a multimillion-dollar, platinum-selling power pop group / staple of classic rock music playlists. But he left REO and joined Starcastle, playing bars around Champaign, Illinois, doing renditions of Beatles, Stones, and Yes songs—while watching his former band shoot to superstardom. Starcastle's big hit record, *Lady of the Lake*, sounds exactly like a Yes song. Google it. As for me? Mr. Luttrell personified a showbiz lesson—know a good thing when you see it.

Maintaining my own "Greek tragedy" theme I took a class in mythology from a professor named Scanlan who inspired me beyond whatever I learned about Dionysus and Apollo. This man—a *teacher*—would dress up as one of the Muses and give his entire lecture in character. He told great jokes: "This week is homecoming, which means half the freshman class will think they are required to go home! Let them! By the way, we'll be losing the football game by so much they're going to substitute a wet T-shirt contest for the fourth quarter! *See you there!*" He was brilliantly funny, smart, inspiring, and fun. His class alone was worth whatever tuition cost that year.

I joined a rock band called The Janitors. The leader was a professor's kid, a teen-aged boy named Wes who played guitar. I played piano. And a local (a "townie") named Combine (like the tractor) was the drummer. I pounded a travel piano that Combine's dad had modified—it was an old spinet, electrified, and tricked out with a little monitor and a mike. It weighed about five hundred pounds, so packing it in a van and hauling it to gigs was preposterous and absurd.

A foreshadowing of things to come.

We'd load in to some bar and sound check and then change into authentic janitor wear—gray coveralls. Then we'd wait for the doors to open to the public. As the place filled with people, I'd walk around the bar, picking up garbage and emptying ashtrays and collecting empty cans. After thirty or so minutes, I'd walk up on stage and pretend to play something badly on the keys, picking out notes as if I had never touched an instrument before. The drummer would walk up on stage after me, sweeping the floor and then drop the broom and go over to the kit and bang on the snare and the high hat and the kick. The guitarist would be mopping and then grab his ax and play weird out-of-key stuff. We'd finally reach a cacophony of stupidity.

And then we'd rock. The bar crowd would be puzzled at first, catcalling and jeering us. But then we'd hit a chord in sync, and soon those same people were cheering and acting like we were really good (we weren't). It always amazed us how anyone could be "surprised." The name on the marquis, the promo on the flyers we stuck to lampposts and bulletin boards in Champaign was purposely clear: "Come see The Janitors." There wasn't an effort to hide anything, and we might have had five to six jobs total over the course of two months that fall. Our playlist totaled fourteen songs including a thirty-minute jam on Bachmann-Turner Overdrive's "Takin' Care of Business" (three chords and a lot of shouting on the chorus). We'd just started to get some real bookings when I broke ranks and joined the Sigma Chi fraternity.

It was spring 1976. Two football teammates had convinced me to join their fraternity. I told them, "I don't have time. I already got thrown out of a frat. I'm in a band." They said, "Your band sucks. Come to the house."

> Note. Had I not joined the fraternity, I would have changed the name of the band to "This Band Sucks." Just FYI.

The symbol was a simple white cross, which greatly appealed to the son of a church deacon. They had a grand piano in the living room. They had a library. And there was a certain swagger about them.

There wasn't any hazing. The keys to success seemed to be get grades, make each other laugh, and have a certain amount of cool without promoting it.

> As an adult, I revised that concept - "a certain amount of cool without promoting it" - to this: "enjoying all the perks while at the same time conveying a regular guy disregard toward them." Same theory, better execution.

I joined at the end of that football season, attracted to the camaraderie and support. My former band? The Janitors got a new member in about three minutes, changed their name, and moved on. My friends from the Armory House couldn't believe what I was doing. The women went nuclear when I told them I was checking out a fraternity. They scolded me. "Don't conform! That's not you!" they would say. "Don't give in!"

But I did.

> Years later, the great Ben Folds kind of told my story with The Janitors in his song "Army," which includes the lyrics, "Citing artistic differences, the band broke up in May / And in June reformed without me and they'd got a different name."

The Sigma Chi house itself was a three-story Tudor structure, and in the center of the large living room, surrounded by floor-to-ceiling windows and dark wood walls, was a baby grand piano. Two older guys—"Mak" and "Ragu"—intrigued by me, a football playing pianist doing Elton John impersonations, were doing a duet the day I moved in. It was something like a waltz, on the piano. I was drawn in immediately. We talked music for an hour during my first visit. Funny and smart and genuinely interested, Mak and Ragu had an attitude that anything is possible. Success and fun and an exciting future were one dominant seventh chord away.

> Greek life—fraternities and sororities—is under the microscope of social change as I write this in 2018. The idea of all-male and all-female "houses" might be coming to an end. I don't know if that's good or bad. But I saw two sides of Greek life as a student, and I don't regret either one. And living away from a fraternity was a good experience, in my case, as well. I am forever grateful to Sigma Chi and the many people I lived with I still call friends.

I sustained a severe football injury in the fall of my junior year on the new "synthetic turf" at the football stadium. The team doctors had to reconstruct my left knee, and I spent September to December in a hip-to-ankle cast.

> My knee surgery was prehistoric by today's standards. They opened up my leg, retied a damaged ligament, scraped off the kneecap, and sewed me back together. I rehabbed for seven months. I have a ten-inch scar and a lot of swelling still. In 2018, the same surgery would have be done with a laser, and I'd have been back on the field after a week or two.

Reader alert! Something life changing is about to happen!

It was a Saturday night at Sigma Chi in the fall of '76. I was sitting by the record player at an "after-hours party" with a fraternity brother who is acting as "deejay." In other words, he was doing nothing more than putting dance songs by KC and the Sunshine Band or Stevie Wonder on a turntable and letting the song play through. There were often thirty-second-to-three-minute breaks between songs because nobody wanted to be stuck doing the deejay work—everyone wanted to dance and talk to girls.

This night, with my leg in a heavy cast and the thought of dancing at least four months away, a man named Curly (his real name is Mike Allen, but they all had nicknames here—Colonel, Bosco, Fugues, Squid, Zemo, Baby Huey, Lurch, and so on) handed me a microphone he had plugged into the sound system. "Say something while I find another record," he directed.

There were couples standing in the dining room, which had been turned into an ersatz dance floor, with chairs and tables pushed back against the walls and giant speakers hanging from the corners of the room, producing ear-crushing noise befitting the sensibilities of the 1970s.

Nobody was paying attention. Nobody. I sat, pity partying off to the side with my cast and crutches, miserably holding a microphone while people milled around waiting for a song so they could dance. Nothing was going on—no sign, no bolt of recognition, no burning bush.

I spoke into the mike. "Hey! Welcome to the Sigma Chi after-hours party, where you're allowed to dance even if you have the rhythm of a furnace! Like most of these guys here tonight."

The music kicked in, and I hopped around on my one good leg, doing an ersatz Chuck Berry duckwalk and—*hello!*—people were giving me smiles and thumbs-ups and telling me to do more. I spent the night talking between songs, killing time, making people laugh, and enjoying my newfound power. It was easy. I picked on what people were doing, what they were wearing, how they danced, and how they reacted. The laughter was intoxicating. My little "raps" got longer and longer as the evening wore on. The room filled with dancers and people drinking beer in red plastic cups waiting for my next monologue. I was having a blast.

It got better.

A student I recognized, someone from campus but not a Sigma Chi or football teammate walked up to me. "I'll give you fifty dollars if you do this act at my fraternity tomorrow night."

Cut to the Movie In My Head.

> Cue the choir. Close-up of Taylor's face. Stop-motion shot of Taylor as the room spins around him, the lights flash, and cartoon dollar signs appear in his eyes.
> I can get paid to make people laugh? *What have I been doing with my life*!?

And my career was born. For the rest of my time at the University of Illinois, I would spend every weekend (unless I had a road game with the Illini, which wasn't often) performing at some campus or fraternity/sorority function. I begin buying LPs (long play vinyl discs) with dance songs and disco hits from a Chicago distributor called Dogs of War Music.

This was the beginning of "scratching," where live DJs / record spinners in Chicago clubs had started imitating the trend in New York. They had two turntables and would use their fingers to stop and start one record, while beginning a song on the second turntable. I was the only white customer at Dogs of War. They showed me some of the tricks of the trade. I wasn't interested. I was doing comedy.

Ah, the late 1970s. Disco was king. Live bands had been replaced by dance music recordings. Comedy was not only "hip," it was a mainstream part of the zeitgeist. *Saturday Night Live* was rocking the world. Steve Martin was performing to sold-out audiences in basketball arenas all over the United States of America. Combining those two worlds—disco and comedy—made Taylor Mason a "name" in Champaign.

And whoa! I was making money. I was booked months in advance. I wasn't even looking for a career, but the stars aligned. I joined a popular fraternity that threw huge parties. A microphone was hooked into a sound system. I had a severe injury that kept me sedentary.

Unknown to everyone, I was a "closet ventriloquist." Remember? The self-inflicted skill I had rehearsed alone for years? Now, getting paid to entertain people, I had to give them a show. I had to *earn* my money. Desperate for material, performance content, and some substance, I resuscitated my old pal Ted, and I wrote a routine about college dormitory food, roommates, and our bad football team. ("I'm a running back for the Fighting Illini," said Ted. And I said, "Right. I bet you're a tackling dummy." We took a beat and then Ted hit the punch line, "If you're a running back for the Illini, you *are* a tackling dummy!").

I wrote jokes about the university president, hippies, dormitory food ("Ahhhh! Make it jump back on your plate!"), the bookstore, and dorm life versus Greek life.

Kismet! For the next two years, I got booked doing three-to-four-hour dance/comedy/party shows for audiences all over the campus. I didn't have to advertise because the campus was so interconnected that, once the word was out, I become the first call when someone is having a "formal" dance or party and wanted something other than a band.

I applied basic marketing concepts from my Ag Business 101 class, and my performances evolved quickly into a little business. I used the Sigma Chi fraternity sound system for the first year, dragging it to parties at every kind of Greek system function that hired me. Dances, Christmas bashes, Mother's

Day weekend shows, and an occasional gig for the university all fell into my lap. I bought a top-quality turntable and then another one, so I could "mix" the music. My final year there, I bought a mike and monitor and would set up my equipment an hour before the events started.

Ted would sing bad versions of pop songs to girls (off-key and with ribald lyrics that I'd make up on the spot—always a crowd-pleaser). I did a version of *The Brady Bunch* theme song as done by Chicago Cubs sports announcer and living legend Harry Caray. This I had actually started doing in the trainer's room at football practice, and it had made my teammates laugh. "Here now is a man named Brady. He's bringing up three young men on his own. Four guys living all together, and ... Hey! A base hit by Buckner!" It worked every time.

This was my first foray into business, and it had little to do with the classes I was taking at the university. My bookings came from word of mouth and being seen around campus. One promotion gimmick I used came between Thanksgiving and Christmas break. I would go to every sorority during the last week or two of the semester and bring Ted, walk into the dining room, and do a short Christmas skit. Usually it included a holiday song with parody lyrics: "He knows if you've been sleeping; he knows when you're awake; he knows if you've been bad or good. Hey, this guy is a stalker! Somebody call the cops!" Those short "teasers" would get me ten to fifteen bookings for the following couple of semesters without having to do any advertising at all! Then I'd do the same thing the following Christmas and get a few more.

To write the jokes I would put myself in my vent buddy Ted's shoes. What would it be like to have someone literally holding you all the time? What would it be like to live out of a suitcase? What is the personality of someone dealing with that? It led to sophomoric punch lines my friends laughed at:

Me. So how do you like living at Sigma Chi?
Ted. It sucks.

Me. Why? It's an awesome house! It's big, a classic example of Tudor architecture, well-maintained.

Ted, *with a long look at me.* Sure. For you. But where do I stay?

Me, *nervous.* Okay. Okay. Let's not get personal.

Ted, *looking around.* Yeah. He keeps me in the dirty clothes. Folks, this is no lie! I'm sleeping in underwear that looks like the helmets of the Cincinnati Bengals!

There is no irony or coincidence. I was meant to be in Champaign, Illinois. I played Big Ten football. I had amazing teachers (thank you, Dr. Evans and Mr. Curley and Professor Scanlan). I dated the dean's daughter (to Dean Wessels and daughter Kathy, wherever you are, thank you for putting up with me).

Sigma Chi turned out to be another one of many lucky breaks I cannot repay.

I spent hours playing that piano in the living room, trying out jokes, and rehearsing my act. I played when I woke up, I played late into the night, I played when there were people packed in the room, and I played when nobody was around.

I still do college shows all over the place because, believe it or not, the requests keep coming in. Whenever I show up on some leafy campus quadrangle or at a university auditorium, I stop and time travel. For just a moment, I'll be back at school. Drama. Excitement. Intensity.

By the time I graduated in spring 1979, I was making money as a live entertainer. There were no classes in comedy writing, no labs for ventriloquism, and no professors teaching how-to-get-booked. But there is no doubt—I majored in show business. Forget the words on my diploma.

Oh, yeah. I almost forgot. I majored in agriculture.

The diploma from the University of Illinois reads, "Bachelor of Science in Agriculture Communications." I majored in the same business my father was in—farm broadcasting. I even had job offers right out of school. But I didn't answer the letters.

Farming played a big part in my life and the Mason family is an apropos representation of the *original* business of the United States. Many Masons began as farmers, but most of us have moved into other professions. The holdouts are my Uncle Art and cousin Matt and family who still farm in Grand Ridge, Illinois. My cousin Leanne bought a dilapidated farm and farmhouse over in Indiana and turned it into a winery, growing grapes and saving the land. Another cousin, Mark, works in ag-related business. My father spent a career in farm news and farm broadcasting.

Me? I majored in it and, on occasion, find myself in front of audiences that include agri-business people, ranchers, food marketing professionals, and growers of all sorts of produce. Not to mention livestock managers, grocers, wholesale food distributors, veterinarians, and so on. I'm always happy to work for these people because I *get it*.

At the very beginning of this nation, from the first Thanksgiving through the Thirteen Colonies and the Revolutionary War, 90 percent of the US population farmed. Today, everything is reversed. Maybe 10 percent of the population does some kind of farming in the current millennium.

Today's US agribusiness person accomplishes as much as fifty farmers did in the middle of the last century. They're in one of the world's most competitive businesses. That $150,000 combine you see on TV commercials is essential in this environment (I used that word on purpose). It's farmer versus farmer, farmer versus state, and farmer versus foreign governments.

> I maintain there are *millions* of people in cities all over the world who are farmers at heart—they just don't know it. They're growing kale and cilantro and peppers in their garden. They're raising chickens in the backyard. They have a penthouse in the city, but they grow strawberries and raspberries on their roofs.

Farmers, inexplicably, get very little respect. On both coasts and in the big urban areas of the United States, in the suburbs and nonrural parts of the US of A, Americans see the farmer and the business of agriculture as a song: "E-I-E-I-O."

Go ahead. Ask someone from Hollywood or the Upper East Side in Manhattan about farming, and you'll get Charlotte's Web references. "A farm? Oh, isn't it the wild place where sheep, rats, spiders, and pigs live together and talk in a secret language and the spiders write words in their webs?" Great.

Agriculture is where you still find the "free market," a concept that's a myth everywhere else. Well, everywhere *except* your local farmer's market. There, the laws of supply and demand, price points, and service still hold true. The medium-size American farmer is a true hero in this modern world, using all his and her skills as mechanics, agronomists, veterinarians and accountants to expertly guide modern farm biz and feed the United States of America, if not the world. See all those in-country farms from your window seat as you fly across the United States to "work" or take a vacation? If they were given free reign, these American farmers could feed the world—three times over, every year.

As someone who's spent a career in this business we call "show," I've always wondered, How come there are no awards, no trophies, no special televised events, and no cultural recognition for *the people who grow and harvest and raise the food*!?

Wait. I know why. Because it's really, *really* hard work that most of us take for granted and have no clue how it happens.

Fave quote from a newspaper reporter in Miami when I told her my family once raised hogs: "Really? How do you grow a pig?"

> Farmers don't know it yet, but rural areas are merely colonies from which cities suck the wealth, particularly those big urban areas on both coasts that make outrageous demands of the medium-size ag folks.

By the way, I'm not talking about corporate farms, which I like to call "groundhogs." They buy up lots of land, and they took traditional farming in a completely different direction. In their perfect world, there are twenty rows of corn from Ohio to Florida, and every year, they plant going north in the spring and then turn around and harvest going south in the fall. Corporate. Like factories of the field. We did this on a smaller scale back in the 1920s and '30s. It was called "the Dust Bowl."

DEFINITION: Dust Bowl. The Dust Bowl was three periods of severe drought during the 1930s. Once-in-a-lifetime dust storms did massive damage to the environment and ecology of the American and Canadian prairies during this time. Insufficient farming practices and a complete failure on behalf of farmers, researchers, and the government helped cause the ecological debacle and helped further the Great Depression. A failure to apply dryland farming methods to prevent wind erosion (aka, the Aeolian processes) caused much of the disaster.

> Ken Burns, the iconic filmmaker, produced one of his finest movies about the Dust Bowl. Burns, by the way, has tackled pro baseball, the Civil War, jazz music, and cancer, in addition to his reportage on the Dust Bowl and other consequential subjects. He and I were in negotiations to do a four-episode take on ventriloquism, but things hit a snag. I wanted a six-figure advance. Mr. Burns would not take my calls.

But that's one of the points. The American farmer has not only learned from mistakes, but he/she has improved, dramatically, the way we create food. The mid-size people I'm talking about can turn a profit on the same amount of land it takes a "groundhog" to turn his giant tractor around on. Google no-till plowing. Created in Ohio, this is the way to grow crops year to year without disturbing the soil by plowing or "tilling" the field.

Ever wonder how the Amish turn a profit on a parcel of land the size of your Hollywood millionaire's front yard? Hmmmm.

> By the way, I have performed for the Amish. Yes. I've worked shows in Pennsylvania and northeast Indiana for Amish audiences, and if that sounds like it might be odd, *you have no idea*. Still, they were respectful and attentive, and they even laughed (sometimes).

Here's an annoying truth: There is only one way to have twenty-seven varieties of apples and three cuts of T-bone steak. Something has to be used that will ward off disease. At the same time, nobody on the planet is more aware, more cognizant, or more careful than American farmers when it comes to making yields bigger, beef better, and poultry and pork healthier. There is a good reason that organic food is more and more available—and more expensive.

Ag business people invented no-till plowing. They apply that same intelligence, care, and attention to *every* part of their industry.

> The Mason family never had "mad cows" (Think the "mad cow disease" from the 1990s). But there were some very well-read swine. Sometimes we'd walk in on them in the barn as they were reading a Stephen Hawking treatise or some obscure piece by Neil deGrasse Tyson. Once, while giving her a shot (to protect her from disease), a sow told me, "You need to understand this: There is an alternative reality superior to our own. That and the idea that nature is intrinsically incomprehensible, which means that actions and outcomes are not dictated. Likelihoods can be projected. That is, they can until they are observed, and even then, they can only be solved and illuminated by standard equations of quantum mechanics." In addition we kept finding stolen library books in the pigpens. Complex formulas and scientific data, explaining the very building blocks of life, atomic energy, and quark theorems had been written on the pen walls. Those swine, by the way, became bologna and bacon and hot dogs, which, clearly, is the original "brain food."

Here are three solid reasons to support mid-size and small farmers: 1) In all cultures throughout history, the denser the population the smaller and more numerous the farms—until now—so maybe that should change. 2) It's cheaper—*much!*—to raise zucchini yourself rather than buy from some megafarm. 3) People realize, more and more, we are what we eat (apparently I've been eating unknown hack comedians for years). If that is true, which I believe, then we must take what we put into our bodies very seriously.

I point this out because I worked for my Uncle Art when on his farm, where I learned to drive a tractor. I walked soybean fields picking milkweed. I hosed down and cleaned out pigpens and then studied agronomy and hybrids and livestock at the University of Illinois, where I earned a degree in agriculture.

How did I put that experience to use in a career in comedy?

I added a couple of pig puppets to my act, which made sense from a personal point of view: Uncle Art raised hogs, and I worked for him.

Moreover, directly related to my creative/workaday life, I find I get the best results when I use careful, orderly, slow, semi-agricultural processes. Like writing this book, as an example.

Chapter Eight
The Theory of Relatives

*A man who doesn't spend time with his
family cannot be a real man.*
—Don Vito Corleone (Marlon Brando), *The Godfather*, 1972

In defiance of all that is holy, and in direct opposition to whatsoever is good and right in this world, I was given a degree by the University of Illinois School of Agriculture. It was a supernatural surprise to myself and (I'm sure) anyone who knew me, considering that, by May 1979, school was a complete afterthought, an annoying part of everyday life that hindered my thriving comedy/ventriloquist/deejay business.

By far the best part of my final year at the U of I? My brother Tony came to campus. He joined the fraternity, and we spent a lot of time together. While my brother Locke had turned me on to underground rock music albums, Tony took piano lessons with me. Where I was ashamed to show my ventriloquism "talent" to the general public, Tony was my audience for many years as I practiced with Ted. At Illinois, we walked around campus together, talking music, sports, and show business. On rare occasions, we even talked school. That closeness would change both our lives in the coming years.

College was over. Everything and everyone moved on. Friends and teammates from the university would spend the next couple of decades mimicking life as we knew it. There were marriages and grad school and children and divorces, heart attacks and near-death experiences, followed by grandkids and bankruptcies and successes beyond what anyone could have predicted. There was epic individual achievement (example, one good friend swam the English Channel). Some worked with presidential administrations. There were inventors who turned dreams into patents and moneymaking ventures, and there were affairs and suicides and countless stories of successes and failures. Someone became the most sought-after gynecologist in the Chicago area. A close buddy went to prison for five years. Yet another saved the Boston Public School System millions and millions of dollars the day before a stock market crash.

The year I graduated, 1979, was a pivot point for the country. The nuclear power plant at Three Mile Island in Pennsylvania had a major, future-of-the-planet-altering accident. Michael Jackson released an album called *Off the Wall*, which went platinum seven times over and is still played regularly on the radio, in clubs, and in remixes and mash-ups forty years later. The popular Chicago radio personalities Steve Dahl and Gary Myer were changing the format for AM and FM, turning "disc jockeys" into "personalities" and—along with someone out east named Howard Stern—reinvented radio.

> Steve Dahl and Gary Myer hosted "Disco Demolition Night" at Comiskey Park on the South Side in the summer of '79, which resulted in a riot, and the Chicago White Sox had to forfeit a pro baseball game. Our paths would soon cross.

John Paul II visited the United States of America at the same time gay rights marches and demonstrations were taking place in cities on both coasts. The Iranian Ayatollah Ruhollah Khomeini took forty-four American hostages, introducing the Middle East to the United States up close and personal—the Iran hostage crisis.

I, of course, only knew about these current events in a vacuum. I was happily secluded in Champaign, Illinois, with no job and no idea what I was going to do. I took flying lessons with the university, in a Piper Cub airplane, and had nine solo hours as a pilot before I left. It's the perfect metaphor because my head was literally in the clouds. Fear of failure kept me from doing anything for three months after graduation. I briefly considered hanging around the university for another year, making money with my little deejay/comedy operation.

I finally did what most middle-class college graduates do when they can't (or won't!) find a job.

I moved in with relatives.

My Aunt Ardie (real name, Ardelle, which I have always loved, but she started calling herself Ardie at a very young age) had married my Uncle Gene Baroni, a hard-nosed, hardworking accountant from Michigan who had become megasuccessful with a well-known firm in Chicago. They lived in a beautiful house in a secluded part of Oak Brook, Illinois, a tawny suburban home to wealthy business people, a designer mall, and the McDonald's Corporation. They gave me my own room, and I became a kind of "big brother" to three cousins—Peter, Danny, and Michael.

I'm sure that experience traumatized them for life.

Aunt Ardie was my de facto big sister. I had spent countless holidays and family get-togethers at her house. She let me watch the Smothers Brothers Comedy Hour on television when I was a boy (my parents would *never* allow that kind of noncomformity and social rebellion at our house), so I saw Steve Martin before he became Steve Martin. More meaningful to me, the patter between Dick and Tom Smothers seemed like what I could do as a ventriloquist. It was state-of-the-art and timely comedy.

The Smothers Brothers TV show only aired for a couple of years in the late 1960s, but it's still a major influence on comedy as we know it. I would meet Tommy Smothers years later, performing at a golf club in suburban Los Angeles. I'm still a fan of that show and the roster of talent that worked behind the scenes.

Irreversible

My aunt and uncle watched *The Tonight Show.* More than just watching, they got the jokes. Where my folks were in awe of Bob Hope and Red Skelton as examples of "good comedians," Aunt Ardie liked David Brenner and Tom Dreesen and Robert Klein and Dick Gregory, not to mention Johnny Carson (who Bill and Patricia found "a little much").

> As stand-up comics were becoming more and more acceptable in society during the 1970s, it would be at least fifteen years before "ventriloquist" was accepted in the same way. Until at least 1985, using the word "ventriloquist" resulted in an indictment and an affidavit, plus jail time.

This is important. I grew up surrounded by family and good people, all of whom were supportive, loving, kind and fair-minded. My aunts and uncles all took interest in my accomplishments. They helped me through my failings. My brothers and cousins and in-laws have followed my career and have paid to watch me perform. To this point, I have not paid anything back. Or forward. Or sideways.

Uncle Gene Baroni and my Uncles Art and Phil, are the most honest people I will ever know. Gene Baroni's reputation and trustworthiness had earned him lots of high-end clients in the Chicago area. Business people from all walks of life came to him for help with their tax "situations." He dealt with each one personally, professionally, and without pretense, which earned him the kind of reputation very few people know. His funeral would draw thousands of people from all over the globe to salute a man who made a difference in their lives. He, like my father and other uncles, was someone to look up to. They were heroes.

Gene Baroni had a client who ran a popular, iconic Italian restaurant in Chicago—The Como Inn. It was being run by the sons of its founder, Joe Marchetti, and the family trusted my uncle with more than their taxes. That relationship was good enough to get me a job as a waiter with The Como Inn Banquet Service, beginning with a big party at a mansion on the north shore of Chicago, in the uberwealthy suburb of Winnetka.

Early autumn 1979, and there I was (Mr. College Graduate) in a waiter's outfit—white shirt, black bow tie, vest, and slacks. I was a catering drone at a well-heeled dinner after a society wedding, so I was "on location" at an estate with an impossibly spectacular view overlooking Lake Michigan. After walking through the umpteen hundred rooms in the joint, serving hors d'oeuvres on a sterling silver tray to a countless number of people who looked like models for hire in tuxedos and evening wear, I found a large music room. It was the size of a small airplane hangar, with giant windows looking out over the lake, and in the center was a Baldwin grand piano. The top was open, the keys pristine and perfect (untouched?), so I could not stop myself. I put the tray down on what must have been a priceless antique desk, walked to the piano, and began playing.

What ensued was no different than Sigma Chi at a Saturday night after-hours party. I was just four hours north, and the crowd was a little older. So? I played a Beatles medley. I did my Jerry Lee Lewis impression of "Great Balls of Fire." I played "Werewolves of London" by Warren Zevon. And soon there was a crowd of people standing around me, shouting out songs and singing along, laughing at my jokes, shaking their heads, and booing good-naturedly when I said something stupid. I did some Rolling Stones and "Saturday in the Park" by the group Chicago. The room was soon packed with people cheering and clapping with the music and having a party. I was very comfortable. This was the kind of stuff I was *good at*. So I performed for maybe forty-five minutes.

Soon one of my bosses entered the room, wondering what all the excitement was.

Stefano Marchetti didn't get mad. He let me play a couple of more songs and playfully interrupted my concert saying, "If you think you're going to make extra money for entertaining, you will need a lawyer."

Everyone laughed.

He rolled his eyes and smiled and said, "Would you please get back to work now? We are catering a major event here!"

As people filed out of the room, some patting me on the back and shaking my hand, a very large man with a martini handed me his business card.

"Call me first thing Monday," he said. "I have a job for you."

His name was Arnie Morton. He owned a restaurant.

You could say my professional showbiz career started as a lark. You could say all my first jobs in show business were pure luck. You could say that I had a bunch of breaks fall in my lap. And you could also say that, had I never hurt my knee or taken the job at the caterer or joined Sigma Chi or watched Shari Lewis or looked at those socks in the drawer with the smiles, I would never have walked on a stage to do a performance or even tried to make a living in entertainment.

You could say those things, and you would be right.

But the beginning, the start of my life in show business, came directly from my Aunt Ardie and Uncle Gene.

Arnie Morton gave me a half-year contract to play piano in his establishment. Morton's Steak House was already a Chicago institution when I walked into the popular waiting area/bar on a Tuesday night in October 1979. For the next six months, I played a clear plexiglass, see-through piano Tuesday through Saturday nights, making a salary and tips. The crowd was upscale. Older. Refined. They liked boogie-woogie, so I played a lot of that, plus Sinatra and show tunes. I was really a form of live Muzak—background music, playing for folks who waited to be seated in the restaurant. Sometimes they'd give me a big tip if I played a song they'd requested, and I bought a "fake book" so that I could please as many folks as possible.

After that, I took another piano bar gig at the Tip Top Tap in Chicago, because the owner offered me fifty dollars more a week.

I went in to tell Arnie Morton I was leaving. When I told him why he said, "Taylor, you do a nice job, but you're too good for this. You don't want to be a piano player in a saloon. Set your sights higher, kid." He gave me a hundred-dollar bill in a handshake with a smile.

DEFINITION: fake book. A "fake book" contains chord charts and lyrics to a couple hundred popular songs. The arrangements are sparse but usually you get close to what the song is supposed to sound like. I often wish there were fake books for other things—joke writing, for example. Or parenting. How about a fake book for life?

The Tip Top Tap was paying me more money, but it was one of the most depressing places I had ever been. Where Morton's was a very popular Chicago hotspot, always full and always hopping, The Tip Top Tap drew the same group of men every night. They sat on stools at the bar and drank the same drinks while I tried to entertain them. It was on the top floor of the Allerton Hotel on Michigan Avenue, so when I first walked in, I thought I'd be playing for a similar crowd as Morton's. Instead, I was living the lyrics to "The Piano Man" by Billy Joel. I made the mistake of playing that song near the end of my first night there, as my big "closer," and one of the regulars requested it every single night for the next six weeks—which was exactly how long I lasted.

From there, I got hired by Henrici's in Oak Brook, Illinois, minutes from Aunt Ardie's house. This became another home for me, where I felt like I was getting better as a live performer, musician, ventriloquist, and comedian. By fall 1980, I had a solid hundred-song repertoire, along with a small following of drunks and shoe salesmen from the Oak Brook Mall who would listen to my Barry Manilow and Elton John renditions. Plus, I added my wooden ventriloquist sidekick JP to the mix.

Who was JP?

In lieu of a graduation gift from college, my father found a woodenheaded "professional" ventriloquist dummy at a magic shop in Chicago. It had been built by a puppet maker from Michigan, Robert Scott, who had only started making the dolls as a hobby; he wasn't a vent himself. These generic kinds of "figures" cost $200 to $250 at the time and featured a balsa wood-and-composite head on a stick. There was a lever on the stick that was controlled by your thumb, so it was very similar to the figure my father had made (Ted). I had not touched this new professional ventriloquist figure since taking the job for Arnie Morton. But after getting the gig at Henrici's, I was in a similar position to the one at college, where I needed more material, and I needed it fast.

Enter my vent character, JP, so-named for the person in those live radio commercials heard Pervis do when I was a boy.

> Decades later, I met Robert Scott, the man who had built the first real ventriloquist figure I used for years. He had moved to Las Vegas and was living with family there. I was working on *Children Talk* a kids TV show filming in Sin City. Scott had built many figures as a hobby. I thanked him. It was a pitifully small acknowledgment and credit for what his handiwork had done for me. So here is a better one—*thank you, Robert Scott*!

My gimmick at Henrici's was to put JP on the piano, as if he were a little person or child sitting next to me, his head covered by a white straw hat, looking down. As folks gathered around the bar, stuffing my tip jar and singing songs, I would start a ventriloquist act. JP began by interrupting me, or the guests; making wisecracks; and generally being a nuisance. It was very spur of the moment.

A bonus was the bartender, an accomplished out-of-work actor named J. Burton Reynolds. (He's not out of work any more!) We quickly formed a working relationship. Burton treated JP as "real" and would play along as we performed little vignettes and scenes. I'd pull the straw hat off JP and do a short routine, and those impromptu presentations got longer and longer and worked well enough that sometimes I did more performing with the puppet than at the piano. There was no break, no "set" to the evening. I'd come in and sit down at the piano, and someone at the bar would sidle up to me on the piano bench.

"Can you play 'Mood Indigo'?" he or she might ask.

A voice would come out of nowhere. "He tried to play that yesterday. He can't. Besides, I hate that song. Get real. This piano player doesn't know any music written before 1970. He's a lost cause."

It's a ventriloquist trick: I swallow my voice, so it's audible but not very loud, and I look, intently, where I want the listener to "see" who is talking.

There would be a pause. The person requesting the song would look at me, but I was looking at the little figure sitting on the piano, who was not moving. I'd gesture toward him and say, "I'm so sorry. This is JP. He's obnoxious." I'd grab the wooden doll, pull his hat up to reveal his face, and my inanimate partner would come to life, looking right at the patron and making a wisecrack: "Taylor does a really good version of Chopsticks. Wanna hear that? Anything but 'Mood Indigo.' *Puh-leez.*"

Ventriloquism, done right, is a mash-up of performance skills. The illusion that a voice is coming from someplace other than the speaker (not unlike a magician using misdirection); the ability to act, as in theater, so the 'character' of the puppet/figure is 'real' and there is tension, dynamic, story, and so on; and the technique—talking without moving one's lips—that pulls it all together.

Some nights, I'd do my forty-five-minute musical set and then head to the bar with JP. Mr. Reynolds would put a bar cloth down. I'd put the wooden molded puppet hand on the cloth—the fingers were really just a part of one unit—and I'd move the body enough so it appeared that JP was cleaning or dusting the bar.

People would gather around to see what was going to happen. Eventually, after some bits of business where Reynolds and I would try and help JP move the rag a little bit, dialogue ensued:

J. Burton Reynolds. "JP, are you okay?"

JP. "Nah. Feeling kinda punk today, J."

JBR. I'm sorry. What's wrong?

JP. Well, for one thing, I'm sick of my molded hands. I don't have any dexterity. Look at this! My fingers are carved together. It's like a club, not a hand. It's hell, man. Pure hell.

JBR. Must be tough.

JP. You don't know the half of it. It's a Fellini-esque nightmare I'm living in. Finger food? Are you kidding? Plus, I can't dial a phone. And if one more person tells me to *point something out*, I'm gonna hit 'em. Believe me, this hand feels like a solid piece of wood. Wanna know why? *Because that's what it is*!

Those nights at Henrici's were like going to comedy and music and performance class. It was a working lab for beginning showbiz. When evenings got boring, I'd just switch from music to ventriloquism. When people got tired of that, I would sit and tell jokes. Reynolds was a wonderful foil, always happy to play along, while teaching me the number one rule of improvisation comedy—*always say yes. Always agree.*

> Eighteen months is the over-under as a piano bar player. Playing for a year is nice, but you don't get the full effect, going through all the holidays' busy nights—not to mention the many, many agonizingly slow nights where it's you and two loners at the bar. Do this more than a year and a half, and it becomes toxic. You play for the regulars. You get to know them. There is a reason they're oozing into the bar at "happy hour" four times a week, requesting "Lazy River" or "One More for the Road" and downing heavy-on-the-vermouth Manhattans.

> What's with the term "happy hour"? It's the penultimate oxymoron. There was nothing "happy" about the hours of 4:00 p.m. to 7:00 p.m. in the joints I worked. It seemed like the saddest time of day in a suburban bar.

> Frankly, a "happy hour" for me would be a nap.

There are people who have built careers as great piano bar entertainers, of course. And there is one great thing about playing a piano bar for more than a year, five hours a night, six nights a week—you get better. You don't have a choice. You're playing the same songs over and over until you know them! It's rehearsal in many ways. And the great bonus is you're getting paid!

By spring 1981, the too much had long gone out of the fun for me in the piano bar scene. It was dying before I got into it. The old-guy-at-the-piano-singing-Sinatra era had run its course, soon to be replaced by two-guys-at-two-pianos-doing-sing-alongs-in-franchises phase that would spring up all over the place.

Henrici's would die of natural causes, a restaurant that had been very popular for a few years until it wasn't. I arrived as its menu changed from dinner only to lunch and dinner and then cut the extravagant items from the entrees it offered. The piano bar was dark and kind of seedy, dimly lit booths of brown leather with red tablecloths, a long bar, and tiny tables throughout. A year after I started, the manager announced it was closing. I've never really missed it.

Sigma Chi buddies who had gone to graduate school right out of Illinois were getting jobs for huge amounts of money. Some of them were buying houses. My peers were becoming bankers and attorneys and engineers, all off to dynamic careers with a cool corner office and a secretary and a guaranteed salary. One guy bought a yacht! I was struggling along pounding out Tony Orlando's "Tie a Yellow Ribbon" for drunk divorcees in a saloon.

It was time to make a change.

Still living with my aunt and uncle, I had crossed the Rubicon of "lovable cousin Taylor" to the inevitable "when is cousin Taylor gonna *leave*?" They were dropping hints and "encouraging" me to get out and live on my own. "Don't most of your friends have an apartment, at least? Don't you want a girlfriend? *How much longer do you plan on living here*!?!?"

Just before terminating my piano bar career, I started hanging around the Second City theater in downtown Chicago.

All I have done for 5 days is eat. I'll bet I weigh 200 lbs. (I've studied for the GRE, also.
Why all the drawings? I dunno...
Am I ever gonna get squared away?
Am I ever gonna grow up?

Dear God;
    Guide me. I just need a chance...

It's almost like everything in my life comes down to some make-or-break moments... maybe there are 10 or 15 of them in my whole life... maybe 100 or 1,000, I don't know... but in a lifetime there are only a very few... and I only hope that it all works for the best for me and everyone else. I'm not here to waste time. I'm here to make a difference... in many peoples lives.

FROM TAYLOR MASON'S PERSONAL DIARY.

Chapter Nine
The Second City

Chicago: The Second City, by author A. J. Liebling was a satirical look at Chicago published in 1952.

Before moving in with my aunt and uncle, I had gone to a prestigious office in Chicago and met with a woman named Shirley Hamilton. She ran the biggest/baddest/best talent agency in the city, and she had cast my dad in a couple of TV commercials back when he was at WGN. He introduced me to Ms. Hamilton, who in turn got me in touch with another major player and showbiz power broker in Chicago, a woman named Joyce Sloane.

"I'm sure you're familiar with The Second City," said Ms. Hamilton.

I shook my head, no. The Second what?

She gave me an incredulous look, like Meryl Streep looking at the ingenue Anne Hathaway in *The Devil Wears Prada*—as in "you have to be kidding me."

DEFINITION: the Second City. The Second City theater is a Chicago landmark and must-see event. Yes, many of the original *Saturday Night Live* members got starts there. The theater's name came from author A. J. Liebling's caustic three-piece story for *The New Yorker* magazine (later published as a book). I won't bore you with the many television and movie actors who are part of the Second City roster. The productions are hip, funny, and spot-on, reflecting current mores, lifestyles, politics, and trends in the United States. Everybody who has even dabbled in comedy and or theater from the Chicago area knows about the Second City. Only a complete knucklehead could be oblivious.

I, of course, was oblivious and knew nothing about it. I would ask people about the place in passing. No matter who I asked, people spoke of it with over-the-top, positive, five-star-review-like anecdotes: "It's amazing!" and, "I have never laughed so hard!" or, "Those actors are all going to have their own sitcoms!"

Based on Hamilton's introduction, I met the Second City theater executive producer Joyce Sloane, ostensibly for an audition. It was really more like a personal interview, and she was very sincere, very positive, and very nice. Afterward, she wrote me a personal letter, encouraging me to keep working and "start reading the paper so you can keep up with the news."

I immediately signed up for an improvisation class, known as a "workshop," being led by one of the theater's founding fathers, a local legend in performance and comedy and Chicago-style improvisation acting. His name was Paul Sills. As with many of the people I've worked with over the course of a very long career, Mr. Sills, I'm certain, often wondered, *What is* this *person doing here?*

> Eric Forsberg was my first director for a theater production. He wrote a children's musical, for which I ended up writing the music and performing the lead role—something called *Jimmy Sweeter Visits Candyland*. Eric has gone on to some notable success in Hollywood and is responsible for *Snakes on a Train*, among other films. His mother taught acting. Eric wrote and directed. I benefitted! See? It's the Theory of Relatives!

Mr. Sills, whose biggest commercial success was a Broadway production of "Story Theater," for which he earned a Drama Desk Award and had a good run, was back in Chicago. His hair was wiry and gray. He wore glasses that made his eyes appear twice their normal size. And he cast me in a Bertolt

Brecht sociopolitical statement-come-theatrical play called *The Caucasian Chalk Circle*.

How to describe this experience? An acting stretch? A psychedelic drug trip without the psychedelic drugs? When I would tell theater people in passing, say outdoors on a street in Chicago, "You'll never believe it! I just got cast in *The Caucasian Chalk Circle*," birds would stop midair and fall to the ground, dead.

I played the roles of Azdak and Shalva and tried to understand the underlying story of a woman who would raise a child better than the real mother of that child.

DEFINITION: *The Caucasian Chalk Circle*. *The Caucasian Chalk Circle* is one of German playwright Bertolt Brecht's most celebrated works. It's actually a play within a play, and it's way too complex to describe here. It deals with social class, communism, agriculture, folk music, Nazis, parenting, and love—not to mention politics. The question most asked about it is, "Why was Taylor Mason ever cast? Isn't that like giving a guitar to an elephant and expecting a Beatles song to come out?"

> There is no sense in trying to make sense of anything in the beginning of my "career." I was a ventriloquist who could play piano, a wannabe comedian who was given an acting role in an avant-garde play, all while living with a well-to-do accountant and his family in the suburbs. Top that.

It was not easy to please Paul Sills, and he could be very biting in his critique and assessment of one's "skill." So what? I didn't care how insulting he could be. I'd been yelled at by football coaches and called all kinds of demeaning things. It rolled off my shoulders and didn't affect me.

Besides. After a while, I wasn't going to his "workshops" to be an actor. I had met someone.

She was very pretty and very smart. She was a professional actress, one of the very few of us who actually had been cast in a *real* play and made *real* (union) money. She was not from the Midwest, and she was as funny away from the theater as she was performing in it. She had a bunch of friends, lots of them men, most of whom had something to do with the ever more popular Chicago theater community.

I took for granted one was her boyfriend.

I didn't care. Things were better when I was around her. I was comfortable. Where my life and workshops and work felt disconnected and indefinable, with her, there was a definite sense of excitement and possibility. Every day seemed like an I-can-do-anything day, bright blue skies over the city, big fluffy white clouds floating over the lake and Wrigley Field, and the buildings in the loop. I looked for ways to be near her, just because it felt so easy. I didn't care that we were not, could not, be boyfriend and girlfriend—or something more. I was very content in her company. It was one of the happiest times in my life.

It stunned me when one day she left.

As in left the country.

She went to Brazil.

I had to get serious.

I showed up one day at Second City, hoping to audition for the main cast. I didn't completely understand the premise (improvisation acting), and I was totally lost as to what was supposed to happen on stage during a scene without a script. I waited in the bar outside the show room, wondering why anyone even wanted to be in real show business, shaking with pre-audition angst. The director, Del Close, burst through the door and called out something like, "Okay, whoever is next!" And I was teamed with a woman more nervous than me, someone even more frightened and intimidated by the whole process.

The first drill was "Four through the Door," a basic format for improvisational comedy.

"Four through the Door." What is that? It might be a basic format for improv, but I'd never heard of it. "For the door?" I asked. Del Close was exasperated and had to explain, which he did in very clear and concise terms, the concept: The actor (me? Oh, right! *Me*!) comes through the door on stage four separate times, and is required to be a completely different character each time. The actor performs a "scene," which ends when a natural ending is reached, or (as he said), "I can't take it any more."

He told the woman I was working with that we were to improvise. We were allowed lots of leeway, he told us; pretty much anything was acceptable, and then it was time to start.

As we walked backstage, I asked my partner if she knew anything about "Four through the Door."

"Yes," she said, visibly shaken and apparently so terrified of Del and the circumstance that she couldn't speak more than one syllable at a time.

Essentially one of us was onstage; the other was backstage. The person backstage would come through the door and begin a "scene" in some way. This person would either say something or act as if he or she were doing something, and the other actor—the one on stage—took his or her cue from that and continued the scene. This happened four times for each actor—hence, Four through the Door.

I laughed out loud. *How can this possibly work?*

My first pass through the door I walked on stage right up to this poor girl, standing by a stool—the only prop allowed. She wore a blue T-shirt and jeans, her hair was black and perfectly styled in early 1980s curly-swept-back glamour, and she was staring at me with a look of complete panic.

She'd told me backstage that I—the actor coming through the door—had to make the first move. So I held my right arm up with my left, letting it dangle lifeless, and then I let it lay on the stool in front of her.

"It doesn't work," I said to her.

She didn't get it. I persisted. "I bought this yesterday right here!" I was holding my arm as if it were damaged goods. "See? It doesn't work!" I let it fall to my side. I held it up again and let it fall.

My acting partner was totally flustered and didn't know what to do.

"I have a receipt!" I said, letting my "broken" right arm fall, and I mimed pulling a receipt from my pants pocket. I acted righteous, the way someone brings a purchased item that doesn't work back to the store: "It says right here—date, amount, new right arm. But it doesn't work!"

She finally caught on. "What do you want me to do about it?"

Great opening for me!

"Well, I'd like you to repair it. Right now. I don't want a new one. I like this one. See how it perfectly matches my other one?"

This got a laugh from Del, and he shouted, "Next!"

I had only done the one character and was feeling thrilled I got a laugh, while at the same time wondering how in the world I would come up with another "character" in thirty seconds.

I was saved by Joyce Sloane.

Joyce, the executive producer, who had just months before written me a personal letter of encouragement, walked into the theater wearing her trademark long black dress and holding some papers. She shouted, "Taylor Mason!" I raised my arm. She walked up to me, right in front of Del Close, and held out her hand.

"I want you to come with me."

I nodded and shook her hand. "Hi, Ms. Sloane. Nice to see you again."

Joyce, I would soon learn, was not just a producer. She was the mother of Second City. She knew everyone, she controlled everything, and she knew whatever was going on—from the writing of the shows to the bartenders and the waitresses and their children to the actors and their issues with boyfriends and girlfriends and personal peccadilloes and everything else. Our meeting this day was the beginning of a nice relationship, although I think she always thought I was going to leave soon.

"Do you know how to read music? I'm looking at your résumé, and it says you played piano bars. This is music for improvisation. It's very different. You have to listen to the actors." We were standing among the chairs and tables where the audience sat, and she was holding my résumé as if it were a stale sandwich. She was looking directly at me.

"Yes. I can read music. I only did the piano bar gig for a little over a year, and I was always planning to be a comedy actor. And I am a ventriloquist and—"

She interrupted. "Good. Look at this. Can you play this?" She shuffled papers around and grabbed a one-sheet chord chart for something called "I Hate Liver." The opening lyric was: "I hate liver. Liver makes me quiver. Liver makes me curl right up and die." I laughed.

It was a six-chord song in 4/4. "Yeah, I can play this."

We stood there for a moment. Close was visibly unhappy, arms folded in a pose that read, "*No!*" He was wearing a black beret, big black-rimmed glasses, a flannel shirt, and jeans.

Joyce said, "Del, I need the piano for two minutes."

Silence.

Eh-oh. Maybe a line had been crossed? Del was auditioning actors. Now there was a music audition? Nobody said a word. At the point where the awkward silence became an oh-I-get-it! I'm-supposed-to-play-right-now moment, I went over to the grand piano by the side of the stage, sat down, and played a few bars.

"You're hired," said Joyce. "Thank you, Del," she said over her shoulder. And she guided me back into her office.

With that, I had a job with the Second City as musical director for the touring company.

> It's a running joke in the business—"I worked at the Second City." If someone is in the business from Chicago, more often than not he or she has the Second City on his or her résumé, whether the person *really* worked there or not. I've had people tell me they were in the same company I was in, even though I have *never* met them or seen them before!

The Second City Touring Company, or "Tourco" as it was known, played all sorts of gigs around the United States. There was a steady run in Dundee, Illinois, a former dinner theater located in a "resort" hotel called the Chateau Louise. The cast included two women and five men, the classic Second City grouping. Looking back, I realize that most of those men and women have worked steadily in theater, television, and film for some thirty years. My roommate on the road? His name was Dan Castellaneta, who would gain fame in the next decade as the voice of Homer Simpson. Yes, him.

The theater in Dundee was typical in every way except for one. The seats angled up from the floor, away from the stage, the last row near the ceiling. The strange thing was the space between the first row and the lip of the stage. The audience was looking *up* to the stage from Row 1. There was a ten-foot drop from the edge of the stage to the floor.

If the actors weren't aware, this could be a problem. One time, an actor working Dundee for the first time went to jump out into the audience, thinking the floor was maybe two to four feet from the stage. Instead, he disappeared from view, dropping out of sight and shouting in pain when he hit the cement floor.

The Second City and Tourco approached comedy far differently than the way I had back in Champaign doing those Sigma Chi parties. The approach was a lot different, too, from my forays into ventriloquist comedy in venues around Chicago and at Henrici's. This was professional and well directed, focused and perfectly executed. The scenes and the jokes and the premises worked on more than one level. The actors were highly skilled and fun to watch.

On Monday nights, the main company had its day off, so Tourco performed in the main theater. I got to play the same piano that Fred Kaz, the genius in residence, had used since the beginning of "improvisation comedy" in the 1950s.

As a fallback, I applied to the Medill School of Journalism at Northwestern University, just in case the showbiz thing fell apart. How suburban of me. How careful. How typical upper-middle class. It's the always appropriate response for when a kid tells his or her parents, "I'm going into show business." Their answer is, "Yeah? And what will you do if that doesn't work out?"

> A quick word of advice to wannabe showbiz types. Do not go to the University of Something-to-Fall-Back-On." Commit to what you want to do and do it.

Chapter Ten
Moonlighting

I like to say that journalism is the graduate school from which you never graduate.
—Pete Hamill, journalist

Northwestern University, Evanston, Illinois—I was accepted into the advertising master's program at the Medill School of Journalism in summer 1982. The reasoning behind the decision to apply and then enroll and take out thousands of dollars in student loans was, in hindsight, complete lunacy.

So it fits with the story line and my own personal character arc!

A fellow Sigma Chi had gone to NU right out of Illinois, earned a master's in business from the prestigious Kellogg School of Management, and was making oodles of dollars. "Andos" has gone on to become an influential businessman working in environmental finance. He's not the only classmate or fraternity brother who accomplished impressive career success soon after graduating. There were bankers, like the one who saved the Boston school system millions. Fred, a brilliant man my age, would become a judge. In fact, some two years out of college, lots of my Sigma Chi buddies were making money hand over fist. Those doing particularly well had continued their educations in graduate school or law school. Some studied medicine. Many were destined for long careers and success in chosen fields, where they would attain prestige and honor and the fortune that goes with them.

While they were making the world turn on its axis, I was playing piano bars and talking to a wooden puppet. I met a girl, Annie, who I dated briefly. Our relationship was overtly one-sided—I needed a car to drive up to Evanston, Illinois, where I took a year of piano study with Alan Swain. These were my first real lessons in years, and Mr. Swain, an accomplished teacher, pianist, and accompanist, had a studio just a few blocks from the Northwestern campus. Twice a week, I would drive Annie's car up to Evanston, and Mr. Swain would critique my playing and offer career advice. "You're a survivor," he'd say. "Now it's time to succeed!" He had a complete and thorough knowledge of the keyboard and pointed out all sorts of techniques and ideas that would shape the next thirty years of my life. I still have his textbooks and call on them every once in a while as a refresher.

One day, I walked in and sat down at the piano for the lesson. Alan didn't take his usual seat next to me. Instead, he stood at the window of his second-floor studio and waved at me to begin. I played a few measures of a Bach invention we were working on, and he interrupted me.

"You should apply to the Medill School of Journalism," he said, still staring out the window. "They offer a degree in advertising. I think you could write commercial jingles. In fact, I think you'd be incredibly successful!"

I walked out of his building that day, went directly to the admissions building, and got the application. Six months later, I was a student again.

> The girl who let me use her car, Annie, never got a proper thank you. She deserved a lot more out of me for a lot of reasons. So here it is—thank you, Annie Hirschauer.

Classes started in June 1982. I moved into the Sigma Chi fraternity house on the Northwestern campus because they let me stay there rent-free for the summer. The school year at NU was divided into quarters, and money was tight. I was funding this part of my education on my own—where my parents had helped with half the cost for my undergraduate education, they didn't have the money to put me through grad school. I was still working evenings for the Second City and doing some solo comedy spots as a ventriloquist, but that earned me $250 a week at the most. I took out a loan that would cover the entire tuition through spring 1983. What I earned as a comedian/musician/ventriloquist had to pay for everything else. To have a place to live rent-free the first quarter of my graduate school year—at the Sigma Chi house—was critically helpful.

I only used it as a place to sleep. The guys who were living there for the summer were much, much younger. I was twenty-six years old to their nineteen, twenty, or twenty-one. I had been out in the working world, I'd been knocked down a few pegs, and I had some real life experience. I wasn't doing the "college thing." Between gigs, I worked on weekends. With that and the incredible amount of reading and concentrating on grad school projects, there wasn't time to forge friendships and hang out with these new "brothers" anyway.

The advertising program was intense. It was difficult. From the beginning, I had to concentrate, formulate thoughts and ideas, and defend my work. It was a daily challenge. On the first day of class, Professor Fryburger said, "We're gonna work ya!"

And they did.

Some of it was fun, and I loved it. Some of it was painstaking. I asked myself daily, *What am I doing here?*

I'm sure those professors wondered the same thing: *What is* he *doing here?*

The year I spent studying advertising just happened to coincide with major advertising breakthroughs. The Coca-Cola Company put the word "Diet" in front of the word "Coke" on a can and forever changed the way the carbonated drink business would operate.

Mass media, the vehicle driven and financed by advertising, was rocked when newspaper machines that looked like television sets appeared on street corners in every major city. The *USA Today* newspaper became a sort of town crier for the country while I was a grad student and, at fifty cents a copy, proved all the big news publications wrong because people were willing to pay more than twenty-five cents to get their daily news.

Not to mention the Home Shopping Network and MTV hit cable in 1982, both of which began a new trend toward "niche marketing," which has become more prevalent and focused today.

My classmates were, in a word, smart. Dave, Sara, Jeanie, Andrew, and Mary all came from the deep end of a gene pool in which it was a struggle to stay afloat and keep my head above water. Then there was Paul Wang, who had come to the states from Taiwan. Paul walked into that first class and sat by himself, staring at the teachers as they babbled. He looked like someone from the eighteenth century trying to use a cell phone. I had to talk to him, so I did.

Which was impossible, because Paul Wang barely spoke English.

It's beyond the scope of any imagination how he managed to get through that summer with a barely comprehensible accent and no understanding of the language. It was a miracle that I observed firsthand. By September, Wang was speaking fluent English. By the time he graduated, he was getting job offers.

Mr. Wang, as of this writing, is a professor at the Medill School of Journalism advertising program. For his part, Dave Kasey made Chester Cheeto, an iconic character in the world of advertising and TV commercials. Jeanie Caggiano beat the odds for our generation, thriving at the Leo Burnett Advertising offices in Chicago. Once again, the people around me have had sterling outrageously successful careers.

When the first quarter—the summer quarter—ended, I found a room in a house six blocks from campus, on the top floor (what had been an attic). I only had it for a couple of months, but that's where I started my fall semester. I couldn't afford books, so I was using anyone else's who could lend me theirs and spending a lot of time at the library.

The library. The biggest difference between Northwestern University and the University of Illinois, besides the fact that NU is one-fifth the size of the state school, was the library. On any given Friday night in Champaign-Urbana, the campus bar scene was the only place to be. It was wall-to-wall humanity in those joints. It was far different in Evanston; on any given Friday night, the library, not the bar, was crawling with humanity. It was a different mind-set.

Near the end of fall, I moved in with two underclassmen who needed a third roommate and extra cash. Thank God for them. Doug and Ned put up with a lot of my bad influences (staying up way too late at night, always playing loud music, and so on).

The truth is that Northwestern was a lark.

I had hit the snooze button on the syllabus of life and got myself some kind of reprieve on responsibility. The old joke, "I didn't know what to do, so I went to grad school," defined me. How did I pass the classes? How did I complete any of the (ambitious and fervent) work? Between the constant performing at the Second City and occasional jobs as a ventriloquist, I somehow completed the ever-increasing amounts of classwork. Life was fast and exciting and out of control—in a good way.

Some of the professors and I didn't see eye to eye. Don Schultz had no time for the weird guy who tried to make everyone laugh all the time. We clashed often, in class, usually because I was wrong. He was hard to please. I was obstinate and arrogant enough to challenge him on a daily basis, which was insane since he ran the program for all intents and purposes. There were times my classmates came to my defense, but for the most part, I was allowed to dangle and fail, hanging myself in a noose Mr. Schultz allowed me to make.

When I graduated (barely) in 1983, I was glad to get out. I was relieved to have been given a degree from a prestigious graduate school and ready to stake my claim in the real world of show business.

But graduate school served its purpose for me. Like in Illinois, classes there had had nothing to do with ventriloquism or performing or stage presentations. But there was a good chance I got more out of the curriculum at Northwestern than the entire student population. For all the pain and mind games I endured (and put other people through), there were particular skills I learned that played directly into my career and success for some thirty-plus years of writing and performing a comedy act.

Professor Schultz was all about efficiency of thoughts and words and making a point. Why use two pages when you can say what you want to with one? Why answer one of his hypotheticals with a paragraph or two when a short sentence can get the job done? Applying that to comedy, why go through wordy and endless "setups" to a joke when a couple of words might lead to a punch line? Taken to an extreme, why not try for "one-word punch lines"?

This technique—get to the joke as quickly as possible—was invaluable knowledge. I know the way I work and execute punch lines is very different than many of the men and women I have worked with in comedy for all these years. I use Mr. Schultz's techniques and models in my work to this day. He's since become the head of the Medill School of Advertising—for good reason. He gave me a solid background and understanding—and very good tools—to write a professional comedy act and put all the pieces together, resulting in a set that would make audiences laugh.

Thanks, Dr. Schultz.

The last project of the year included "saving" a defunct or soon-to-be-defunct business. My group got Dad's Root Beer. I worked my tail off on the concept.

Mr. Schultz hated it.

That was another valuable lesson. Who cares how hard you worked on something? Who cares if you made your "best effort"? Who cares what your opinion is? In the real world, all that matters are results. Moral victories are meaningless in the competitive world of success. Deal with it. Failure means learn from your mistakes and do better next time.

Speaking of failure, the most unforgettable part of my year in Evanston came during the fall. The Northwestern Wildcats varsity football team, languishing at the bottom of the Big Ten at the time (along with my alma mater, Illinois) had lost some fifteen games in a row. During the beginning of the 1982 season, the Cats played a home game against Northern Illinois University. Late in the game, it became apparent NU was going to win.

The Northwestern student body couldn't believe what was happening. They hadn't won a game in *years*. The students didn't know how to act. *What do we do if we win?*

I was in the upper reaches of the stadium, hanging around for no good reason, when I realized these people didn't have a clue. So I ran down to the edge of the stands, near the same football field where, a couple of years before, I had recovered a fumble. Now I stood at the foot of the student section and began chanting, "Goal posts! Goal posts!"

The crowd picked up on my suggestion, and a surge began in the stadium. I, laughing deliriously, sprinted onto the field just before the scoreboard clock went to :00.

I instructed people who joined me around the goal at the eastern edge of the gridiron how to make a goal post break off. I'd seen groundskeepers at the University of Illinois, installing and uninstalling the same kind of thing at the stadium in Champaign. "We need someone to get up on the crossbar!" I shouted.

Moments later, there was Dave—yep, my new friend at Medill—standing on the crossbar and holding the goalpost, while I screamed at a bunch of fraternity boys, "Push! You have to *push!*"

The goal went over. The kids stood around. *What now?*

"We take this to the president's house and dump it on his lawn!"

I walked with the student body to the president's house, and they dumped the equipment in his front yard.

The president himself came out on his front porch, clearly concerned. He looked confused. What was all this racket? What was going on?

I had the feeling there was a good chance he didn't even know there had been a game that day. He stood in front of the students gathered in his yard holding a broken goal post. He said, "I hope you're proud of yourselves. That's a very expensive structure."

I laughed in his face. "Yeah ... and that's why you have won just this game in the past two seasons, sir!"

The crowd around me cheered.

I walked back to campus to study.

By the winter of the year up in Evanston, I was barely pretending to be a student. I was completing assignments and papers at the last possible minute, causing lots of angst with the study groups I was part of, and rarely completing assignments until minutes before they were due. I was way behind the rest of the class.

But my career in show business was all A's. When 1983 started, I had begun to work around the Chicago area in clubs and cabarets, performing musical comedy and ventriloquism. I started getting prime performance spots at small comedy clubs. What I really wanted was to work at a joint just one block down the street from the Second City. It was a full-time comedy club that brought in national touring acts, men and women who had performed on *The Tonight Show*, people who had recognizable names. The club was called Zanies.

I got an audition.

Chapter Eleven
Trainspotting

DEFINITION: trainspotting. The desire to be able to understand just a little part of the world—a manifestly controllable part.

If it sounds like life was chaos, I'm not giving you the complete picture.

My life as I got ready to graduate from Northwestern was a daily free-for-all of pure pandemonium and bedlam. Pretending to be a grad student at a prestigious university but concentrating on a career in comedy had created a holy mess. I was running a hundred miles an hour without a destination.

Note to the young and impressionable: I don't suggest following this strategy.

> When people asked me, "What are your goals? What is your schedule? Do you even have a plan?" I had a ready answer. "Yes," I'd say. "The plan is: *There isn't one!*"

The biggest issue was the obvious—my full-time, real, practical education was happening at the corner of North and Wells in Chicago, where I was taking advanced courses in comedy, music, improvisation, joke writing, and performance. There were nights when I would play piano for the first show at a small theater behind the main stage at the Second City and then race down to a club called Zanies and do a short twenty-minute spot there and then race back to the Second City and perform as a musical director.

When things got really dicey and I absolutely had to do schoolwork at Northwestern, I had to find a piano player to take my place at the Second City. I called the one musician I knew who could handle the songs and the improvisations.

I sent the musical score to my brother Tony who was still at the University of Illinois. He filled in for me (and probably did a better job).

> My brother Tony took my place for some travel gigs and ended up dropping out of school at Illinois and working full-time with the Second City. He would later return to school and get his degree years later.

There are only two ways a lifestyle like this can go—a total nervous breakdown or an acceptance that, whatever happens, that's what's supposed to happen. For me, the world was exciting and fun and dramatic. Local booking agents called and asked for my availability. My classmates from Northwestern would come and watch as I worked with touring comics from New York and Los Angeles. I was having fun. I was getting paid. It was a daily rush of adrenalin and craziness as I became more and more comfortable with the process of being in "showbiz."

Graduation in spring 1983 wasn't so much an accomplishment as it was a relief. Finally. I could go out and work at the job I'd been hiding from the professors all year.

My mother had started at Northwestern but had run out of money. She organized a small graduation party for me—proud to show me off to friends and acquaintances back in Ottawa, Illinois. I didn't know any of the women who came that sunny June day, but my mother was beaming. To see her talking with people, offering them cake and cookies, and talking about me was such a highlight, such a great moment in my life that it made the year of struggle at Northwestern entirely worth it.

I did give the world of advertising one last chance.

I had taken a job at the Kappa Alpha Theta sorority at Northwestern, working as a dishwasher and waiter for the school year. In return, I got free lunch and free dinner—which was incredibly helpful since I was living on a shoestring.

I naturally spent part of my time at the sorority showing off, playing the piano, and "performing." While I was serving lunch late that spring, one of the girls approached me.

"I heard you're studying advertising. My dad runs an advertising firm in New York City," she said. "I told him about you. He said to give him a call."

I did. Her dad was the kind of person I would come in contact with for the next four decades—busy, professional, and to the point. We spoke for thirty to forty seconds about school and his daughter.

Then came the questions. What did I want to do? Why should he hire me? Why was I studying advertising at all? It was all very straightforward and appropriate. I stammered through answers that had to sound a little bit inane, if not laughable.

But I was given a job interview after he asked, "What is the biggest thing you learned about advertising at Northwestern?"

I said, "I learned you don't need an advertising degree to work in advertising."

He laughed out loud. I was given a day and time to meet people in his Chicago office.

My first and only job interview went extremely well.

It did not start out that way.

I have summed up the way people in the real world see me. It's an acronym—WASYAG—pronounced *WAZ* (rhymes with has) *YAG* (rhymes with hag), WAZ-YAG. It stands for "We Are Serious, You're a Goofball."

I didn't follow the protocol. Where most of my fellow grads were going on interviews with résumés and professional portfolios packed with experience and examples of concepts and plans that marketed a broad range of goods and services, I walked in to a wood-paneled office in a posh Michigan Avenue office building with two grocery bags filled with drawings and notes. I didn't have any real examples of my "work." I had not taken the time to get artist renditions of ideas and concepts for advertisements.

Example, a TV commercial for a business newspaper, based loosely on a fictional competitor to *The Wall Street Journal*: My commercial idea was a cartoon of city buildings, each a different color, three to four stories high. The buildings "eyes" were windows on the second and third floor; the doorways were "mouths." My childlike sketches showed a breeze blowing copies of a newspaper—in other words, my dreamed-up competitor to *The Wall Street Journal*, which I named *The Takin' Care of Business Journal*. And this breeze would blow the copies of the paper past the cartoon buildings. The buildings would "read" the copy as it flew by. They'd bounce and groove and then quickly grow into skyscrapers. The concept was that small businesses that read this "new business newspaper" would quickly grow into giant corporations. At least that was the idea.

The woman conducting the audition took one look at me when I walked in. She saw my paper bags and said, "This better be really, really good, or I'm throwing you out of here. I don't have time for this."

I said, "I don't blame you." Joking aside, I said, "But I want you to know I stayed up all night drawing these pictures."

Her response was folded arms and a blank stare. She didn't have to say it. *Not funny.*

Even I understood. You've heard the saying, they can smell fear? Well, with me it's not that they smell *fear*, they smell something completely different.

I think they smell the truth. Maybe some angst and a hint of regret that I didn't prepare things the right way. The way that everyone does. *The way I am supposed to*!

I presented my material—and for this presentation I had done some prep work, rehearsing a performance during which

I included my hand-drawn advertising copy and ten to twelve "ideas" in which I attempted to sell the unsellable.

That was my pitch. I wanted to convince her I was a clever, smart, tuned-in copywriter who could sell stuff that could not possibly be sold. I wrote an ad for rotten peaches, individually wrapped in expensive-looking gold foil, a set of six for $29.95. I had a line of expensive, fine-tailored suits that were to be marketed to farmers (a demographic that doesn't spend a lot of money on clothing), using the Hank Williams, Jr. song title, "A Country Boy Can Survive"—as in a country boy can survive an evening in a major city as a fashion plate.

Each of my ads—except for the business journal—was its own version of a "Pet Rock."

DEFINITION: Pet Rock. The Pet Rock was created by ad writer Gary Dahl in the mid-1970s. The premise—a customer bought a rock or two or three, which came in a box, but instead of having to feed and train and deal with the trappings of a real pet, the pet rock was responsibility-free. The real joy of the purchase was the accompanying booklet ("how to care for your Pet Rock"), which was filled with funny instructions and jokes.

She allowed me to complete the entire overture. When I finished, she said, "I was skeptical, but you won me over." She asked where I was from, why I went to grad school, and how I knew the executive in New York City who had gotten me this special job interview. She said the firm was not hiring people but, "We might be able to find a place for you here as a copywriter."

Finally she asked me to tell her something about myself that she couldn't possibly know—something that would be a surprise.

I said, "I'm a ventriloquist."

She laughed—an honest, oh-my-gosh-that's-the-funniest-thing-I-ever-heard laugh. It was the kind of laugh people give you when you say something really cutting edge, on-point and ultrahip.

I never told her that I was being honest. Or that her laughter was kind of insulting.

That's a modus operandi I use to this day. My job is to make people laugh. If they laugh at something they're not supposed to or in the wrong spot or for the wrong reason, I don't stop them. Laughter is laughter. I'll take it.

I never went to work for that agency. I walked out of the office building and had an epiphany. It was an out-of-body dream where I watched myself going through a revolving door year after year, aging badly, becoming fat and bitter, meandering into an office cube farm for the rest of my life. Like livestock. One of Uncle Art's hogs in Grand Ridge.

I still had my résumé in hand. I was sleepwalking, moving in a daze, walking north on Michigan Avenue on a warm summer day in 1983, coming to grips with the fact that I was no longer a student. I couldn't sponge off my aunt and uncle any more. I had to make a decision.

I had no strategy. There was a question: Was I going to work in advertising or would I be a ventriloquist?

I came to a restaurant—the Magic Pan. It was dark. Empty. Closed.

I pulled the handle on the heavy wooden door. It opened.

"We're not open."

The place was dark. The voice came from the back, somewhere in the shadows behind the chairs turned upside down on tables, speaking not so much to me but at me—as in *please leave*.

"Ummm ... I'm looking for a job." The words came out of my mouth, unplanned and unrehearsed, with a certain sincere urgency. I surprised myself and held the door open, the sounds of the street spilling into the restaurant. It was midmorning, an hour before lunchtime.

The voice said, "We aren't really hiring."

"Can I just apply?"

A body came out of the darkness, dressed in jeans and a T-shirt, a towel over his shoulder, a grown man with dark hair and stubble.

"Fine." He gave me the once-over, shook his head, and went back into the shadows. I walked down two steps into the place and sat down at a table. The smell of something good and wholesome, something healthy, hung in the air. And from the darkness, again, came the man. He sat down, falling into his chair with a thump. He leaned across the table and held out his hand. We shook, and he looked me in the eye. He checked out my oxford shirt, black tie, and haircut. I wore a job interview uniform, but not for a waiter. I thought he might start laughing. It was awkward, and he clearly didn't understand what was going on.

Acting as if there was a camera watching our every move, as if this were some dumb prank, he gave me an application. I filled it out with my own pen, by the light of the sun coming in the front windows of the place and handed it back to him.

It was over. I would be a ventriloquist for a career. My signature on this application was a commitment to that.

He studied it for less than a minute. He looked away, smiling and shaking his head.

"You just graduated from Northwestern?"

"Yes."

"You have a *master's degree*?"

"Yes."

"*And you want to be a waiter*?" The words came out with a laugh. "Why on earth would you want to be a waiter?"

The guy was maybe ten years older than me, in his midthirties, trying to make a go of it in the food business in Chicago. I gave him the best sell job I could: I wanted to work in show business. I would be performing at night and auditioning regularly for other work, and a full-time job would hinder that. I was good with people. I understood marketing and pleasing the client, and I thought a waiter job would be ideal. He was not convinced.

But he accepted my application, and I started a waiter job there, a crepe eatery serving pretty good food. I lasted ten days and moved on.

It was June 1983. There were twelve million unemployed Americans. I wasn't one of them. I had all my comedy jobs, and right after the Magic Pan, I took a job at Redamaks, a burger joint right down the street from Zanies. I would sometimes make a hundred dollars in tips.

That's a hundred dollars in one day.

The place had a bar, and when the actors and staff from the Second City would come down for lunch or early dinner, I figured a scam to get them free beers. For every one they bought, I got them a freebie, which led to astronomical gratuities and meant I had money in my pocket all the time.

> People who've waited tables have great respect for service business employees—not just the servers and the bartenders, but the cooks and dishwashers and hotel cleaning staff and all the people who do those thankless jobs the rest of us take for granted. Ex-waiters "get it."

My career became more focused. I began working the comedy circuit in Chicago. There were precious few clubs, but there was still a certain amount of work, and after getting a couple of weekend spots at Zanies, my phone began to ring.

Zanies was *the* joint. It featured comics from across the country, and the best local acts got to perform on a regular basis. There were good audiences, the admission wasn't too much, and the drinks were cheap. Many nights the place would sell out.

I was living a nonstop schedule, working at the Second City and Zanies on a regular basis, while my waiter job kept money in my pocket.

Ronald Reagan was president; Martin Luther King, Jr. was given a holiday we've celebrated every year since; and some guy named James Watt, the secretary of the interior, started the "PC movement" with a comment about minority representation on some government panel. He said something to the effect of "I have a black, I have a woman, two Jews, and a cripple." It was the beginning of political correctness, every comedian's worst enemy.

The Chicago mayor was one Harold Washington, the first African American to be elected in that city, and he flourished even in the shadow of Richard Daley, the man who had run the Windy City for many years. Chicago was polarized as never before. There were hilariously corrupt and funny Illinois/Chicago politicians like Dan Rostenkowski ("Rosty the Snowman" was an early bit I did on him) and Ed "Fast Eddy" Vrdolyak. The city was losing population (which meant low rent!). And the battles between the city council and the mayor were dubbed "Council Wars" by an incredible talent I'd worked with at the Second City, Mr. Aaron Freeman. Mr. Freeman turned the political machine of Chicago into his own muse, combining the hypocrisy and corruption of Chicago politics with characters from the first *Star Wars* movie. Aaron has done very well over the years, building an act around the battles at city hall.

By the middle of October, I was approached by the Zanies club manager, Bert Haas. "Ricky wants to see you. He's going to offer you the job of emcee."

Bert, my age and similar background, had helped me from the start. He gave me a chance to audition one night in front of a small audience, and my "set" went well enough that he had me back.

He would give me short, to-the-point, and very detailed critiques: "You went too long. Sometimes it's better to keep your time tight. Get off on what you think is a big laugh."

"Try some other way to walk on stage. Don't have the puppet out first. Maybe carry it up in a bag or something and then reveal it, kinda like a surprise."

"You talk too fast when you get nervous. When it seems like things aren't going well, fight the urge to speed up. Slow down. Give the audience a chance to hear you."

Without Bert Haas I would not have a career. There were some tough nights in the beginning, nights when I thought show business was a dead end, going nowhere; it was already over before I had really begun. Bert Haas was all business. He was very intense, and he operated solely on what he had seen that worked or didn't work. He made pointed critiques about what he saw as opportunities to build my act. More than anything he allowed me to fail—a lot.

I can't thank him enough for that.

Rick Uchwatt owned Zanies Comedy Club. He was a shrewd businessman, a huge fan of comedy, and a great friend. Ricky would soon become the go-to person for comedy in Chicago, working as a personal manager for some of the acts, booking huge shows in the big theaters, and running the business of comedy in the country's third largest city. He was bigger than life, he was a lot of fun to hang out with, and he didn't suffer fools gladly.

Our first meeting took place in the back of the club, by the bar, after a Saturday night second show where we had made a lot of people laugh and the drinks had flowed.

"I want to offer you a job," he said.

"Thanks!" I beamed a smile back at him and waited for what I knew was coming.

"I want you to emcee the shows, every night, starting Thursday. You might have to do thirty minutes a show; you might only get fifteen. You might have to do thirty-five. But it will be a chance to grow and write and become—"

I cut him off. "Ricky, I accept. It's an honor. I'm thrilled that you're giving me this chance. I won't let you down."

"Don't get cocky," he said, and we shook hands.

Bert walked into the room from behind the corner, where he had been listening. "Great. That solves that problem. Rick, I need to see you."

The two of them turned to leave, the boss going first around the corner and up the stairs to his office. Bert looked at me from behind his wire-rimmed glasses and smiled. "Do you remember the first line you had when you started working here last year?"

I shook my head.

"You used to open every set with this: 'As you can tell, I have no stage presence at all.' You've come a long way. This is a big deal for us. And for you. Don't blow it."

Ricky would talk to me a lot over the years, usually about business and other comedians and his clubs. Unlike with Bert, Ricky and I had very little in common. But our boss-employee relationship was excellent.

You could be a "starving artist" in Chicago circa the mid-1980s and actually live fairly well. Rent wasn't over the top. There was work if you hustled. The Steppenwolf Theater Company that would send many of its actors and writers on to international fame and fortune was booming. The cast at the Second City included Jim Belushi and Tim Kazurinsky, both of whom would join *Saturday Night Live* a short time later. The touring company I worked with at the time included the aforementioned Dan Castellaneta, and Julia Louis-Dreyfus, who would become a household name on the still-running-in-perpetuity *Seinfeld*.

Oh, yeah. Then there was this girl.

Marsia Turner had returned from her yearlong hiatus in Brazil, visiting family in the city of Recife. Back in Chicago, she had taken a job working in production in the front office of

Second City, reporting directly to Joyce Sloane, as well as to Bernie Sahlins, the producer and director of the juggernaut. I saw her regularly in the office on my way to a gig or between gigs or (more often than not) just because I wanted to.

I wasn't really looking for some kind of relationship. She was outta my league. I had missed her. Now she was back, so I tried to get close to her any way I could, which meant playing on the Second City softball team, pretending to be part of the theater scene, and hanging with the people she did. And Marsia knew people. She was connected, and I took for granted she had a boyfriend. Or someone else. Or something else. I didn't care. It just seemed like things in my life were better, life was easier, and everything was more comfortable when I was around her.

I just wanted to be with her for whatever reason.

It's an odd segue.

The Chicago Bears, Bulls, and Cubs were, are, and always will be my hometown teams. My favorite player in any sport—to this day—is Ernie Banks, number 14, the always positive Cubs first baseman who never got to major league baseball's playoffs, much less a World Series, yet somehow played far above his lot in life with baseball's lovable losers.

My father worked for WGN, the Cubs broadcast partner for decades, and so my brothers and I spent many summer afternoons in Wrigley Field, watching Ernie and his team lose ball games.

I spent much of my youth pretending I was playing football, baseball, or basketball in stadiums around the country, wearing the uniform of my heroes. Never mind that I was lacking in pure athletic ability.

I'm one of the thousands who has worn the scars for a lifetime from the collapse of the 1969 Cubs team. My hero Ernie Banks and the rest of the team somehow let an insurmountable lead escape them and gave the upstart New York Mets a chance to win a World Series.

When you live and die with losers, you become a world-class daydreamer. You make yourself believe anything is possible. The Bulls can win an NBA Championship! The Bears can win the Super Bowl! *The cubs can win the World Series*!

Anything can happen.

Marsia Turner asked me to see a Cubs baseball game that July. The first word that came into my head was "kismet!"

Get it? She liked baseball! She understood the Cubs! She knew what it was to sit in the right field bleachers at Wrigley on a do-nothing day in the middle of July with someone you care about, kind of paying attention to the game but not really (who went to a Cubs game expecting them to win in the '70s, '80s, and '90s?), while low-hanging white cotton ball clouds floated in from Lake Michigan and hovered over the ballpark—the colors and sounds and vibe of a we-can-do-anything summer afternoon intoxicating you and the girl and everyone around you.

We went. We sat in the right field bleachers. The Cincinnati Reds won the game. I rubbed suntan lotion on Ms. Turner's back, and we walked through Chicago's North Side after the Cub's loss (whatever), talking about comedy and theater and the people we knew, what had happened yesterday, what had happened today, and what could happen tomorrow.

By Labor Day, I had moved in with her, a first-floor apartment on the Near North Side, just south of DePaul University. Our biggest investment was a VCR, and we spent many Sunday afternoons sprawled on a couch, watching videotape movies and shows. We had become a couple, and we're still together thirty-plus years later.

Not to get personal or anything.

Chapter Twelve
Zanies Comedy Club

Got a call from an old friend we used to be real close / Said he couldn't go on the American way / Closed the shop sold the house bought a ticket to the West Coast / Now he gives them a stand-up routine in LA.
—Billy Joel, *My Life*

My act in Chicago was based on observational humor, satirizing local sports teams, politics, and locations and landmarks known to people who had grown up in "Chicagoland." The Chicago Cubs were an endless supply of jokes because they were lovably bad—even when they got into the postseason, it turned out to be a disaster. All Chicago sports teams lost on a regular basis, so a joke wrote itself at the beginning of every autumn: "This is the time of year when a Chicago sports fan can turn on sports radio and hear that the Bears, Bulls, Cubs, White Sox, and Black Hawks all lost today!"

DEFINITION: Chicagoland. The great expanse that starts just south of Milwaukee, Wisconsin; stretches west to Illinois towns like Elgin, Aurora, and Oswego; and then extends south to northwest Indiana is called Chicagoland. The person most credited with the word is Colonel Robert R. McCormick, who was the editor and publisher of the *Chicago Tribune* for the first half of the twentieth century. From the time I was very young, it has always held the aura of something magical and mystical and otherworldly. Like Disneyland or Alice's Wonderland, Chicagoland will always hold the promise of something special; something amazing; something truly breathtaking, spectacular, and fantastic.

Chicago is racial animosity and the Rainbow Coalition. Chicago is all the romance of the Cubs, but it's also the Bulls and Michael Jordan and Mike Ditka and "da Bears" and the Blackhawks. Chicago is Michigan Avenue and the South Side; it's the blues and jazz and Chess Records and the symphony and WXRT. Chicago is "da machine" and Richard Daly. It's the band Chicago and the rapper Common and The Staples Singers. It's the Metro; Lake Shore Drive; Oak Street Beach; and those expressways with the funny names—the Dan Ryan, the Edens, the Ike.

If you're an adult and you live in the Windy City, you are by definition "political," whether you know it or not. It's in the DNA. It's in the filthy Chicago River water, it's in Oak Street Beach, and it's in the loop. Chicago is to politics what a parasite is to a host—a symbiotic relationship that keeps one another going and going until …

The Chicago of 2018, as I write this, is far different than when I lived and worked there.

For me, Chicago will always be Northwestern University and the "el" and the Second City and Zanies Comedy Club and Bert and Rick and all the great comics. It'll be the Park West and WGN and thousands of hours at the piano rooms in the music building at DePaul University. It's where I studied the business of comedy—which was a stroke of luck I don't take for granted.

Chicago is where I met my wife.

I was doing my Shari Lewis-style sock puppet routine, following in Shari's footsteps and, later, the footsteps of a brilliant ventriloquist named Ronn Lucas, creating all sorts of "characters" by changing the hair or eyes or clothes on a sock. In a four-minute routine, that puppet could be a confused taxi cab driver ("Soldier Field? Never heard of it!"), a blues singer (aptly named "Bertha D. Blues"), a student at only-geniuses-need-apply University of Chicago ("I am the standard deviation!"), and a variety of other parodies of Chicago life. JP was still the main focus of my vent routine, the classic wooden slot-jaw puppet that buoyed me through the first eight years of my professional comedy career. The jokes with JP dealt with girls, clothing, jobs, and music. As time went on, his character began to take on a composite personality based on many of the "middle acts" that came through Chicago and worked at Zanies Comedy Club.

> It is no secret that the popularity of ventriloquism waned during the 1960s, '70s, and '80s. There were some professionals who managed to keep the "art" alive during those meager times. Jay Johnson starred as a ventriloquist on the popular television sitcom *Soap*. He was very good live and kept vent somewhat viable in comedy clubs. Another was Ronn Lucas, the amazing performer and sound manipulator who could do unbelievable effects with just his voice. Those two acts saved ventriloquism from going into the wastebasket of public approval, and there are many of us who owe them much gratitude.

The best local comedians—T. P. Mulrooney, Larry Reeb, Judy Tenuta, Emo Phillips, Jeff Schlessinger, Tim Cavanaugh, John Caponera, Paul Kelly, and Teddy LeRoi—were the ones I studied. I worked with them on a weekly basis, and though they didn't know it, they had become adjunct teachers for me. I learned the little things about comedy stagecraft—how to "take the stage," for example; how to deal with hecklers; and how to "work with the crowd."

Working with the crowd—aka, "Where are you from and what do you do?"—was particularly important for me as the full-time emcee at Zanies Comedy Club. Since I only had a thirty-minute act—and only ten to twelve minutes of it was any good—I had to learn how to talk to people from the stage and kill time, all the while making people laugh. This included having to think on my feet; finding the humor in someone's job or college major; and doing so without making that person feel mistreated or exploited. The jokes couldn't be personal. The jokes had to be about something the person did or things out of their control. Instead of making fun of someone who was a mini-mart clerk, I would make fun of the clientele clerks at mini-marts had to deal with. Instead of persecuting someone because he or she worked in a government job, I made fun of the government. It was a winning formula then, and it is a winning formula today.

Most stand-up comics don't want to be emcees. It's considered a low point in the hierarchy of the comedy world—headliners make the most money; middle acts, sometimes called "feature acts," make a little less, the opening act makes the least, and the emcee is... well, the emcee is considered a necessity—but for someone else to do. Because being an emcee is considered a hindrance to career advancement.

I saw it differently. I saw the emcee as an extension of everything going on at Zanies—from the waitresses to the bartenders in the back of the room to the bar managers and especially the show itself. And that included the comics. I tried to make myself the glue that held a show together every night. I wanted to be an integral portion of the entire experience from the audience point of view. There were nights when I only did about fifteen to twenty minutes of material because the headliner didn't want me doing more. Sometimes I had to do an hour because the comedians who were booked for the show struggled or baled out of their sets early or didn't show up on time.

> This concept for emceeing was a logical progression of what I had learned at Northwestern—people don't buy something for the product itself. They buy the *experience*. So Zanies Comedy Club made people laugh. This applies directly to the most successful solo acts. People follow a comic because they like the way he or she makes them *feel*.

Obviously influenced by the local comedians, all of whom were funny and supportive and very professional, I learned how to deal with hecklers, how to take a set that was tanking and save it, how to open a performance, and how to close it. Their influence and their expertise were—and still are—essential to my work.

It was the touring comics who gave me insight to the world of show business on both coasts and how things in the big time work. Some of these men and women were stars from the TV world, particularly those who had appeared on *The Tonight Show Starring Johnny Carson*.

David Sayh was a classic example. Sayh was a New York comic who had done more than ten appearances with Carson and played Zanies a couple of times a year. Sayh was older than the rest of us. He had a wife, a couple of kids, and a mortgage. His career might have peaked, but he was still very good. His set was tight, honed, and well rehearsed. He could do it in his sleep. He had lots of work and the most pristine credit. "Please welcome *Tonight Show* veteran David Sayh!" gave him immediate viability. I'm guessing that he still works—a lot.

At the other end of the spectrum was the new school, the Lenos and Seinfelds of the world. They drew a huge audience to Zanies, and sometimes there were so many reservations the club would add shows. The local TV affiliates would drop by to interview these new stars, and I watched them handle the questions and their celebrity with the kind of confidence and aplomb defining the megastars they would become.

Rick Uchwatt began to book this new breed of comedian. Stand-up comedy had become *the* hot showbiz ticket in every major city across the country, with comics getting TV shows, cable specials, and movies. Rick was no longer booking all local guys with an occasional star when he could afford it. Now there were guys with real credits and a following he could book every week. Larry Miller, Marsha Warfield, Jackie Martling—the room was full every weekend. There was excitement and drama almost every night. And I was in the middle of it.

The big radio personalities who "everyone listened to" in Chicago had changed with the times as well. When my father had been at WGN the big name, the *only* name in the radio personality world, was Wally Phillips. Like the change in comedy, radio had gone to a different style as well. For Chicago, the team of Gary Meier and Steve Dahl were dominating the ratings and the airwaves. It was only a matter of time before they decided to perform in a comedy club and make some cash off a live performance.

They were crowd-pleasers, giving their fans exactly what they wanted. Dahl and Meier talked a lot, told some stories their fans knew about, and gently chided me for being a ventriloquist. As happens with acts who aren't used to the comedy club world, they only did about forty-five minutes. Rick told me, "Go back up there and do another thirty!" I did.

The rest of the weekend—another show Friday, two shows Saturday, and a Sunday night show—went the same way. Dahl and Meier would go on (genially poking fun at me). ("Wait," they'd say, seeing me walk on stage with JP, "you're not gonna do ventriloquism! *Nooooo!*" And their audience would laugh. Then they would laugh. And even I would laugh.) Their set would last a half an hour, and I'd go on and do my act. These kinds of shows were the best thing to ever happen for Taylor Mason. Working with the radio stars was fun, because they were on the air every day and had a legion of fans. But this was also the first time I actually "headlined" a comedy club.

Dahl and Meier ended up being a sort of middle act for me, and while they had their audience laughing and applauding for their time on stage, they were the perfect "set up" for my fledgling material. Comedy club audiences want laughs, regardless who the performer is. An act, or in this case a duo, can get by for a while on celebrity and notoriety, but there has to be a big payoff in the end. So while Dahl and Meier's fans were thrilled seeing their idols live on stage, I followed their presentation every night with my best possible set of music and comedy and ventriloquism, getting big laughs and lots of applause.

Stuff like this would happen every few months at Zanies. A well-known celeb would come to the club, sell a bunch of seats, and then bomb as a headlining act. But I had grown to the point where I could fill in the gaps and finish off the shows.

> I learned this about celebrity: Being well known for being well known does not necessarily imply intelligence, talent, or worthiness.

The club itself had a story. Zanies had been built as a strip joint sometime in the 1950s. The ghosts were everywhere, from the weird mirrors on the walls to the oddly shaped room and the psychedelic art on the walls. The front window was huge, no doubt built so that passersby could look in and see the girls strutting their stuff. When the club switched to comedy, the window was covered and used as a billboard promoting the upcoming performers.

The front door was on the immediate right of the stage. People didn't walk in so much as get sucked into some other world, something far short of exotic but way off the beaten path.

The Second City, just one block away, had a charming artsiness, and the immediate feel of "theater" as you walked upstairs to its main room, greeted by staffers and a history of entertainment. It was a Chicago landmark.

Zanies was a block down the street. It was rough around the edges. The room was long, front to back, like a railroad car. The catwalk that had once been the center of the club was gone, replaced by tiny tables and chairs. The bar was in the back, all the way at the end, hidden from view behind a makeshift sound booth and a shaky dividing wall separating the miniature bathrooms from the audience. The ceiling was low; the lighting was haphazard and dim; and it smelled of a thousand nights of hard drinking, perspiration, and musky humanity. It was tiny, seating only 150 people max, but because the room was so tight and so close, laughter would rebound and carom off the walls and reverberate back and forth, off the ceiling to the floor, shaking away the ghosts of strippers and lonely men. When Zanies was rocking, the laughter literally went right through you, regardless of where you sat. There was nothing cute about it, nothing "homely but lovable." It was dark and seedy and a little bit lewd. It reeked of improbability, diversion, and surprise.

Zanies was hip.

Behind the bar was a small storage area for the booze, a popcorn machine, and an ice maker. Not an inch was wasted. There was a door in the back, heavy built and substantial, locked every night. And it would be months before I was actually allowed to go in and out there, instead of walking in the front door. It led to a narrow walkway along the side of the club, where beer and liquor were carted in. Chicago's finest would occasionally stop by for reasons I wasn't privy to, knocking on the door and asking, "Can we talk to Ricky?" It was a perfect place for elite acts to keep away from their fans by sneaking in the back door.

A rickety stairway led to the second floor, and there was the office of the clubs owner and main booker. Everything upstairs was some kind of deep brown wood, with a large desk and artwork from the strip club days. There was shag carpeting, right out of a 1960s Rat Pack movie, brown and red and yellow and the absolute definition of "tacky." Rick's office was off limits to me, so I would visit only when he invited me in. Bert had an office up there, too. In later years, they remodeled the entire second floor and made it into a "green room" with a bath and couch and refrigerator.

There were old-timers who would come to the shows, sad old men in beat-up winter coats and those definitive Chicago hats with flaps that covered their ears, eyes watery from five hundred too many scotch and sodas. They'd sit front and center, looking around at the walls and the young people and this club where they used to watch "da girls." They'd order drinks. They'd sit, silent and staring around the room, while the people sitting around them—younger, vital, alive—would laugh and cheer the act on stage. The old guys would look around, slowly get up from their chairs, and leave.

Marsia would come down from the Second City where she worked every once in a while to see my act, especially when one of the superstars came to town. Of Jay Leno, she said, "Everything is funny." Jerry Seinfeld: "I didn't laugh once. Boring." Emo Phillips: "So clever." She gave me one bit of advice, one simple piece of wisdom from my friend and lifetime partner on an obscure night driving home to our apartment in the Mazda.

"You can't take so many breaks," she said, looking at nothing, just making a comment as I drove through the dark city streets.

"What do you mean?" I wasn't mad or hurt. I wanted this—data, critique, information.

"Sometimes it seems like you don't know what you're going to do next, and it's uncomfortable for the audience."

Whoa.

"That makes sense," I said, "because that's the way I am working. I have no idea what I'm going to do."

She waited to respond until I realized I was supposed to look at her, and then she said, "Okay. Well, just don't let it be so obvious to the audience that you're searching for your next thought. You have to be in the moment with them. It's fine not to know. Just don't let the audience know."

If you get that kind of intuitive advice from someone, you should seriously consider making him or her your bestie.

Or marrying him or her.

Show business is like most businesses—a hierarchy where, at the top, you find the leaders and owners and people in supervisory positions. The stars. Next are the driven ambitious workaholics trying to get ahead. And finally there are people with a job, doing their best, showing up for meetings and sessions and coordinating the day-to-day operations that make any given enterprise successful.

There are two major differences. One is that, to be successful in entertainment, you need some kind of talent. Not that a career in sales or manufacturing or banking is devoid of talents. But entertainment is different because not only are you working to please the public and impress people, but you are also offering a skill they do not have. In other words, for someone like Taylor Mason, showbiz is just like every other business except that I have to be *funny*.

The other major difference is that in my business the coworkers change on a regular basis.

This wasn't true in the beginning. At the piano bars and at Second City, there were the regulars. For example, Henrici's in Oak Brook had its bar with a good man working behind it—J. Burton Reynolds.

As a musical director for the Second City touring company, I worked with a set cast, so Steve Assad and Vince Waldren and Ron Dean were my coworkers, the people I got to know best.

Zanies was another world, with different headliners and all kinds of acts coming in on a regular basis. There was the staff, including Bert the operations manager, Fernando the bar manager, Brant Harris the bartender, and all the waitresses—Brigette and Dee and many more. This was my family for a couple of years, and the precursor to a career in the business.

This is showbiz, remember, so your friends are the people you're working with. My friends and coworkers have changed and intermingled for some thirty-five years. With some, it's been a one-night fling, where we did a sound check and a rehearsal in a theater or a church or a club, never to meet again. With others, it's been a single TV shoot for a commercial or promo of some kind. Maybe it's a couple of nights in a club somewhere. We work together for those short evenings, connected in a visceral way.

I always try and thank coworkers, let them know I appreciate their work and what they have done for me. The personalities are different, but the expectations are the same—they'll help as much as they can, but I have to do the job. With that understanding, I come in to each setting without attitude or emotional baggage. I try and lighten the mood. I try and set myself up as approachable, flexible, and easy to work with.

When I have done television shows or major tours, the people involved—and I mean *everyone* involved—become my friends. So friendships and relationships are always in a state of flux and change, drastically, from year to year, month to month, and week to week. A two-year run with a children's TV show (*Taylor's Attic*) meant I formed strong bonds with camera operators, producers, directors, writers, actors, and staff. When the show ended, so did those bonds. A tour with Southern gospel singers and the hundreds of people who made the arena-to-arena concerts work, meant I had great friends and pals for a couple of years. When I left the tour, I left those friendships behind.

Over the years, as an icebreaker, I used this line right after my sound check: "Sounds great. Now, when I get up on stage, please turn the *talent* knob all the way up as high as it will go. When anyone else is on stage, turn it down a little bit ... just so there is obvious difference between my skill and theirs."

Today this line can be found on T-shirts! Hey! I *want my residual*!

DEFINITION: residual. In showbiz terms, residuals are the royalties or postproduction payments that come long after you wrote or performed or worked on a TV program, motion picture, or theatrical play. I like to call it "mailbox money," because it's impossible to predict but always a welcome sight.

There were lots of good nights at Zanies, lots of fun shows and electric crowds. My memories are good, and there probably was no other place in the country where I could have been allowed the opportunity to grow and improve I was given there.

I met some incredible acts. The comedian John Fox, unknown to most of America, came in three to four weeks every year. His act was vulgar, raunchy, and crude; he defined "X-rated." He was made for the toughest show in all show business—the late show Friday night in a comedy club. Mr. Fox was also very, very funny and had been compared, laugh for laugh, with the Eddie Murphys and Richard Pryors and Robin Williamses of the world. Fox was a true road warrior. He had a forty-five to fifty-minute act that never wavered, beginning to end. He could do it in his sleep (and the wait staff could do it, word for word, after six or seven shows in any given week). He often went on stage drunk and got drunker as he worked, but the booze seemed to amplify his performance, and he would leave his happy laughed-out audiences drenched with sweat and physically exhausted from the experience.

"Big Ed" was a three hundred-pound gay man who couldn't sing, played the piano poorly, and used every garish sexual prop you could think of in his act. He drew a wild crowd and gave them exactly what they wanted for ninety minutes every show. The same went for Ollie Joe Prater, a fixture on the comedy club scene in the 1980s with his full beard, cowboy hat, and boots. These two had knockdown, drag-out hilarious shows that would blow into town, rock the club every night, and head off to the next gig. I had very little in common with what their act was on stage; but their work ethic, their ability to give the audience—and the club—what it wanted was unmatched. They could be much funnier than the "name" comics who had TV credits and power player agents. These artists had a chip on their shoulder the size of Mt. Everest, and they wore it proudly. I always felt I had more in common with them, those hard-working and ever-creative comics who were trying to become stars in the business - even though our live sets were ideologically opposed; I worked "clean" and they worked "blue."

Comedy clubs in the '80s and '90s were everywhere. Outside Los Angeles, New York, Boston, and San Francisco, the clubs ran a three-person operation for the most part—an emcee, a feature act, and the headliner. For any given show, there could be one to two "guest sets," where someone would come in and audition or work on a set or just ply his or her chops with the blessing of the club owner or other comics on the shows.

These "road clubs" were open from Tuesday or Wednesday through Saturday or Sunday. The Tuesday and Wednesday night shows were smallish crowds; Thursdays were usually "specialty nights" for ladies night or radio station promotions and so on. The "money nights" were Friday and Saturday, particularly Saturday. And Sunday was a wildcard—if Monday was a holiday, the Sunday night shows would be jammed.

The weekend was when comedy clubs made their money—two shows Friday and two or three on Saturday. The Saturday shows had the best audiences, energy-wise, because people were not coming from a long workday. This was a real night out, classic "date night." And the shows, for the most part, were fun and fast-moving. Since there were multiple shows, the start to finish times had to be kept tight, as the staff had to get the drinks out and the comics had to get off stage on time to get the next crowd in.

The late shows on Saturday were often free-for-alls. The week was coming to an end. The crowds were happy and ready to laugh. The comics had been honing their stuff for some five to six shows, and they had it down to a crystallized set.

But the Friday late show was something else.

Friday late show is where a comedy act grows up.

Friday late shows could be a zoo. Think the Cantina Bar in the original *Star Wars* movie—that collection of aliens, half humans and ne'er do wells. That is the definition of second show Friday in a comedy club, an audience of people who had been at work during the day and now had come out to the club to end a workweek. There was probably some drinking before the show (it *was* 11:00 p.m. after all). So there was alcohol, maybe some drugs, or a combination of both in a lot of bodies. Sometimes for the audience, it wasn't a planned event, just something to do late at night on a Friday in a given city.

It was place to go for no other reason than to have a place to go.

Given those parameters, the Friday late shows could be bizarre, venturing into a black hole of deviance and oddity. Groups of young people might come in and start heckling before the evening started, yelling at the waitstaff and demanding things that were not on the menu. There was an aura of danger, an underlying vibe that the show could be a disaster. Worse, someone might get hurt. And most problematic, a comic might have to deal with an aggressive, unreasonable, and very inebriated paying customer combining the possibility of physical confrontation with booze.

At the late show Friday, you might have to deal with one numbskull.

Or a hundred.

When I first started at Zanies, I feared the Friday second shows. They were nightmares. That condition—total fear of what might happen—continued for months, since I worked clean and didn't do the "insult comedy" that worked well in that setting. I tried not to let it hinder me because Friday second shows were not my goal in business, and second show Friday was certainly not my audience. It took a lot of second show Fridays to find the way to be successful.

By the time fall 1984 rolled around, Marsia and I had carved out a little life for ourselves. The wonderful thing about being some sort of creative artist in Chicago during the mid-1980s was the quality of life. Our little one-bedroom apartment on Kenmore, just a block south of DePaul University, cost us $175/month in rent. We ate out a lot, Chicago being one of the best restaurant cities on the planet—Chinese, Mexican, Italian, and Chicago-style pizza. There was a florist around the corner, and since we were earning a little cash, I would get flowers every week or so for my girlfriend.

Marsia's dad sold us his car—a 1982 white Mazda, and the night it was officially ours was huge. It was as if we had become adults. We got in and drove around the city, laughing and not believing our luck. *We had a car*!

> One night, walking home from our favorite Greek restaurant, I suggested to my live-in girlfriend, "Let's cook out tomorrow! Let's get a grill, and I'll charbroil some meat!"

Marsia laughed and said, "Okay!"

"In fact, there is something I wanted to ask you. Marsia?"

She looked at me. We had been living together for almost eighteen months. We had made a commitment of sorts. So I asked her this: "Would you …"

She was holding my hand, and now she squeezed it really hard.

"Would you … marry … nate some steaks with me?"

Zanies jumped on the franchise bandwagon that year, opening a club in Nashville, Tennessee. I had very little experience "on the road." Marsia got me a gig one night out in Rock Island, Illinois. Someone called the Second City looking for a "comedy host," and she booked me over the phone, sight unseen, so I drove out and did it. The show was highly forgettable for a bunch of reasons. They were disorganized beyond belief (shades of the future!). The featured speaker was golf legend Lee Trevino who gave a short talk that was hard to hear because he didn't know how to use the microphone. The only things I remember: I got paid $500 (*a lot!*); it was only three hours from the Near North Side of Chicago to the Quad Cities on the Illinois-Iowa border (I'd thought that was light-years away back in high school and college); and I didn't mind the driving.

I'd driven to gigs before. The trips out to Poplar Creek and the Mill Run Theater took planning and some knowledge of what road to take (this was pre-GPS). But I was home to sleep in my own bed, a perk I don't take for granted these days, and so none of these jobs qualified as "the road."

Then came the job in Nashville. Bert came to me and said he and Rick wanted a full-time emcee for the club in Music City. It was new. They needed to train the staff, the audiences, and any future comics about the way Zanies did business. Zanies in Chicago had always had excellent emcees. It was part of the brand. So they offered me a four to five-week run. It was steady money. I took it.

I'd only been living with Marsia for a year or so, and now I left. It was her first glimpse of what life would be like as my wife.

The day I left, she hugged me and said, "This is a big opportunity for you."

She was right, and I'm proud to say I didn't waste the time. It was a great primer for what was to come.

Ricky bought a condominium, and all the comics stayed there during the day and then headed to the club as a group every night. This was my intro to the "comedy condo" culture that became the stuff of backstage late-night chatter in comedy clubs for years to come. The Zanies condo gave me my own room. Cable TV had just started, and we all spent a lot of nights sitting around watching the new channels—MTV and HBO being the most popular. The place had a kitchen, four bedrooms, and two baths and was maintained by a cleaning service that came in twice a week. All in all, this was a very nice, very sane, very *unusual* kind of comedy condo. It was livable.

My comedy condo experiences would be far different in the near future.

The month in Nashville flew by. The club was new, comedy was the hot thing across the United States, and all the big stars came through town. I really enjoyed working with Yakov Smirnoff, the Russian-born comic who drew standing room only crowds for his killer sets. He asked me to play piano for his closing number—where he dressed in full Cossack regalia. And I did it every night as the audience clapped along and hooted and Yakov danced. It was so much fun.

After returning to Chicago, I won a comedy contest. It took place at the Hyatt Regency on Wacker Drive, sponsored by a radio station and a beer company. The station turned the hotel bar into a comedy club for a night, and most of the local comedians, about twenty acts, showed up for the big event. I went on, did some of my stand-up, closed with my partner JP, and absolutely nailed my short ten-minute performance. I didn't think I had a chance to win and couldn't stick around to find out because I had to race back to Zanies and finish my spots there.

I was standing in the back of the club when I got a call at the bar. Brant, the bartender, said, "You have people calling you here?"

I shrugged. I dunno. Maybe. I took the phone and shouted, "*Hello*?" over the laughter and applause coming from the packed room.

On the phone was the woman who had run the comedy contest, excited and shouting into the phone, "You won! The judges said you were the best!"

I drove over after we finished the Zanies set, and got my prize:

Two tickets to Los Angeles
A set at a comedy club in southern California

Marsia and I spent the next day planning our trip to the West Coast—the land of show business. We decided to spend our time checking out the comedy scene, see if we could get some bookings, and interrogate friends who had moved from Chicago to the West Coast. Was it possible to live and afford the prices in Los Angeles? And was there enough work?

If things didn't look good on the West Coast, we wouldn't care. We were making plans, and if LA wasn't a good fit, we'd move to New York City.

Chapter Thirteen
Not Afraid to Fail

*We are here to laugh at the odds and live our lives
so well that Death will tremble to take us.*
—Charles Bukowski

If you could boil comedy—all showbiz really—down to its essential elements, you're left with this: How will you deal with failure?

And after you've dealt with failing, after you've been rejected and turned down and passed over, that's when you come to a fulcrum. You either stop chasing a career in the business, or you get to the place called "not afraid to fail."

Comedy is the business of failure. Jokes fail. You're performing on stage and the mike fails. You memorize a short routine; you go on stage; and; even though you've done the lines a thousand times; your memory fails or you blank on the lines. Or maybe you just panic.

Epic fail.

It's never ending. You audition for a spot at the local comedy club or you get a casting call for an Internet-only commercial or maybe for a role in a major motion picture. You give a great reading of the script, and it all goes well but there isn't a callback. And even when you do a great job, absolutely nailing an audition or performance or interview, the booker/producer/client still might say, "Sorry. No. Next."

DEFINITION: callback. The first step after an audition where the client/producer calls an auditioning artist back for a second audition or interview. Not to be confused with the comedy performer's term, also known as a "callback," where a comic does a joke based on a previous joke in the same performance.

A fact of life: Showbiz will not be easy. I understood early on that I was going to fail—a lot. That has not changed.

It's similar to sports. A pro baseball player who hits .300 is considered "good," even though he *fails* 70 percent of the time! An NBA player is a great 3-point marksman if he makes *half* of his shots! You can be a millionaire as a pass rusher in the NFL if you sack the quarterback once—*once*—per game. That's *one out of seventy plays*!

So, applying that concept to my job, maybe one out of ten jokes I write actually works. That reads pretty bad on paper, but in my "real" world, it's doable.

Here is a personal example.

I appeared on the 1990/91 season of television's *Star Search*. The show, a precursor to the talent search television vehicles that came along in the 2000s like *American Idol* or *America's Got Talent*, was a made-for-TV-competition program pitting singers; dancers; musicians; and, most popular, two comedians against one another in each episode. Both acts would get two and a half minutes to perform, and then the in-studio audience would "vote" for one act or the other. The winner would continue on to the next episode, and the top four winners in those categories would compete for a $100,000 prize.

My personal manager at the time was Rick Rogers, and we came up with this strategy: Try and fit nine to ten jokes (one every fifteen seconds) into each of my sets and hope that outdid my competition.

It was a simple concept. If I "hit" on seven of the ten jokes in my show, and my competitor hit on all six of his or her jokes during the presentation, I still won! By attrition! Even though my competitor was right 100 percent of the time, I would get to move on in the show because I had more successful punch lines: 7–6.

It worked. I ended up doing a few weeks in a row on *Star Search* and then went to the finals and earned $100,000 for my efforts. Not only was it a career-enhancing opportunity, it also enhanced the value in not being afraid to fail.

> The jokes wrote themselves. "I won $100K on *Star Search*! We invested that money for our kids to go to college. They'll be able to afford ... books!" And my partner Romeo said, "We won $100K on *Star Search*. That money's gone. We played Vegas." He did a long take, looking directly at me, and then shouts, "Three is not a color!"

That was the entire premise for my work—setup, punch line, laughter. Put three of those together and you have the beginnings of a "routine." Put ten together and you have a monologue. Put thirty minutes of those in a row, and you're going to get paid by someone, somewhere, to tell jokes as a professional.

The opposite of that is the failing part. Put three bad jokes together, and you have sentence. Put ten together, and you have a paragraph. Put a couple of paragraphs together, and you're getting booed off stage, you're running through the parking lot to your car, and you're spiraling into a depression that will take an entire bag of Doritos, a liter of ... whatever you like to drink, and weeks of soul-searching to overcome.

My little trick is to advance by failing. I'm falling upwards. I write and perform so many jokes that, sooner or later, something is going to work. So let's say I succeed 10 percent of the time. I write ten jokes and put them in my act. One of the ten works. Did I fail nine times, or did I win one time?

Who cares!

The issue is I have to write a hundred jokes to get ten that work.

By 1984, I was doing seven to eight shows a week as the Zanies emcee. I was working with all the best acts in Chicago, who were supportive even though I was (ahem) doing a ventriloquist act.

There was an old spinet piano on the tiny stage, banged-up and out of tune for much of the year. I used it a lot when I started. It was an easy time filler. My impressions of Elton John, the Beatles, Billy Joel, the Who, Stevie Wonder, and Aretha Franklin got big laughs. I had closeted my favorite "skill," because to perform a ventriloquist act in a hip comedy club in a major city smack-dab in the middle of a stand-up comedy boom looked like evidence of career suicide.

Or failure.

Eventually I made a marketing choice. One night, I asked Bert, "Who else is doing ventriloquism in the comedy world?"

He didn't have an answer.

In Chicago there was one, Bob Rumbaugh, who I knew and admired. But ventriloquism was not just passé. It was shamed. Ridiculed. Disgraced.

Perfect!

It was a risk, because it was considered so passé. But ventriloquism would make me unique and separate me from all the other (very talented and funny) stand-ups who came through the club every week. From the start, it felt natural and right. My act changed regularly because I was experimenting with routines (JP as a cab driver, JP as a Chicago politician, JP as a sportscaster) and jokes based on ventriloquism ("Taylor, please stop putting words in my mouth; you have some deep-seated control issues, man. You need a therapist").

I started getting attention from showbiz people with big connections in the Chicago area, usually referred by Bert or Rick. I shared the stage nightly (as emcee) with superstar touring comics of the day—Leno, Seinfeld, Sinbad, and Richard Lewis. I would often have JP, my vent character, introduce the act.

Unless the act specifically asked me *not* to introduce him or her "with the puppet."

I needed to bridge the gap between ventriloquist, emcee, and stand-up comedy. Before taking the emcee job, I had watched Chicago comics work as the show host at Zanies. Those acts often started the show by "going to the crowd," asking people where they were from, what they did for a living, what movies they liked, and so on. It's a great skill. There are comics who have based careers on being able to make audiences feel comfortable, gently making fun of jobs and hometowns and the immediacy of the moment. I began using the audience in my act, especially when I emceed. "Who's from the suburbs?" People who got up to use the restroom got interviewed: "Do you really have to go now? Are you gonna come back? I'll save your seat!" Talking to the audience made the next step easy: I began telling jokes.

I turned my act into a tri-headed comedy vehicle, perfect for a comedy club and instrumental in getting through a tough second show Friday. I could perform a funny music parody act, where I did "Meet the Flintstones" as a reggae jam or a rock opera. I could switch to ventriloquism, bringing back my socks routine from childhood and my woodenheaded muse JP for some fast vocal interplay. Or I could do a six-minute stand-up routine about driving into the hinterlands of the Midwest. ("I was in the middle of Iowa. It looks serene and friendly with all those fields of soybeans and cows standing around, but don't be fooled! There is a dark side. I turned on the radio and the announcer said, 'There will be a public stoning in Des Moines this Saturday. Bring the kids! Free rocks for the first fifty attendees!'")

Sometime that spring, Rick Uchwatt put me in contact with Jam Productions, a Chicago agency that handled rock music tours, and the agency began booking me as an opening act. This led to some twenty-five to thirty dates in big arenas and large club settings for a variety of performers from all walks of the pop music world—Spyro Gyra, Warren Zevon, Chaka Khan, and Herb Alpert and The Tijuana Brass. Every one of those opening act spots was a thrill, and something offbeat and weird seemed to accompany every gig.

Chaka Khan let me do a set before her show in April, but when she returned in October and saw me, she looked at Scotty, the Jam Production agent, and said, "I told you I had to have a black act. I'm not working with any more white comedians."

Scotty turned to me, laughed, and said, "Sorry."

I didn't care. I understood. There were a lot of African American comics in Chicago, and they didn't have the same access I did. Ms. Khan was helping the people in her community who needed help. I wasn't mad. If anything, I admired her.

I got a two-show night with Canadian folk rocker Gordon Lightfoot, performing at the Mill Run Theater in Niles, Illinois. The Mill Run, which had been state of the art when it was built, was nearing the end of its life here on earth by the time I started working there sometime in the mid-'80s. The funky thing about it was the stage, called "theater-in-the-round," which rotated 360 degrees as I worked, so I was moving as I performed, the audience passing before my eyes in slow motion.

DEFINITION: opening act. The opening act is supposed to "warm up" a given audience. The idea is to galvanize and encourage the crowd to enjoy the "headliner" or main act for the evening.

The first night I did a show at the Mill Run, I worried I might get motion sickness or that the audience would see my hand in JP's back. But nobody said a word about that, and I didn't ask. I was often introduced by someone off stage: "Please welcome Taylor Mason." I would go up in front of 1,200 people with to no applause, no recognition, and no feedback. It sounds like a lose-lose proposition for an unknown entertainer, but the truth is it worked. The Mill Run was intimate and friendly. The staff was cordial, and the audience, regardless of the headliner, always seemed to be attentive and responsive once I started.

> Sometimes the opening act is better than the headliner. In that case the headliner is actually *closing for* the opening act.

I had rewritten an old country ditty called "The Auctioneer's Song." I changed the melody and added my own lyrics, and I would perform my rendition of the song a cappella with JP. It wasn't so much funny as entertaining, showing off my ventriloquist skills nicely, especially in a small club like Zanies. The tune worked even better in the big Mill Run theater. And when I nailed the auctioneering part perfectly—done by JP, of course—I would get a long applause break. Those kinds of crowd reactions are essential to big arena and theater shows because it eats up time. I banked a couple of those applause-inducing bits in the act so that I could take a breath at the ten- and twenty-minute marks of a thirty-minute set. One I counted on was my "Auctioneer Song." The other was a wordy routine about going to heaven or hell. The punch line of that one was:

Taylor. But if you don't get to heaven, you might end up in hell!
JP. That wouldn't be so bad!
Taylor. How can you say that?
JP. Because, Taylor, *all our friends will be there*! And a lot of folks in this audience, too! (*That line would earn laughter and applause, so I tagged it with another punch line*: Just think, we'll get to meet the president, the mayor, the governor, Keith Richards.")

The references to local politics, sports teams, and locations has always been a staple of my live performances. And the hard-core work I was doing in front of various audiences has proven to be a good formula for my entire professional career.

After a strong opening set in show one for Gordon Lightfoot, I stayed in the wings of the theater to watch the star perform. I had always been a fan, having learned "The Wreck of the

Edmund Fitzgerald" by ear on the piano down in Champaign. And his million-selling "If You Could Read My Mind" was one of the favorites I'd played while doing the piano bar gigs. So I watched in earnest as he strode to the microphone to a huge ovation and started in with a song I didn't recognize.

Mr. Lightfoot's set was uneven and choppy. He would start a song with his guitar and then stop and turn to the band. He'd shout something, and they'd start over. This happened a couple of times before he picked up a bottle—could have been water, could have been something else—and took a swig. He started the chords to the pop song "Sundown," recognizable and familiar like a pair of shoes that slide on when you wake up in the morning. The fans clapped and whooped. Gordon began singing.

Then he stopped.

The band kept playing. He was waving his right arm over his head, I think in an effort to get the band to stop. But they kept going. The bass player walked over and said something to Gordon, who stepped to the mike and then stepped back.

He had forgotten the words! The band kept playing! I couldn't stop watching.

Today, in the twenty-first century, the big music acts all have teleprompters and media devices on stage telling them what to sing. Heck, lots of the tracks are on digital playback machines, so if the singer isn't in key, he or she just lets the track do the work and lip-synchs.

But in 1984, there was no teleprompter, no digital playback, and no tracks. There was just a frustrated bass player trying to help a superstar get through another night on the road as a career came to a soft landing in a now-defunct theater in the Chicago suburbs.

I'll say this in Lightfoot's defense: It didn't matter because the audience was singing the words as if it was part of the show. The band and its leader, off balance and out of kilter, joined in with the crowd—some 1,200 of them, singing his own song back to him as the stage spun in its steady circle.

During the break between shows, the stage manager came up to me as I was eating my dinner, sitting alone at a folding table with a paper drop cloth on it.

"Good food?"

Recognized by someone with clout? I was ecstatic. "This is great! Catering? Unbelievable! I wasn't planning on eating anything between shows."

He laughed at my over-the-top-excitement and sat down.

"We have a problem."

I stopped eating. I felt the panic come quickly into my throat, and I visibly swallowed, like a cartoon character who knows he's about to get flattened by the big cement roller. "What did I do?"

The stage manager put his hand on my arm and looked around the room as if he were going to give me the code to a bomb that was under the theater, which I was supposed to defuse. "You know that auction song you do?" he asked.

"Yes? You want me to drop it? Change it? Make it longer? Whatever it is, I'll do it!" I was practically shouting at the guy, half-relieved that I hadn't been fired or told my check had been held because I had done something wrong.

"Well ..." He looked down and shook his head. "Uh ... Gordon is going to do that song in the second show."

I stared at him. "You're kidding."

He laughed and shook his head again, fully aware this was awkward and said, "No, not kidding."

He patted me on the shoulder and walked away, over to the stage manager, and spoke to him briefly. The stage manager, used to dealing with celebrities and their peccadilloes, went to the sound and stage crew and spoke to them as they were sitting and eating dinner. They laughed out loud and looked at me. I laughed back. They gave me thumbs-up and shouted things like, "You have to give him your puppet, too! And when he's finished singing you can put him in a suitcase!"

Lightfoot did "The Auctioneer" in the second show.

> Gordon Lightfoot recorded "The Auctioneer" on his album *Dream Street Rose*.

I opened for Conway Twitty, the venerable country music star who had, by the time I was lucky enough to share the same stage with him, been in showbiz some thirty years and had a legion of devoted fans. He also owed the State of Illinois some umpteen thousand dollars in back taxes. So when I arrived at the Mill Run, there were police cars everywhere, surrounding the theater and making their presence felt by standing around and eyeing everyone who entered through the backstage door. The authorities were determined to nab Mr. Twitty after his one-night engagement. I couldn't see how it would be possible for the man to escape Chicago's finest, who stood at every doorway as I worked.

I don't remember how my set went. I do know that, days later, I got word that Conway had eluded the grasp of the cops, ferreted away at the end of his show by his adoring followers, who apparently mobbed him at the stage, whereupon he changed clothes and walked out without being detected.

Maybe the most memorable act I opened for was the iconic Tina Turner.

It was 2015, and I was standing in line with assorted moms and children at the guest services desk on the *Disney Dream* cruise ship. There was a two-person band playing in the giant lobby. The "band" was really just a pretty blond girl wearing a red-sequined gown and singing pop tunes in a shrill voice. She was accompanied by a much older bald guitarist, wearing a bright blue blazer and an open-collar shirt and playing his guitar, along with a big karaoke-style machine that supplied backing tracks and vocals.

They were loud.

They stood on a riser in the middle of the room, under a spectacular chandelier, matched only by a beautiful concert grand piano that sat elegantly silent by the guitarist. The songs they were doing were pop hits from the '80s through today. They weren't bad musicians, staying in tune and in tone and in time, while people milled around them enjoying the vibe. Small children were dancing or doing somersaults on a plush red carpet. Some of the adults were wearing evening gowns and tuxedos. I was caught up in the family-ness of it all, watching the scene as I waited my turn to confirm a flight home.

I was in hide mode, wearing a baseball cap pulled down over my eyes so I wouldn't be recognized and then feel obligated to make small talk. A mom behind me had already given me the "I know you!" smile that expects a return look. I pretended to check my iPhone for "important" messages.

The band started a new song. It was easily recognizable to people of a certain age.

It was the Tina Turner hit single, "What's Love Got to Do With It."

Time travel kicked in. Poof. I was no longer standing on a cruise ship in the Bahamas:

> My memory is clear. I am racing up the Tri-State Tollway north of Chicago, my girlfriend in the passenger seat of the white Mazda we bought from her dad, my future father-in-law. All the windows are open wide as we head from the city to suburban Niles, Illinois. The girl—soon to be my wife—is happy and laughing. We're shouting over the loud music blowing out of the speakers, competing with the traffic and the wind. It's the kind of pristine moment that will pop into my head for the rest of my life whenever I hear Ms. Turner on

the radio, at the gym, or being sung by a duo on a cruise ship.

It's 1984. I pull into the parking lot behind the Mill Run Theater. My partner/puppet JP is in a nylon bag in the backseat. I grab the bag. I take the arm of my girlfriend, Marsia, who follows me as I strut assuredly through the backstage entrance ("See? I've been here before!") and through another doorway with a big sign that says "stage" on it. Then I'm in the dressing room with all the crazy drama and excitement and very definition of living the dream.

I'm wearing a solid blue shirt and a 1980's-style red power tie. Scotty the booker is there, hobnobbing with tour managers and personal managers and theater staff and the myriad of hangers-on that show up for nights like this. He smiles at me, gives me a confident nod, and saunters over.

"She wants you to do thirty minutes."

"Great."

Tina Turner was in the beginning stages of a history-making career comeback, with a monstrous hit single ("What's Love Got to Do With It") playing in rotations on every pop radio station in the country.

The Tina Turner experience was far different than all the other Mill Run acts I worked with from country and pop and jazz. She was a bona fide rock star who had built up a history that played perfectly with celebrity stardom. She had been abused by her ex. She had suffered through civil rights. And she had come through personal and professional hell more focused, more talented, and more *incredible* than ever.

She did not need an opening act.

But there I was! I did my set, walked off, and stood with Marsia in the tunnel leading to the stage. The crowd had been polite during my little presentation, laughing and applauding when appropriate. But I was little more than a time waster, and

I knew it. When Turner finally appeared to us, underneath the seats in the dark shadows behind the stage, she was in a world of her own.

Two bodyguards held her up with their hands in her armpits. Her head, with the trademark brown shag hairdo, was thrown back, and her eyes were closed. She looked as if she had passed out or was being dragged from the scene of a horrible accident. Marsia whispered to me, "She's in a trance!"

As if on cue, the band began the recognizable chords to "Nutbush City Limits." The Mill Run Theater transformed in a drumbeat from mundane suburban theater to rock 'n' roll fantasy. The lights went out; a spotlight exploded right in front of us; and Tina Turner, in all her Tina-ness, came to life, a time bomb of energy, strutting to the stage in a white-hot light, her painted-on electric blue miniskirt revealing everything as the crowd surged forward, standing, screaming, and waving. She was the definition of superstar—beautiful, confident, focused, and totally in charge. She was forty-four years old, and she rocked with more energy than artists half her age.

Two days later, I was with Ms. Turner again but in a very different setting. Turner had contracted a series of dates with the McDonald's Corporation, doing shows for their yearly management conference in different locations around the United States and Canada. Although she had now reappeared on the pop culture scene and was once again a major touring artist, she was honoring her agreement with Mickey D's. She would do the remaining management conferences, even though she could have been out raking in the dough at all sorts of big arenas around North America. The vibe at the McCormick Center was very different than that of the Mill Run. Turner put on a great show, at least what little of it I saw. But the lesson learned has stayed with me all these years—honor your contract.

The Mill Run was a venue that served me well, with its revolving stage that cut the audience into quarters, so that a crowd of 1,200 became 300 people per revolution. My act played well there, me with my woodenheaded partner JP and the occasional sock puppet à la Shari Lewis. I worked with jazz greats like Spyro Gyra; pop stars like Neil Sedaka and Bobby Vinton (who offered me a full-time job opening for him in Branson, Missouri); and the occasional country act (Ronnie Milsap among others) who were on the downside of their careers.

It was just one of many places Jam Productions used me. The Park West Theater in downtown Chicago was a real rock 'n 'roll club, one of the nicest in the city. I learned quite a bit as the opening act for the likes of Warren Zevon, Chuck Berry, Jerry Lee Lewis, and a Chicago band called Off Broadway. The Zevon show was unforgettable.

I've always been a Warren Zevon fan, having picked out the piano chords (there are three, total) to "Werewolves of London" while playing the piano in the front room at Sigma Chi. There were many of these acts I worked with whose songs were part of my repertoire either during my piano bar run or with my comedy act. It feels awkward all this time later that I shared the stage with these people at all. No doubt I was, at least to them, a throwaway part of the program. I was a never-known, immediately forgotten entertainer who killed thirty minutes of show time one night in some city—in a life of one nights in many cities with never-known, immediately forgotten entertainers.

But I knew them! I knew them through their songs! I could play the Jerry Lee Lewis songbook front to back ("Somewhere over the Rainbow" being the only tune he recorded that had more than a couple of chord changes and a chorus in addition to the verse). I learned lots of Jerry Lee's music by listening to my brother Locke's collection of Chuck Berry records (and his piano player, whom I would actually get to meet in person one day a decade later, Johnny Johnson).

On occasion, I'd get to meet these stars and feel as if I was part of the whole event. And with most, I could have said, "I'm a big fan! I use your music in my act!"

Mr. Zevon was a hard-drinking, hard-rocking, hard-living stereotype of 1970's rock, and that included all the effects and trappings that go along with the life. You could make a case that he needed an opening act like me because his body, ravaged by a certain lifestyle, couldn't handle a two-hour show on his own. Why else have an opener?

His crowd imitated that essence. I call it "the Stevie Nicks effect." Fleetwood Mac, the iconic classic rock band, came to Champaign, Illinois, while I was in college. I didn't see the concert, but the day after, all the sorority girls were dressed like witches—the Stevie Nicks effect.

The people who bought tickets to see Warren Zevon had become Warren Zevon. They wore black leather jackets, chains, tattoos, tattered jeans, and an attitude. They were playing their part, looking like the dysfunctional and world-weary characters that inhabited Zevon's songs, so that, when I walked on stage to a muffled, "Please welcome Taylor Mason," I was immediately heckled and cursed by some bikers sitting right in front of the stage.

The flop sweat started gushing before I reached the microphone.

It had to have looked like a joke to them. I was wearing a pink button-down oxford shirt, a pair of gray slacks, and loafers.

"We've seen a lot of comedians," one of them shouted.

"You ain't gonna make it!" A hand appeared out of the darkness at the foot of the stage and into the spotlight, like an arm coming out of a grave in a horror movie. I was startled by a tattoo of a sword running along the beefy forearm. It set a beer right there, right on the stage, as if daring me to kick it off. The hand slinked back into the darkness. I could make out bodies sitting and standing in front of me in the inky blackness on what was a dance floor some nights but had tables and seats for concerts like this.

I was completely intimidated, and I felt my mouth go dry.

Someone shouted, "Get off the stage, moron!"

I had thirty minutes to go, staring into an abyss of impatient anger. I looked around. I was alone. There was nobody standing in the wings; nobody doing "crowd control"; nobody giving me an encouraging, "Go ahead, young sir! Show us what you can do!" I looked around at the monitors, the mikes, the amplifiers, and the guitar stands set up in the helter-skelter formation a rock band uses.

And there, in the middle of it all, was a Steinway concert grand piano, black and shiny and perfectly lit for the coming master.

I didn't need a prompt.

I walked over to the piano, sat down, and said, "You guys wanna rock 'n' roll?"

I got heckled, as I should have (what a dumb thing to say): "Ha ha ha! Right! This isn't Barry Manilow land! You have to be able to play it to do it!" some drunk shouted.

So I started. Simple. Easy. I played through "Whole Lotta Shakin'" by Jerry Lee Lewis. I segued into "Little Queenie" by Chuck Berry. By the time I changed the song to Little Richard's "Tutti Frutti," I had people singing along. They sang drunkenly and out of pitch, but at least I had their attention. I finished the medley, there was some applause, and I stood up to get into my act.

Bad move. The crowd started jeering me again: "Where're you goin'? You ain't done! Play some Skynyrd!"

So I sat right back down and played "Back in the USSR," the Beatles song. I changed that to "Honky Tonk Women," a Rolling Stones classic and something every one of the nine hundred Zevon devotees seemed to know by heart. Why not? I stayed with the Stones and started "You Can't Always Get What You Want," which was thankfully the perfect tune for this drunken bunch. They were singing along! I could picture them out there in the void, arms around each other rocking back and forth, one big family, singing, "But if you try sometimes, you just might find you get what you need!"

I played the chorus for some five minutes, doing every showbiz trick I could think of:

"OK, just the women!"

"Now just the guys!"

"What about the bikers? Lemme hear the bikers!"

"Just the people from Wisconsin!" This got a laugh and a contingent in the back of the room made a game effort, shouting out the lyrics as best they could and getting a distinctive "clink" of beer bottles and a rousing cheer from the audience around them.

"Just the bartenders!"

"Okay, just the cokeheads!"

I did "Hey Jude," the Beatles again, and the perfect sing-along song for hard-partying rockers everywhere. "Na-na-na-na-nah-nah. Na-na-na-nah. Hey Jude!"

I was doing my old piano bar act, but now I was in a big-time joint!

By the time I played the last chorus and looked at my watch, I was done! Hallelujah! My time was up! I had done my thirty minutes. So I said, "Thanks everyone!" And I walked off to inebriated cheers and yelps and applause.

I was met just behind the curtain by a stage manager who, just a few minutes earlier, had given me an evil eye when I sat down at the keys and screamed over the singing audience something like, "You better hope that piano stays in tune!" As I walked toward him, big dopey smile on my face, he said, "Don't ever do that again." I kept smiling and moved past him and past the band waiting to go on. He shouted after me, "Nobody plays Warren's piano!"

Scotty appeared with my check and the smile of someone who knows where all the bodies are buried. "That was the best set I've ever seen a comedian do!" he yelled over the audience—now cheering for their hero Zevon, who had walked on stage.

I thanked him. I headed for Zanies, where I would perform for a smaller very different crowd that same night. I was ecstatic. I had just rocked Park West for a half an hour, was told by the booker that I had done the best comedy show he'd ever seen, and I had not told one joke!

I rarely met the celebrity acts I opened for. It was an in-and-out deal for me. I'd arrive two hours before showtime, do a short sound check, and wait around for someone to say, "Mason! You're on!" I'd do my job, get my check, and go back to Zanies or to the apartment and sit with Marsia as we'd watch TV and go to bed. It was a quick rush, a brief brush with celebrity and fame, and then I'd go home. I loved that.

There was an outdoor arena called Poplar Creek in the 1980s as well. As I became a regular opening act in Chicago for big-name entertainers, I was also booked for outdoor shows in this suburban setting. Poplar Creek was very different from the Mill Run Theater, sitting on a few acres of land and exposed to the elements. People could sit in the seats under a pavilion, or they could sit a thousand feet away under the sky, on the grass. This was a challenge because I had to "play big." It was a cavernous venue, as if someone had carved a concert hall out of a cornfield (which is probably close to what happened), seating a few thousand folks. Every time I worked there, it was sold out.

Herb Alpert had scored a late-70's hit with an instrumental called "Rise," and his name still packed these places across the country. He toured with a large band, so smaller joints like the Mill Run were impossible for his show. Aunt Ardie had one of his albums, something I listened to mostly because the cover art was unforgettable—a woman giving the camera a come-hither look dressed in nothing but whipped cream. It was probably cutting edge at the time. But now, in the mid-'80s, it had entered into what could loosely be described as "wholesome." His crowd was mixed, people of all ages, and it turned into a special night for me. It was the kind of night that sticks with you and makes you believe more success is coming if you keep your focus and your ethic; you have to be patient because it's on the way, and it's coming soon. Nights like this prove you made the right decision and nothing can stop you now! I had the kind of moment that makes you feel affirmed. You've arrived.

In the middle of my set, as I bantered with someone in the crowd, a man way out in the darkness, shouted, "You should be on Johnny Carson!"

The crowd erupted in spontaneous applause.

I floated off the stage and glided back to Chicago in the Mazda, the stereo cranked up as loud as it could play. George Clinton and Parliament cheered me on, singing "Can You Get to That." My predestined life and career as a successful entertainer flashed beside me with every car I passed.

I would be the opening act for lots of stars in the coming years, but these first experiences put a thumbprint on my career, a sort of rite of passage that helped turn me into a performer who could work any kind of venue, for any audience, in any way. Some of these acts were on their way to the top of superstardom, like Tina Turner, who would be starring in hit movies and selling out major arenas just three or four years later. Some were forgettable when I did the show with them, ghosts of AM "hit" radio in the early 1960s, still looking for one more chance at the top. There were the Bobby Vintons, who moved to Branson and got his own theater and held on for years. If these first years after Northwestern were a master's program in the business of show, I learned a lot seeing these ex-stars, current wonders, and future celebs as part of their concert appearances.

Years later, I worked with a band from New Jersey called the Smithereens at a college in Pittsburgh. I had to perform while they were five feet away, behind a curtain, doing their sound check. I tried to tell my jokes and do my ventriloquist act over the kick drum. I worked with the Temptations at a college in Colorado and REO Speedwagon and Trisha Yearwood in Chattanooga, Tennessee. Those were outdoor shows on muggy summer nights in Chattanooga, Tennessee. Legions of giant bugs were flying into the stage lights, and one flew right into Yearwood's mouth as she was singing. The pro handled it really well, downing a bottle of water and going right back into the song.

In Lake Tahoe, I opened for Kenny Loggins, Crystal Gayle, and Reba McIntyre. (She said, "Someday I'll be opening for him!" It was a line I stole and use to this day.) I was on before the BoDeans and the Gin Blossoms at colleges in Wisconsin.

One night, back at the Park West in Chicago, I opened for Chuck Berry. The band was made up of Chicago musicians, who were rehearsing when I got to the club. They stayed on stage, playing rock music as the audience filtered into the club. They were still on stage when I was introduced, and they stood and laughed and watched my act and started playing again the moment I walked off.

There, in the backstage dark, between the cases and the soundboards and the boxes and the stuff you see in any theater off the main set, was Chuck. And Scotty. Mr. Berry was being paid, right in the open, in cash. Scotty counted it out. The band was playing. Chuck recounted, blasted a smile that looked radioactive in the backstage dusk, and walked on stage. Scotty handed me a check.

"He gets paid before he goes on?" I asked.

"Always," said Scotty.

Lesson learned.

I walked outside. At the curb right in front of the club was a Park West bouncer arguing with a policeman. "This is Chuck Berry's rental car. He's gonna leave as soon as his show is over!" The bouncer, short and stocky but clearly built for his job, had been given orders and probably tipped very well.

Chicago's finest didn't care. "Can't park here," said the cop.

The bouncer said, "Well, I don't have the keys. Mr. Berry does. He's on stage. He's working. He told me he would leave in exactly"—the bouncer made a show of raising his right arm and pulling back the sleeve of his jacket to reveal a watch on the underside of his wrist,--"exactly fifty-two minutes from now."

The policeman said, "Okay. Have it your way. I'm calling a tow truck."

The bouncer pulled his sleeve back down to cover his watch, brushing it with a certain aplomb. "You do that, officer. You call the tow truck. I wonder how long that will take? *Two hours*?" He laughed.

The policeman left.

To this day, I follow that Chuck Berry model. I fly in; I get a rental car; I drive to the gig; I get my check; I do my job, meet my fans, and drive back to the airport or the hotel for the night. Lesson learned.

If it's good enough for the superstars, it's good enough for me.

Opening act is not the easiest, not the most fun spot to be in. The star is the person everyone came to see. The reason for the opening act comes down to this—the star doesn't have enough material to cover a full show (say ninety minutes) and needs some filler. Or the star *can't* do a full show on his or her own. More often than not, it's a time killer. Gotta justify those $50 to $100 tickets! Enter the opening act.

> Professional boxing has another name for it—"the undercard." Which sounds like the place a magician hides the "missing" eight of clubs from the deck. Being the opening act is a little like boxing; you have to take some figurative punches.

Sometimes it doesn't work. Marsha Warfield, an African American woman from Chicago who had a very strong headliner career in comedy clubs and went on to star in *"Night Court,"* the great sitcom, rejected me as her opening act. So did *Saturday Night Live* impressionist Darrel Hammond. But I've had great experiences. I met the Four Tops at a college in Indiana as their "support act." They didn't need me, but it was a blast.

I had spent my teen years and countless nights in college learning the chords to hit songs by REO Speedwagon, Tina Turner ("Proud Mary" was one of the first pop tunes I learned by ear), Gordon Lightfoot, Jerry Lee Lewis, Warren Zevon, Chaka Khan, the Beach Boys, Neil Sedaka, and more. Here in the mid-1980s, I was realizing my ambitions on the same stage with them, telling jokes and singing songs before they gave their live performances. I'm still overwhelmed by those experiences. The retelling feels as if I'm trying to recount a movie I love that I haven't seen in a long time—something that happened, something that I vaguely remember being part of, but something that could not possibly have happened to me.

Opening act is a risk. Nobody goes to see the opening act. The opening act is like hors d'oeuvres at a society dinner: What is this? Is it any good?

Can I get some more?

Believe it or not, these days, I have comedy acts and musicians asking to open for *me*. Sometimes, just to make things easier, I'll go on first and do some of my act, and after fifteen minutes or so, I'll introduce the "opener." I learned this trick from the great Ken Davis. It improves everything.

Look man... no matter how tuff it gets, no matter how hard they make it... keep fighting! There is no defeat, there can't be a loss, you will win! There can be
NO SURRENDER!

I'm dancin' to the beat of the drummer in my own head that nobody else can hear!

FROM TAYLOR MASON'S PERSONAL DIARY.

Chapter Fourteen
New York City

It takes $200,000 a year to be poor in New York!
—Bernie Sahlins, my wife's boss at the Second City Theater, when we told him we were moving to NYC

Marsia had been planning for a while to leave Chicago. Her job working for the execs at Second City was not glamorous, but it gave her some cachet in the world of entertainment. She was a Jersey girl, had left everyone and everything she knew to move to Chicago. She had no fear. It was time to move on.

Me? I was kinda letting things lead me by the nose. Chicago had been better than I could have hoped. But if Marsia was going somewhere—LA? New York? Boise?—sure, I'd go!

Winning the comedy competition in Chicago felt like the universe had sent us a message: It's time to leave the Windy City and get to the next big thing. First stop, Los Angeles. The competition prize gave us free airline tickets and three free nights at the Hyatt Regency on Sunset Boulevard, so we had free travel, and we took full advantage. There were lots of Chicago transplants working in Hollywood, so we got some vital data from people who were living in SoCal. We looked at a couple of apartments and got a feel for what monthly rent was (expensive). I canceled my spot in some comedy club where I was scheduled to perform as the Winner of the Chicago Comedy Contest. Instead, Instead, I got on stage at the world-famous Comedy Store in Hollywood, which had a lot more cache. Then I did a few minutes at a little club called Igby's, thanks to a phone call on my behalf from Bert Haas and some connections I earned from those nights emceeing at Zanies. I didn't need to perform somewhere I'd never heard of. I needed to get a feel for the scene in Los Angeles.

> Igby's Comedy Club was one of the best rooms I have ever worked. The crowds were always attentive and responsive, and I had a lot of good nights there. Igby's will be mentioned again. I'm sorry it no longer exists.

What we learned in our short stay was that Los Angeles can be very expensive and ultracompetitive, and comedians flowed like water. Most of the acts living on the West Coast traveled "in country" for two to three weeks of every month for comedy club or college shows to be able to pay for living expenses. The one to two weeks not on the road were spent auditioning and begging for spots in the elite comedy clubs.

Everyone was in show business. You stopped at a gas station, and it might turn into an audition. The attendant asked, "What can I do?"

"Fill it up, regular," you answered.

The response was, "Based on your suggestions *fill it up* and *regular*, I'm going to improvise a short comedy monologue as I put gas in your tank!"

On the four-hour flight home, we huddled together in our seats and discussed the future. Our future. What to do? Where to go? We came to a mutual decision not to move to Los Angeles, at least not yet. We'd go to New York City first. Marsia had family in New Jersey. There was a lot more work for comedians in New York and the surrounding area. And it seemed we had more business contacts and friends out east as opposed to the West.

As if to affirm our choice to move east instead of west, just before the move, I met a man who would pave the way to a career in show business.

Joey Edmonds was unassuming and sincere, a little shorter than I am with short brownish curly hair and a friendly smile. He approached me at the end of a typical Zanies night, people milling around the club after the show, paying their bills and hobnobbing with the comics. I was heading back to our little Chicago apartment, walking past the bar to exit out the back, and Joey reached out and touched my arm.

"Nice job tonight."

To be singled out by anyone after working as an emcee was more attention than I usually got. I've never been averse to flattery. I stopped. "Thanks."

He went into a pitch. He was an agent. He had worked as a comedy act for colleges and was now booking colleges and was always on the lookout for "new talent" to do college shows. He said I had been recommended. He liked the fact that I worked clean and stayed out of the bathroom and bedroom for my premises. He asked if I had done any college shows. I had. He asked if I'd like to do more. I said, "Yes. I'm always looking for work."

For the next sixteen years, Joey Edmonds and I did some hundred plus (often as many as two hundred!) college shows per year. In all, Joey Edmonds booked some two thousands shows for me in every kind of post-high school education environment you can name. I did Ivy League schools. I played all the "power conference" colleges and universities. I worked private schools, public schools, military schools, religious and faith-based schools, some of the historically black colleges and universities, and community/junior colleges. I worked culinary arts schools, prep schools, flight training schools, law schools, med schools, adult learning centers, and every other school you can name. East Coast, West Coast, wherever, whenever—I did it.

Joey Edmonds kept me working and helped me pay first the rent and then the mortgages and then for my children's clothes and early education and vacations. His professional suggestions, from what to use on stage (and what *not* to use) were the kind of thing that can only come from experience. And experience he had, having been a comedy act with partner Thom Curley for many years. "Edmonds and Curley" had performed on *The Tonight Show Starring Johnny Carson* in the 1970s. That performance had led to thousands of shows for the duo at colleges all over the United States. He is directly responsible for the NACA (National Association for Campus Activities) "showcases," where comedy acts get seen and booked.

Joey, married to an excellent stage actress, decided to stop touring in the early 1980s. He and wife Lynn had two children, both of whom work to this day in Joey's still vital and successful agency.

He was kind and thoughtful and decent. He understood my lifestyle and the fact that, like him, I was not just my job; I was a husband and father who did an act. Celebrity and notoriety didn't scale as compared to treating people with dignity and sincerity. We won awards. We made a lot of people happy. We helped raise money for philanthropies and foundations and service groups. Joey Edmonds would go on doing that and much, much more for a decade and a half after I left his ever-thriving agency.

DELETED PASSAGE HERE

I felt an immediate connection to Joey that night we met, and everything he said made sense. He talked about the college market. He talked about how an act would fly into a city, get a rental car, and drive to a college performance. He didn't glamorize anything. He was honest and fair and he spoke of the bottom line. The big selling point was money: I could earn three times what I was making at Zanies, and maybe more. I had the feeling he'd been watching me for a while.

> It turned out the very funny Chicago comic Tim Cavanaugh had been working with Joey and doing college shows for a couple of years. "I am seduced by the money," he said. When he first told me about his college tour, I said, "I'd never do that!" So here's my mea culpa, Tim. Feel free to call me Mr. Hypocrite because, within a year of meeting Joey, I was a full-fledged college comedian doing sixty to seventy college shows a year. That would triple over the next decade. Most of those were far from home.

My first road shows in the college world were a blast. Joey got me a job opening for a short-lived TV star named Larry "Bud" Melman, a Brooklyn man who fell into a career on *Late Night* with David Letterman. Melman (real name Calvert DeForest) didn't have an act, per se. He was a celebrity, a made-for-TV icon whose career came and went like unwanted spam in your inbox. His job was to kill forty-five minutes on stage, just being "Bud" Melman. He would walk out on stage with a couple of co-eds from the school (or community—by the third gig I had the feeling his support team hired models or escorts), and that entrance got the biggest response he'd get all night. It was painful to watch. And because his act was so short, he needed an opener.

Enter Taylor Mason. Joey got me three shows with Melman, at the University of North Dakota, North Dakota State University, and the University of Minnesota. I flew from Chicago to the city of the school for each of the shows, did my set, and flew home. For these, I was picked up by a representative of the school, who took me to a hotel, picked me up for a sound check later, and then returned me to the hotel after the performance. I took early-morning taxis to get home.

It was 1985. I was out of Northwestern University just two years. I look at pictures of myself from that era, and I look a lot like the college kids in the audience. I'm sure many thought I was a student at their school.

So my introduction to "the road" wasn't so bad. I got treated very well down in Nashville, with my own bedroom in a nice condo. I flew to the upper Midwest and did shows with a TV celebrity, where I was literally blowing the headliner off the stage and garnering great reviews from college activities counselors, and I was making $750 per show.

Mr. Cavanaugh told me, "Joey is honest and sincere, and he'll get you a lot of work." On his advice, I agreed to a handshake deal with Edmonds. It seemed like a really good opportunity. I'd pick up some college dates, and maybe that would help offset the cost of our new apartment Marsia had found. She had flown to New York and, with a friend, had signed a lease for a second-story flat in Park Slope, Brooklyn.

I got booked on a local television show in Chicago, performing in front of a small audience in a storefront theater. Joey videotaped my act with a camcorder, made a couple of copies on VHS tapes, and sent those videos to some colleges in Pennsylvania and Ohio. To my amazement, the Penn State University system booked me for twelve shows over a sixteen-day period. This little tour—the beginning of a decade and a half of college gigs—would earn me $6,000 in just over two weeks.

It was so off the beaten path of things I thought I knew and things I took for granted to be true that thinking about it now makes me wonder why I didn't quit on the spot.

First, Joey had me do a set at Joliet Junior College in Joliet, Illinois, on a Thursday afternoon just before we moved. He wanted me to see what college shows were like. "It's not all theaters and arenas like the Melman shows." This job was the perfect way for Joey to get feedback from a student activities director he knew well—a way to see if we could work together.

My performance was a precursor of things to come. At Joliet, a microphone and makeshift speakers were set up in a hallway between a cafeteria and classrooms. The concept seemed to be they wanted someone performing as students were going to lunch or taking a break. It wasn't anything like the shows I had been doing for the balance of my career during the past three years, where I was the focus as a featured entertainer. This was uncomfortable, and I had to fight my initial thoughts about the gig because it felt demeaning, insulting, and ripe for problems.

The words of my father and Rick Uchwatt echoed in my head: *Don't be a cynic.*

As a performer in this situation I was competing with young people meeting one another after class; some were intent on studying; most just wanted to get something to eat and move on. People were sitting, standing, walking, and talking. There wasn't any focus. There wasn't any interest. My introduction? There wasn't one.

"You can start now," said the student activities director, a disheveled older man (maybe in his late forties?) who looked to be worn down by a life stuck in the disappointment and myopia of a midlevel job at a community college.

So I went to work. I tried joking with the students. They ignored me. I shouted. I sang. I had JP talk to girls as they passed, making dumb comments and trying desperately to get attention. For whatever reason, it worked. After fifteen to twenty minutes of cajoling and begging and babbling, I had what might be called an "audience." Some 100 to 120 junior college students sat in various positions on chairs and couches and the floor, paying me a slight bit of attention and waiting ... For what?

I did my act. I thought it went horribly.

There goes that, I thought, driving back to Chicago. *I blew it. I guess the bright side is I won't have to deal with that humiliation anymore!*

But Joey called me at home that night. "You were a hit!" he said. "You're going to do very well in the college market!"

Lesson learned. To succeed in the college market, all one had to do was make a sincere effort to do a show, try and engage the students, and not get frustrated. I could do that!

So I moved with my girlfriend to Brooklyn, New York. Marsia's Jersey childhood pals, Ralph and Peggy, helped us bring our few belongings into our new apartment. It was on the second floor of a condo owned by the family we rented from and was very small. There was a front area by big windows looking out on John Jay High School. A few feet past that (there were no walls) was our bed, and on the opposite end of the apartment was a kitchen. There was a bathroom.

Marsia took a couple of odd jobs before her career in show business would also change.

There wasn't time to examine our new life in New York. My first tour—the Penn State University trip—started three days after moving in.

And that's what it was—*a trip*.

My concept of college was based entirely on two of the best universities in the country—the University of Illinois in Champaign and Northwestern up in Evanston.

Illinois was one of the original "land-grant" institutions in the United States—designated to receive the benefits of the Morrill Act of 1862 and 1890. These schools were founded to teach agriculture, science, military science, and engineering. Most, like Illinois, became public institutions across the country. (There are exceptions like Cornell and MIT, but who's counting?)

My private school experience came at Northwestern, one of the top-rated schools in the nation.

Both were members of the Big Ten Conference with stately brick buildings, diverse student bodies, big-time athletics programs, and large Greek systems. To be a student at these schools is to be insulated from the real world as you prepare for careers and lives of personal and financial fulfillment.

Right.

My tour of the schools in the Penn State system was unlike anything I could have imagined while I was a college student myself.

Penn State had a "feeder" college program, not unlike most community colleges. A student takes class at Penn State DuBois, for example, in Dubois, Pennsylvania. For those two years, the student takes his or her core curriculum classes—English, math, chemistry, and so on. If the student completes the two years he or she can then go to state college and join the big school—*Penn State*—and focus on a major. It's not a bad idea, and I'm sure it's worked for thousands and thousands of people.

For many students, this was a much cheaper way to get a college diploma. The system offered a good chance for them to save on tuition, maybe work from home and make money, all the while earning credits toward a degree.

Another difference: As with most community colleges, the student population had a healthy number of older students. Among them were retirees and parents working toward getting a second income. There were people who had dropped out of the workforce and were trying to find their way back in, starting with an education.

Specific to me, the yearly bill at most colleges and universities included a "student activities fee." This might result in all sorts of fun things for a college student to take part in. It could mean a mixer at the beginning of the school year so freshmen could meet one another in a safe faculty-approved place on campus. It might mean movies every Friday night at the student center, maybe a post-athletic event party or a dinner for Valentine's Day.

Lots of schools use this fee to bring major popular recording artists to the school for a concert. It might be used for an author or politician to come and speak and answer questions from the student body.

And, in my case, part of the student activities fee went toward "entertainment." The Penn State feeder schools had, back in 1985, one office and one activities person making decisions for all the schools. So when my video was viewed and approved, I was given a contract through the Joey Edmonds Agency for some twelve colleges all over the state. I started out at the Penn State Berks campus, northwest of Philadelphia in Reading, which had an established campus, athletic fields, and a fairly big student body. It was modern and very up to date, and the school had me perform in the evening in its brand-new theater. It was perfect! *This was gonna be a breeze*! A couple of hundred students showed up, I went on stage and did sixty minutes of an act, and was paid via check (!) right afterward. And, they gave me a hotel room.

I had written some jokes just for college, of course. These were mostly based on my act from my days at the U of I. They were about bad cafeteria food ("You know something is wrong when you see the guy in front of you shouting at some green food on his plate, 'Make it jump back on your tray!'") and books ("It's such a trip to have to actually read books ... and there aren't even any pictures!") and dating ("My college girlfriend really opened my eyes to the opposite sex. I'll never forget: We were sitting at a bar, talking, and I realized ... wow ... you've got, like, your own *opinions*!").

But the next thirteen days were completely different than this first show. Joey had booked the tour across the state in a methodical way, so I followed Route 80 across the state (Pennsylvania is *huge*) school by school, town by town. Most of the shows took place in cafeterias, where I had to compete with kids standing in line for food; announcements over the loudspeakers; students studying; students playing cards or Dungeons and Dragons (yes, this was a big deal during college shows throughout the 1980s); and a lot of people who just didn't want to hear from anyone, much less a comedian and his puppet.

At the Harrisburg campus, I had done almost an an hour when the activities director told me, halfway through my performance, "Oh ... sorry. You weren't supposed to go on until 30 minutes from now." It was 11:00 a.m. "You have to go until noon. Sorry." I had already used most of my act up performing for the twenty or so bored teens sitting in front of me. So I did what any beginner in the business of comedy does when all else fails; I made fun of my surroundings. Pointing at a picture of a waterfall on the wall, I said, "There is the great Harrisburg Waterfall! Anyone know what happened to it?" No response. I realized at that moment that I was really no more than a teacher, and I was now getting exactly the feedback they would give to their Psych 101 or Beginning Rhetoric professors—nada.

I ignored their boredom and pretended that I was having a great time. "This waterfall was actually torn down to build your college!"

This got the attention of one of the students.

"*Really?*"

"Yes," I deadpanned. "There was a five thousand-foot waterfall here thirty years ago. Nobody talks about it. Nobody seems to care. But the truth is this structure could cave in *at any minute!*"

Now I had their attention.

"Yeah. In fact ... doesn't it seem like the floor is sloping downward, right where you guys are sitting?"

I didn't know if they believed me or not, and I didn't care. *I had their attention.*

"I'm kidding, you guys. The waterfall was located over there." I pointed out the window toward a gas station across the street. "Only a matter of time before that Sunoco falls into the earth."

I used this bit of business—making up crazy stuff on the spot, improvising, calling on my experience with the Second City—hundreds of times over the next twelve years in colleges. I often led "tours of your campus" or "stuff you never knew about your community college" and made up stories about the founders of institutions of higher learning from Maine to Arizona. Anything to kill my hour of "comedy" and get my check.

The next performance, this at Penn State DuBois, was memorable for a couple of reasons. I started my little set in the cafeteria for a crowd of perhaps fifty people. Many of them were older, well past the age of fifty, and they sat in groups of two to three, scattered around the room. I was given a small riser for a stage, with a microphone that was amplified by speakers in the ceiling, most of which sounded as if they had been blown for years. The cafeteria wasn't lit very well, but it didn't matter. Showtime was noon, and windows surrounded the modular picnic table-style seating, so there was plenty of light.

I did my sixty-minute show with a modicum of laughter and applause. When I was done somebody shouted, "You have to come back!"

I thanked the person who said this, a man in his seventies. "Do you all go to college here?" I asked, not having left the stage.

Everyone laughed.

"Nah. We stay at the senior home across the road. We're here for the free entertainment!"

This got a big cheer from some of the older folks in various stages of getting ready to leave and disparaging looks from ten to twelve college kids sitting around eating their lunch.

I put JP and my socks in a duffel bag and met with the student activities director. "Thanks for dealing with the seniors," she said. "They've kinda taken over our programming here." She handed me my check and left, and I got ready to head out myself.

That first college run would conclude with a late-August show at Waynesburg University, about an hour south of Pittsburgh. Unlike the Penn State schools, Waynesburg had yet to start classes. I was a kind of welcome-to-college show for incoming freshman and a welcome-back-to-campus act for returning students. This was a four-year university, unlike all the schools I had played up until now. It was small; nestled in a community just off the expressway; and easily accessible from Ohio, Pennsylvania, and West Virginia.

I was performing in the student center, and there was a real stage and lighting, unlike most of the other the shows during this tour. There was even a big old piano I could use. I sat down to rehearse for a couple of hours, having shown up well before showtime.

Students would come walking in as I played the piano, testing the microphones and setting up. Everyone asked questions. And it blew my mind.

"Are you a senior?"

"I didn't even know there was a music school here!"

"Did you take a class to learn how to play like that?"

"Are you gonna be in any of my classes?

I was twenty-nine years old but still looked young enough to be a student. Even more telling, at the end of my show, some of the kids came up to me and asked when I'd be performing on campus again. Did I go to Waynesburg? Was I a teacher? Would I start a band? For the next five to six years there were many shows where my audience at any given college around the country thought I was a fellow student or grad assistant on campus. This worked to my advantage for the most part, because I had an immediate connection with the kids.

I created an act that was easy to perform and fun to watch. And it was one I could do at the drop of a hat. It was mostly ventriloquism in the beginning, but by the time college shows had become just a blip on the schedule of my career, I'd combined music, vent, and stand-up, plus some audience participation, so that I was welcome in just about every collegiate venue.

Joey Edmonds handled all my college shows as an exclusive booking agent. Based on the Near North Side of Chicago, his only job, his niche in the world of entertainment, was comedy for colleges. His career had actually started as a member of a singing group in the 1960s, a folk/rock act that featured harmony and socially relevant songs. Much of the performance of that group was the between-show banter of the singers, which led to Joey forming a comedy duo with Thom Curley.

Curley had left Edmonds in the late 1970s, off to pursue his fortune as a solo act. Our paths crossed a few times at Catch a Rising Star in New York.

The way to get a college to book your act was simple.

There was an organization called the National Association of Campus Activities (NACA). The organization had been around for a while, but before Edmonds and Curley, its live acts were mostly singers, bands, and the occasional magician or juggler.

Now it was the 1980s. Comedy clubs were everywhere. There were comedians on every street corner, and they needed work. Many were young, just out of college themselves, and looking for a way to make money. NACA "showcases"—which were kind of like auditions—began to use more and more comedians for colleges to look at and book.

There were NACA conferences in the four regions of the United States—East, Midwest, South, and West. Every year, there was a national NACA conference, too, which drew four times the number of college representatives as the regional conferences. At each conference, there were three to four or more showcases that featured all kinds of live performers.

These NACA showcases were the bread and butter for Joey Edmonds and myself. After the first one we did, Joey said, "I think you should emcee the showcase instead of perform on it." It was brilliant business and got us a lot of work.

If we played our cards the right way, we could book up to five shows in a three- to four-day period. Since the kids and the directors had seen me do three to four different "sets" during my showcase, it gave lots of schools a chance to say, "Yeah, he did music, and that works at our school," or, "The interactive part is really good for us," and so on.

Joey would book these routings for me, and I'd fly into a centrally located city and then drive to a school and do a show. A given week might look like this:

Monday – Fly to Minneapolis–St. Paul, arriving at 10:45 a.m. Get in a rental car and drive to Bloomington Community College, just twenty minutes from the airport. Do a "nooner" (walk on stage and perform from 11:45 a.m. until 12:45 p.m. Get my check and leave.)

Drive to a gym in the Twin Cities, work out, shower, drive to St. Cloud, Minnesota, and perform at 7:00 p.m. Get off stage at 8:10 p.m., get my check, and go to a hotel. Sometimes the schools paid for the hotel; mostly it was my responsibility. If the school hadn't paid, I'd drive to the next town and stay overnight in a hotel near the college for …

Tuesday—Wake up in Duluth, Minnesota. Hit the gym. Drive across the state line to the University of Wisconsin–Superior and perform at noon in the cafeteria. Get a check and drive back to Minnesota, performing that night at the U of Minnesota–Duluth. Sleep in the same hotel.

Wednesday—Get up late because I don't have to perform until the evening, at the College of St. Scholastica. I do the show. Collect my payment and drive back to St. Paul, stay overnight, and then wake up early.

Thursday—Get up and drive down to Riverland Community College in Albert Lea, Minnesota. Do a show at noon, get paid, and drive down to Waldorf College in Forest City, Iowa, where I finish the week with an evening show there.

Friday—Grab the first flight back to New York and hit the bank with a big deposit.

DEFINITION: nooner. The term for a performance at a college or any institution that starts sometime between 10:30 a.m. and 1:00 p.m. and is over by 2:00 p.m. These usually take place in cafeterias or lounges and are often a surprise to the student body and audience, who were unaware their day would include the guy with the puppet.

From the checks I got from each program, I deducted airfare and rental car fees, and would send 20 percent of the take to my booking agent (Joey Edmonds). Plus, I was home for the weekend to play the clubs in New York City or pick up a local comedy club or just hang with my girlfriend.

Not bad for a puppet act that didn't curse, with absolutely no major television credits and no powerhouse promotion.

During that first college tour—where I learned that Pennsylvania is a very big state and that the cities of Pittsburgh and Philadelphia represent a completely different part of America than the hundreds of little towns in between those two big cities—I got a lesson in show business in Monaco, Pennsylvania.

The Beaver Campus of the Penn State University system was a beautiful school, located northwest of Pittsburgh just off the Ohio River. I was performing a classic nooner in the school cafeteria. It was modern, with large glass windows surrounding the eating area. There was lots of space for students and visitors to spread out, eat, study, or relax. I was introduced and I did my job—a sixty-minute show for an appreciative mixed crowd of young adults and senior citizens.

I was given a check and a thank you by the activities director. I gathered my ventriloquist figures and put them in a suitcase. Then I was walking toward the door, off to my next job.

A short man wearing a white open-collar shirt and black pants stopped me in the hallway. His hair was shiny, thick, and as black as his shoes. I remember wondering, *Does he color his hair?* He gave me a big smile and said, "I really enjoyed your act. Thank you."

He was shorter than me, maybe five and a half feet tall. He stood with hands in pockets and a friendly smile and such an unassuming attitude that I stopped and put the puppet case down.

I said, "Thank you."

He said, "I used to be in showbiz." Before I could stop him or figure out if he was legitimate or not, he launched into his story.

He had been part of the vaudeville world of the 1930s and early '40s. ("I'm seventy-eight!" he enthused. "And I don't look it, do I? You don't have to answer.") He had put together an act with the help of his wife, and they had toured the United States playing long-lost theaters and showplaces, followed by a tour of dinner theaters in the 1950s. "I miss those days," he said. He had two daughters. He'd put them through college and was now a grandfather. He had stopped performing in the late 1960s. "The world passed me by." He worked in a restaurant for a few years and then retired. His wife had passed away some years before.

"I always come here to the college to watch you young guys."

He had my attention. I was familiar with vaudeville—what ventriloquist isn't? I've always felt the "comedy club era" of the 1980s and '90s was its own sort of vaudeville. I listened to his story.

His act did not change over the course of a third of a century. It was perfected down to the second and lasted about seventeen minutes.

He would request to follow an act that brought the house down, usually a great singer or outstanding physical performer like a trapeze act or incredible magician. The audience was still buzzing about what they had just seen when my new friend would go to work. This was his "opening" for years. No introduction. Always following a killer act. The audience never knew what to make of the little man who walked on stage apparently by mistake. He did not look like one of the entertainers, wearing a straw hat, a light jacket with a flower in the lapel, and loose pants. He stiffly walked to center stage, awkwardly looking around, appearing to be in the wrong place at the wrong time.

Eventually people would begin to shout at him.

"Get off the stage!"

"You're wasting our time! Let the professionals do their job!"

"As long as you're up there, you might as well do something!"

His performance included a bit of playacting. He appeared to be nervous, wiggling his fingers and shifting his weight from one leg to the other. The more agitated he appeared, the more the audience egged him on.

"Do something!"

"Dance!"

"Tell a joke!"

Finally he would take the flower out of his lapel. The audience jeered. At least he was doing something. He held it up. He looked at it and looked at the people sitting in the seats waiting for something to happen.

So he took a bite of the flower.

There would be a moment of silence. A collective, "Did he just eat part of the flower?" on the part of the vaudeville crowd.

A big cheer would follow, which emboldened him. So he took another bite. More cheers. He ate the whole flower.

Then he'd point to his hat. The audience would scream. He would take his hat off, examine it, and take a bite. Cheers and applause! So he would eat the hat.

Now he had won over the crowd, but he needed a "closer." He took off his jacket.

He was wearing a belt! He slowly pulled his belt off, held it high for everyone to see, and the crowd, now totally in his pocket, gave him wild applause and shouts of encouragement. He would hold the belt above his mouth, the way he had seen sword swallowers do, and just before he could take a bite his pants would fall down, revealing his garters and knickers. The audience would explode in laughter and cheers as my new friend covered himself, picked up his jacket, and ran off stage.

The flower, hat, and belt were made from a concoction of sugar, flour, and caramel. It was a painstaking daily process that he and his wife started first thing in the morning on workdays and took much of the day to complete. His entire live performance, perfected show after show, took less than twenty minutes.

He finished his story and shook my hand. I didn't want him to leave. I wanted to hear everything—what the theaters were like, who he had worked with, how he'd managed family and career, and how he had not gained five hundred pounds while eating all that sugar! But he was gone, having told his tale, while I foolishly didn't stop him.

I will always wish I could have that day back.

Chapter Fifteen
Catch a Rising Star

If they are not laughing at your goals, you are not dreaming big enough
—Sravani Saha Nakho

We were living on 4th Street in Park Slope, Brooklyn, across the street from what was then called John Jay High School. It was a couple of blocks from Prospect Park, where Marsia and I would jog in the mornings. Using every connection I had and auditioning on a nightly basis, I became a regular in some of the New York City clubs, including Catch a Rising Star, Dangerfield's, Stand-Up New York, and a downtown club called the Duplex. I doubled as emcee at Catch a Rising Star, mostly because ex-Chicago comic Emo came through with a good-as-gold recommendation. This all meant I had fairly steady work in the city. These were "showcase clubs."

Emceeing at Catch a Rising Star was much different than it had been Zanies because I had more to do.

The weekend schedules—two shows on Friday and three on Saturday—were set by the club's manager/agent, Cynthia Coe. During the week, there was more flexibility, and I often found myself juggling what act got to go on when, who got the best spots (between 9:00 and 10:00 p.m. when the audience was "warmed up" and "fresh") and who got the worst slots in the evening. These came after all the really good comics had been on stage, rocked the room, and left the audience "laughed out." I was introducing a lot of people who were on their way to stardom in television and motion pictures. There were names like Dennis Miller, Ellen Cleghorne, Chris Rock, Jon Stewart, Joy Behar, as well as the big acts I'd seen back at Zanies—Leno, Seinfeld, and the like. On occasion, a bona fide superstar would come in, and the club would become the center of the comedy universe as Robin Williams or Rodney Dangerfield would mesmerize an audience for a few minutes.

DEFINITION: emcee. The emcee, or in today's lexicon MC, is based on the term "master of ceremonies." The emcee is a host or announcer who introduces performers and presenters at a particular event. The role actually has its roots in the Catholic Church, dating back to the fifth century, where the master of ceremonies officiated the papal court.

I made some enemies. It's easy to do in a business of celebrity, ego, superb talent, and the ever-present pressure to be funny. My system was simple: There would be a set list of comics' names on a piece of paper posted by the doorway that opened to the two hundred-seat show room. This was a guide, and I could follow it as I chose.

My evening might unfold as follows.

I'd go on and warm up the crowd with some of the tricks I'd learned in Chicago. "Hi, I'm Taylor Mason. I'm the host for the evening and my first goal is to find out as much as I can about this comedy crowd. Who's from out of town?" The key to success in this situation is not to make fun of people's looks, ethnicity, sex, gender, personal life or spouse/date. Everything else was on the table. Someone might say, "I'm from Ohio!" And I'd answer, "Hey! Good for you, Ohio! You're forty-eighth in tourism!"

I'd work for ten to fifteen minutes, getting a feel for the room and maybe working on new jokes for my own act. I'd start by introducing newer less-experienced comics for the early part of the night, saving the best spots for experienced pros. By the forty-minute mark of the night, after having had two to three comics perform, I'd start bringing up the acts who could really get laughs.

The prime-time performers, to my mind, had to have TV credits and some cachet. In this respect, an appearance on

The Tonight Show trumped *Late Night with David Letterman*, which trumped an HBO special, which trumped an MTV appearance, and so on. Using this system, Rita Rudner got dibs to get a great spot on the show, say forty-five minutes to an hour in, since she had been featured numerous times on *The Tonight Show Starring Johnny Carson*. Dennis Miller was a star on *Saturday Night Live* and had appeared with Carson on *The Tonight Show* and with Letterman on *Late Night*. That trumped Brett Butler's spot with Mr. Carson, so she had to wait until after him. It wasn't personal. I was just giving the audience what I thought was the best show possible.

My plan usually worked. Most nights featured fifteen or more comics, and most of them had very, *very* strong performances.

Some acts were demanding—they had some clout, and they would come through the front door shouting, "Who's the emcee?" They would tell me they had to go on right away. Some would sit at the bar, quiet and removed from what was going on, and I'd have to go ask, "Uh, do you want to go on tonight?"

Gilbert Gottfried was always hilarious and outrageous, but after a couple of nights watching him absolutely drain every laugh there was, I would ask him to go on after 10:30 p.m. It didn't seem to matter—he would exhaust every crowd whatever time he went on. There were nights he literally went on for more than an hour and closed the club.

My job, and I took it seriously, was to keep the evening moving. If an act tanked and got nothing more than a smattering of laughter and applause, I had to bring the audience back quickly, so that the next act had a fighting chance at working for a comedy-ready crowd. If someone went on and absolutely blew the roof off the place, there was no reason for me to go up and waste time. I'd bring the next act right on stage so they could continue the momentum. I often told audiences it was okay to heckle me, but let the pros do their job.

I learned that no matter what else happened, if people liked you as the emcee, if they trusted you as a comedian and the host of the show, you could deal with just about every situation that might arise.

When I started doing my act at these major clubs in the nation's biggest city, I only did stand-up comedy. This was the late '80s. Ventriloquism was out of the question—comedy career suicide. No way anyone could do it in the hottest showcase rooms in NYC. But once I established myself, I started bringing JP, defying what was considered acceptable, and using ventriloquism as part of my act. It made emceeing easy. There was an acoustic piano on stage as well, so I had all sorts of ways to bring audience enthusiasm up or quiet a crazy crowd down or bring them back after a comic struggled.

It wasn't perfect. I caught some grief. There were a lot of pros working the clubs in New York who were not happy working with my act. So what? The truth is that, if one is going to be a ventriloquist among the cutting edge comedy acts, one better have a thick skin.

Besides, let's be honest. I'm not doing something vitally important. I'm a comedian. I was (and I still am) thrilled to be working.

I ignored the critics. There were only a couple of them. It helped that I was busy.

There were a lot of comedians I admired as I worked my way into the Manhattan comedy scene. There were among them people who perfected their craft, did exemplary work, and were destined—for whatever reason—never to become a star. I cannot put a finger on any reason one person becomes a star and another languishes in obscurity. Many are still pounding the boards today, playing clubs and small theaters, doing corporate gigs and USO tours or cruise ships, and working wherever and however they can. Our paths cross to this day, and it always feels like a reunion of sorts.

Rich Jeni was a New York comic, very smart and really funny. He had serious heat with the major players in television and film on both coasts. Where most comics would do their ten- to twenty-minute sets and be happy to have not embarrassed themselves in a high-powered comedy workshop like Catch a Rising Star, Jeni had free reign. He didn't waste his extra time, sometimes doing an hour of hilarious stream-of-consciousness observations that left audiences exhausted and happy as they walked out into after-hours Manhattan.

Ronnie Shakes was an older guy, always happy to have his stage time. And like all the real pros, he didn't waste a second. He created six-minute monologues that took a few months to write and perfect in front of an audience. He would then call the bookers at *The Tonight Show* in Hollywood and tell them, "I have a new set ready." They'd fly him across the country. He'd do his *Tonight Show* and fly home, ready to work on his next six-minute set. He didn't do the road. He was busy, but he didn't work any NYC club other than Catch. Someone once told me his family ran a pizza restaurant, but I never asked Shakes himself. My relationship with him could be summed up with this: "Please welcome *Tonight Show* veteran Ronnie Shakes."

Dennis Wolfberg was a joy. Like many stand-up comics in the 1980s and 1990s, he had been working another job (Dennis was a schoolteacher) before venturing into stand-up comedy. His experience teaching children meant he had no trouble getting up in front of people to speak. He had a nervous tic, a comical way of opening his eyes and sticking out his tongue when he made a point or became excited. Instead of hiding or allowing that twitch to hold him back or cause him emotional stress, he had turned it into what comics call a "hook." His punch lines were accentuated by bulging eyes and his tongue swirling around his mouth.

I was honored to be his opening act in Princeton, New Jersey. And the truly amazing thing about Dennis that weekend was not his wonderful performance. His audience was one of the best I have ever worked for. The crowd was engaged and fun, comfortable, and attentive and responsive; I felt as if I was working for a supportive family.

At the end of that short run with Dennis, instead of closing my set with the usual work-to-a-big-finish routine, I told the audience what I thought of them. In closing, I said, "This probably has as much to do with Dennis as it does with you, but it's been the highlight of my year to work with him and to work for you here tonight."

Mr. Wolfberg spoke to me for a brief moment afterward. I never really knew him, other than to know his work. He was a brilliant writer and performer, and audiences adored him. Of all the comedians who have come and gone in my lifetime, of all the people in every part of show business life, Dennis Wolfberg is the single man who probably would have changed the comedy landscape—for the better—had we not lost him. He died at age forty-four as he was negotiating a huge television deal. He truly left a hole here on earth.

Bill Hicks had jettisoned to the top of the comedy pack after he appeared on an HBO comedy special (hosted by Rodney Dangerfield and starring Andrew "Dice" Clay, Bob Nelson, Carol Leifer, and Barry Sobel. This had been *the* seminal "cable comedy TV special." It made immediate stars of at least two of the acts. And everyone on that show went on to solid careers in comedy.) Hicks was "dark," a brooding, cynical, edgy comic describing life in America from an absurdist and surrealistic point of view. The HBO special gained him notoriety and fame, and I worked with him on a few occasions in New York. I played the short-lived Zanies franchise in Little Rock, Arkansas, sometime in the late '80s.

After one show, an older couple came up to me. "We're Bill Hicks's parents," they said.

I was stunned. They were dressed very conservatively, very nicely, especially compared to the youngish rowdy crowd in the club. I almost said, "Don't you mean grandparents?"

They told me how much they enjoyed my act and they left, arm in arm, as if they had just been to church and were heading out for Sunday brunch.

Back in New York, I told Bill about the experience. "Yeah, they know I'm a comedian, and they probably liked your act." That was all he said, and I didn't need him to say any more.

These four men—Jeni, Shakes, Wolfberg, and Hicks—have passed away. All of them, true comedy geniuses and professionals of considerable skill, are sadly forgotten. It's a great lesson. People wrote pages of eulogies about them. They were spoken of in reverential terms for a few weeks, and there were drunken nights in the lobby bars of comedy clubs where comics toasted the memories of their friends and fellow comedy warriors.

But for all of that, I rarely hear their names any more, which is sad but true. Hicks is sometimes still acknowledged for his no-holds-barred persona. The other three get mentions in books like this. None of us are irreplaceable. Comedy is a job, the same as playing piano in a restaurant or coaching or teaching or working in the service industry. So when I work with comedy performers who have major attitudes, acting as if they're more important than anyone else, it's hard not to laugh at them. There are so many people with boundless talent that I can't hold that in any higher regard than I do the skills of any hardworking person in any walk of life. The four comics I spoke of here left a huge impression on me as working comedians, husbands, genuine people, and brilliant artists. I mention them because they deserve to be remembered.

The other emcees at Catch a Rising Star were supportive and helped me along. Bill Schefft was one. He was a fine comic who was eventually employed as a writer for David Letterman. Bill was knowledgeable and generous with words of advice. He always had a cigar and a kind of gruff manner, like a fun uncle. He loved sports. When he found out I had played college football, we talked about the Big Ten and college athletics for an evening, in between me introducing comics and keeping the show rolling at Catch. He's been published in *The New York Times* on a few occasions, writing features about the athletes and teams in NYC.

I introduced hundreds of comics at Catch a Rising Star in the late 1980s and into the '90s, all talented and funny and inspiring in their own rite. Wayne Cotter honed his *Late Night with David Letterman* six-minute routine for a year before going on the show and nailing it. He later moved on to working with Jay Leno when Mr. Leno took over *The Tonight Show*. Lou DiMaggio ended up moving to LA sometime later, having a heart attack, and sharing his story on a national TV spot. I stopped and stared at the TV screen in the gym where I was in New Jersey, recognizing him right away. Rita Rudner, who would do new jokes in her act every time I saw her, became a top act on *The Tonight Show* and then a superstar in Las Vegas. Chris Rock told me, the first night we met, "I want to be the black guy on *Saturday Night Live*."

It was an exciting time.

I've often thought that some of us—maybe I'm just speaking for myself?—would not have been comics in another era. I don't just mean the talented people I emceed for in Chicago and New York. I'm talking about the entire wave of comedy acts in the '80s and '90s. We were the people who seized a moment in time. We "got in when the gettin' was good" and forged our way into careers and lives in the business because we took advantage of what was happening. If it was the 1970s, we'd have been doing underground FM radio. If it was the '60s we'd have been involved in pop culture, folk music, or art. If we had come of age in the '50s, we'd have been the copywriters at the big advertising firms. But it was the '80s. Comedy was king. And nobody benefitted from the popularity of live comedy, deservedly or not, more than I did.

Marsia took on a series of jobs that could loosely be defined as "quirky" when we got to New York City in 1985. By 1988, she had become an assistant to the producer Les Garland at MTV. Soon after, we moved from Brooklyn to New Jersey, getting an apartment in Montclair.

These were heady times for my wife and her comedian husband, working in New York and making a living in show business. The move to New Jersey was good for a number of reasons. We were still close to New York City, we had a car, we wanted to start a family, and there was a lot of work that kept improving our quality of life.

Once ensconced in the New York scene, I began picking up lots of work within an hour's drive of Manhattan. There were a number of clubs on Long Island, including a popular place called the East Side Comedy Club. It was beautiful, with a state-of-the-art sound system, a nice lobby bar, and a show room that sat three hundred people. It was open all week and hired headliners for the weekends.

I had not followed the prototypical comedy format in my career. The standard had been set in the early 1980s—opener/emcee, middle act, headliner. So a comedian started as an emcee, moved up to middle, and became a headliner when he or she had either picked up major TV credits or had a strong forty-five-minute set that could close out those late Friday shows.

I skipped most of that, going from Second City theatrical act to emcee at Zanies to headliner in colleges and comedy clubs. It worked in my case because I had built up enough stage time and material in my performance that I could easily do the required forty-five minutes, which usually became fifty to sixty minutes in the clubs, as audiences expected more for their comedy dollar.

The gigs from Boston to Washington, DC, could keep a comedian working forever. From 1985 until sometime in the late 1990s, there were enough clubs and one-nighters in that northeast I-95 corridor that your average thirty-minute middle-act comic could earn $1000 per week playing one-nighters during the week and a legit comedy club on the weekend.

> There were five different kinds of rooms all over the United States that comedy acts worked, not including the colleges and the corporate jobs:

- ***One-nighters*** took place Monday through Thursday nights in bars and restaurants throughout the United States. The concept was simple—a booker would go to an establishment and sell a night of comedy. There would be a charge at the door, say $10, and that would go to the show. The bar would keep the drinks and food. There were other deals cooked up as well, but that was the paradigm. There were three acts. The first act got $100, the second act got $150, and the third act got $200 to $250. The rest went to the booker.
- Yes, for a five- to ten-year period, the bookers for one-nighters made a fortune. Most of them had three to four rooms, earning them $1,000 or more every night they booked.
- ***C rooms*** still exist and probably always will. A booker goes to a venue of any kind, often a hotel bar or an established restaurant with a conference room or meeting room and sells a Friday and Saturday night package the same way he or she sells a one-nighter. The bar gets food and drink, the comics make $250/$150/$100 per show, and the booker gets the balance. Some rooms did four shows for the weekend; some did three. A headliner could earn $1,000 in a weekend—not bad.
- ***B rooms*** – By the mid-'80s there were comedy clubs in every major and mid-major city from sea to shining

sea. There were franchises (the Funny Bone Comedy Clubs, the Improvs; Zanies; the Punchline Comedy Clubs; the Comedy House Theaters) that shared business plans and comedians. There were also comedy clubs that ran as singular entities in a city (the Stardome in Birmingham, Alabama; the Laugh House in Philadelphia; the Comedy Connection in Boston). A "B room" was open four to five nights a week and served no other purpose in the community than to provide comedy as entertainment along with food and beverage. B rooms paid better (a headliner could earn $2,500 for a Wednesday-through-Sunday run). Ten to twelve times a year, the room would bring in a bona fide star, who would sell out every seat all week and keep the interest and the viability of the club in the public eye. It also served as a way for "middle acts" to make a living and improve their performances.

A rooms – Each major city has an A room. It might be the flagship for a chain (Zanies in Chicago; the Punchline in Atlanta; the Punchline in San Francisco, which was not related at all to Atlanta; the Improv in Miami) or a single entity like Cobb's Comedy Pub in San Francisco and Caroline's in New York. To play these rooms was a résumé-enhancer, especially for new comics. To *headline* these rooms was a *career* enhancer, making you a viable player on the comedy scene. A rooms paid better, had more access to media and interviews on local TV/radio outlets, and drew the occasional agent and casting director. To play an A room is still a big deal. To headline means you're at the top of the heap.

Showcase rooms – Located in New York and Los Angeles, the showcase clubs existed for one purpose (other than to make money). Showcase rooms wanted to be *players*, helping discover the stars and celebrities for major media. Catch a Rising Star, Stand-Up New York, the Improv, and the Comedy Store in Los Angeles featured multiple comics every night of the week and often hosted current celebrities when they "stopped in" to wow the audience and do a set.

The other comedy venues included cruise ships, considered "hackville" by most acts at the time and casinos in Atlantic City and (especially) Las Vegas. At one time, there were eight full-time comedy clubs in Vegas. Atlantic City had two or three.

> Comics of the 1980s and 1990s looked at cruise ship work as a step down. It was considered a desperate move for an act who couldn't "make it" in the clubs or on television. But karma will get you. By the early 2000s, many acts who considered cruise ships a "crutch" were working on cruise ships—and still are.

Combine those clubs and casinos with college work, and a comedian could do some thirty weeks of "road work" during the year, earning him or her around $50,000. Then he or she could live near a city (New York, LA, Boston, or San Francisco, for the most part) and play "showcase rooms" for a few weeks in hopes of getting a TV show or cable special. It was a system that worked well for many in the business for many years.

> The comedy club circuit, which boasted hundreds of rooms across the country at one time, spawned many "middle acts"—comics with thirty to forty minutes of killer stand-up comedy—who booked up a year of work and went from coast to coast, working five to ten shows a week. I'm not sure if that was such a good thing.

I rode the crest of that wave the way professional surfers hang ten on giant waves in Maui.

Most clubs did not have a piano, the way Zanies and Catch a Rising Star did, so I would often have to perform an hour or more of ventriloquism and stand-up to fulfill my role as headliner."

I played a series of one-nighters all over the East Coast after we moved in 1985. Living in Brooklyn and having a car, it was easy to drive to "Yoder gigs" (so named for the man who booked them, Mr. Yoder) in Connecticut. They paid $200 for a forty-five-minute show. There were so many gigs in New Jersey that I didn't have to call agents or bookers; they called me.

The disco era had ended, but the disco—a bar with the colored dance floor and the mirror ball on the ceiling, not to mention a sound system that would make any outdoor rock arena proud—was still open for business. As a last gasp, these dance joints started booking comics. At first, the club would open for dancing and then the comedy show would happen around 10:00 p.m. After that, it would be back to dancing. It was only a matter of time before the owners of these bars changed the program, got rid of the dance floor, and made their "nut" during that one night a week when the comics would show up and fill the room.

There were bars along the Jersey shore that had these comedy nights. The first time I got booked in one, some dive just a block from the beach, I was thrilled. Jersey. The beach. Springsteen. "Greetings from Asbury Park." I got to the club early, drank in the atmosphere, and called Marsia. I was living a fantasy. The show was a blast. The audience was high-energy and responsive. What could be better?

My second night was the other side of New Jersey. The opening act, a girl named Abby, was cursed loudly and booed off the stage. She came off sobbing, hiding her face in her hands. She walked out the door and drove away. I haven't seen her since that night. The middle act was a black man from New

York, a funny guy named Dwayne Cunningham, who got good laughs and walked off the stage with a big smile.

I went on and three minutes in someone yelled, "When does the show start?"

Classic.

This guy was tattooed and wearing a tank top, sitting with his buddies, a pile of empty beer cans on the table in front of him. He was defining stereotype.

Easy.

"Come on, guy. I don't collect shopping carts in the parking lot when you're doing your job. Let me do my act." A favorite (stock) heckler line.

His friends at the table laughed hard, hitting him on the back and pointing at him. He wasn't happy. He gave me his middle finger.

I continued with my act, knowing he'd try and compete with me sooner or later. He did, as I brought JP out.

"No puppets!" he shouted.

JP did a long, slow, deliberate take toward the guy, and the audience laughed. JP said, "Are you talkin' to me?" Another big laugh because the line was a reference to Robert De Niro in the movie *Taxi Driver*, loved by any self-respecting male in the late '80s.

The poor guy fell into the trap: "Yeah! I'm talkin' to you!"

JP looked at me and back at the heckler. "I can't believe you're talkin' to me."

Pause for comedy effect.

"*I'm not real!*"

The audience went bonkers, and the guy was quiet for the last of my forty minutes on stage.

One nighters could be a lot of fun, easy nights where the extra cash fell into your hands for doing nothing. Just as easily they could be obstacle courses of heckling, inattentiveness, drunkenness, and apathy.

> I often stood off to the side of the stage during the first decade of my comedy career. I would watch the audience and get a feel for a person or persons who were most enjoying the show. When I went on, I would play to them. Why not use the "best" audience members to get my own performance going?

Most of these East Coast one-nighters were tough but not unmanageable. It wasn't a night to try new material, but a lot of the shows were fun. You would go on, give them your best stuff, and get paid. It was great in many ways because I could drive out and drive back the same night, and when the shows went well I had the feeling that I was improving as a live performer.

> By the way, there is no such thing as a "bad audience." It is the job of the comedian to find a way to make the audience laugh.

Rick Messina, who had given me his business card one night in the back of Zanies in Chicago, is the penultimate comedy story. His career arc matches the rise and acceptance of stand-up and live comedy in the American zeitgeist, and his story is as powerful as any superstar you can name. He's a movie waiting to be made.

Messina used me once as a middle act on Long Island at a nice club called Governor's. After that, I was a headliner. He had an excellent reputation, and he was working with acts from coast to coast. He booked a room in New Jersey called Rascals. The place was in West Orange, about thirty minutes from Manhattan; it was one of the most fun comedy clubs I've ever played.

His story goes something like this: He began by working for a Long Island club that featured comedy, eventually became the manager. After a short while, he moved into booking the club. The scene was booming. There were lots of Long Island and New York City comics, so finding the acts was easy. Plus the rooms were full, and the money was good.

Messina branched out and began booking rooms outside New York City. That included the comedy jewel of North Jersey—Rascals.

Rascals was in the basement of a large restaurant/bar. The room was huge, seating four hundred plus, and it sold out every weekend show. All the major acts played the club, and sometime in the mid- to late-1980s, the establishment cut a deal with a local cable channel and began production of a TV show: *Rascals Comedy Hour.*

It was a great deal for the club and for the acts. Getting booked meant you were not only getting paid, you were also going to be on television, and you would get a VHS tape of your performance. A VHS of your act was huge—the video was the replacement for the business card in comedy. By 1989, every TV talent coordinator and every agent at every level of the business would ask one question: "Can you send me a video?" Being able to send a tape was half the battle to getting booked.

The club itself was run by the Magnuson brothers, three Jersey guys who managed the good luck of having a comedy club at a time when the crowds were always hot and the room was always full. Messina got them major talent and the best of up-and-coming people, so there was as much energy and star quality in West Orange as there was in any Manhattan or Los Angeles showcase club.

The guy who really ran things is, to this day, one of my favorite people in comedy. Danny McKenna wore a suit and tie every night. He ran a tight ship. He seated the audience, keeping the drunks in the back so they wouldn't disrupt a show; he ran the sound system and gave everyone a light when their time was up. He was as comfortable dealing with the personality of his superstar headliner and all the accompanying personal issues as he was attending to an irate patron who didn't get his or her martini in time. Danny was the face of Rascals, much more than the hideous squirrel logo that adorned the sign outside the building.

Messina, from humble beginnings, outdid almost everyone else on the East Coast in comedy. He parlayed his position as a booker into being a Hollywood player. Picking and choosing the acts he wanted to work with, he eventually became personal manager for Tim Allen, helping Mr. Allen become a cable TV icon before jumping into the stratosphere of the show business universe with a top-rated sitcom and multimillion-dollar grossing movies.

The Rascals Comedy Hour parlayed itself into a deal with Showtime, one of the first cable networks to feature hour-long comedy specials. I did a twelve-minute spot on one of these in the late '80s, filmed at Rascals where I was already familiar with the room and how everything worked. Like many other comedians at the time, getting on television wasn't hard.

The PBS station in New York saw me at Catch a Rising Star one night. I was booked to perform, and I was interviewed on *The David Susskind Show*. I guested on *Robert Klein Time* and had a blast—Klein being one of Aunt Ardie's favorite comics. His dog Moishe was sitting next to me, so I had the dog "talk" using my ventriloquism to close out our episode.

By the end of the decade, I had done a couple of Showtime specials, an MTV comedy special, and more. It gave me some cachet and viability.

By 1989, Marsia's MTV job and my constant work had given us a little money so we could afford a nicer place. We moved to Montclair, New Jersey, living just off Bloomington Avenue, minutes from the city. She took the bus to Manhattan to MTV headquarters five days a week. I started picking up extra work at Rascals, just a few minutes from our place, when I wasn't on the road.

We decided to start a family. We saved some money and bought a house in Verona, New Jersey. I was kind of a regular at Rascals, in addition to the New York City clubs, and the colleges started booking me in earnest.

The era of President Ronald Reagan, hair bands, Magic Johnson versus Larry Bird, Rubik's Cube, and the Space Shuttle *Challenger* disaster would soon be part of history. George Herbert Walker Bush was elected president, promised "no new taxes," and then signed his own presidential death knell by raising taxes. The '90s approached.

My career would move in another direction.

Chapter Sixteen
Back to College

College is fun as long as you don't die.
—Tsugumi Ohba, *Death Note, Vol. 4*, "Love"

I landed at Atlanta Hartsfield on a warm fall afternoon a couple of years ago. Once off the plane, I raced past other travelers in the wide airport hallways, wearing my heavy backpack and swinging a big carry-on bag back and forth as I ran. I got on a train to the rental car facility, got in a car, and drove southeast, away from the urban sprawl and the suburbs. I was heading to that evening's job—a gig in a nondescript town where I would do a show for a little (and little-known) college.

The sun disappeared in my rearview mirror as I drove to the school, passing the red clay, the tall pines, and a trove of tiny unknown rural Georgia towns on the way. I passed little homes and bungalows where the blue light of television sets appeared through the front windows as the day came to an end. Even in the dark, it was easy to find the town and the school, the GPS on my iPhone acting as the perfect guide. It was just as easy to find the venue because, once I hit the campus, there were students walking in small groups, all going the same direction. So I followed the crowd in my rental car, slowly crawling along with them in a sort of disorganized parade.

I parked on the grass in the back of an old auditorium, between a couple of official-looking vans with the school logo painted on the sides. I left my bag of props—the puppets Romeo, Paco, Ramon and Paquito—in the back seat. My travel to a college job had become more efficient and simpler over the years. For the first couple of decades, I would check big bags on the plane for all the shows, even a one-nighter like this. The process has changed significantly. Tonight, I have come ready for work. I preplanned things so that, if I had to walk right on stage, I could. This "new me" packs for efficiency, access, and immediate availability.

There was loud music coming from inside the auditorium. After I locked the car, I walked toward a bright yellow light beaming out of a door to the far left of the building. I bounded up two steps at a time (see? I'm young and hip!) onto a landing where a group of young people—students? a band? other acts?—were standing and talking. I walked up the steps and said a cheerful hi as I passed. They ignored me. I entered the building.

I was immediately backstage. There was a band performing some kind of heavy metal / country / rap music, the pounding drums and bass obliterating any other complaint they might have been making. The *air* shook with each beat. I was behind the speakers, behind the curtain, behind the stage, hoping someone would notice me—the old guy in the T-shirt and jeans—and ask me what I was doing here. My wish came true. Someone clapped me on my back.

"Taylor! We're ... glad ... here! Thank ... tonight!"

The "music" was so loud I could only make out a few words coming from the short, balding, very sweaty man gently hitting me. He had a wide grin and a bad mustache, and he wore a short-sleeved white shirt and jeans. He pointed back toward the door where I had come in. We walked out.

On the landing, the same group of kids ignored us as he introduced himself. He was the student activities director. ("I'm still here!" he shouted. "Can you believe it?") He asked if I'd be ready to go on in ten minutes. I searched the contacts file in my brain but could not remember him, his voice, his mannerisms, or his name.

> For many years I could remember everyone. And I could remember every club, every college, and every stage and theater space. The best way to describe my inability to do so now? I'll use computerese: "memory full." I need to get to an Apple store and buy a thumb drive to stick in my ear and free up some memory.

I smiled and put my hand on his shoulder. "Of course. I could go on in ten minutes! I'll go on whenever you want! I always loved working for you!" It made me sad to think I could not remember anything about this person who respected my work.

Yeah, I think to myself, *what a long strange trip it's been*.

He disappeared for a moment, returning to introduce me to a young African American woman with dreadlocks and a made-for-stardom perfect smile. She was impossibly fit, wearing blue jean cutoffs and a red T-shirt with the sleeves rolled up. She stood at his side. After being introduced, she slid in front of him and shook my hand. She wanted my credits, something she could use for an introduction. I gave her a couple of career highlights, and she started to write a note before I said, "You don't have to write anything down. Introduce me any way you want to."

She stopped writing, gave me a sideways glance, looked at the director, and nodded. Another big smile for me. "See you on stage," she said, and she walked back into the auditorium.

I ran out to the car, grabbed the bag-o-puppets, and ran back to the auditorium.

The band, dressed in black tank tops, skinny black jeans, and black boots, had finished their noise making. Now they were behind the stage, packing up guitars and amps and controllers in big black-wheeled cases. On stage, the woman I had just met was revving the audience up. It was hot in the auditorium, and I began to sweat in the closeness of it as I stood off to the side of the stage watching her. Was she a student? An assistant to the director? A comic? Whatever, the crowd loved her. They were cheering and laughing and clapping.

She went into my introduction. I looked at my watch—9:22 p.m. Time to go to work.

I walked on stage. By the time I reached the microphone—where did the woman who'd just introduced me go?—the applause had stopped. It was my first look at the room. It was jam-packed with students, maybe eight hundred or nine hundred squeezed into chairs right in front of me and sitting on risers to my left and right. The lights were in my face, I could feel the heat from the spotlight, and I delivered my start-of-the-show smile.

I tried, but I could not remember a time when this kind of circumstance might have intimidated me. Maybe before I had kids? I'd been doing this for so long that everything—*everything*—was routine. This was what I did. It could be a club or a casino or a theater; it didn't matter. I knew exactly where I was this night (small college in the south), I knew who my audience was (college students from the south, mostly Georgia and the Carolinas), and I knew pretty much everything I would do for the next hour (a lot of ventriloquism, some music, and an audience participation routine to close my act). My biggest advantage this night?

Not my act.

Not my brilliant material.

The energy in the room was all-powerful.

The vibe had changed from the loud, in-your-face drum 'n' bass pounding from the band to the cheering and laughter that the African American woman had received before bringing me on stage. Now there was an expectant-but-unsure quiet as I took the microphone. Quiet is okay. Working with silence is a great way to gain focus and attention span. There was a lot of intensity and liveliness sitting in front of me, so after waiting for the tension to reach a certain critical point, I asked the freshman class to applaud. They exploded into cheers and applause for themselves (which garnered good-natured "boos" from the upper classes). Then I let all the classes cheer for themselves, finally asking for the faculty members to applaud. There were only about twenty of them, their pitifully soft response so different from the excited students that everyone laughed.

I opened with an old line I'd been using at colleges for years. "Okay, everyone. I'd like to start this evening with some advice. As a college grad myself, I want to give you three basic questions you need to ask your professor the first day of every class. They are: (1) Is attendance mandatory? (2) How important is the final exam to my grade? And (3) what is the *least* amount of work I can do and still pass this course?"

It's sophomoric and sarcastic, and it's perfect for the collegiate audience. These were eighteen-to-twenty-year-olds. As always, my show started with a big laugh.

DEFINITION: working with silence. To work with silence is to use silence as a benefit to one's performance when working live. The key is not to be intimidated or overwhelmed—or worried—that there isn't any audible response from a given audience. Instead, to work with silence is to use that moment of quiet to earn some focus. And you can use it to enhance jokes, stories, and punch lines.

I gave them my best—the way I do every night, no matter who the audience is. There are times I have to find a way to convince myself, wherever I am and whatever the audience, that this night, this performance, this moment is critically important. I *always* find a reason. I might have an old friend or a family member in the audience. There might be someone there who wants to book me in the future. Maybe I enjoy playing the room and the vibe pushes me to do well.

This night I was ashamed I couldn't remember the activities director, so I dedicated myself to making that show go really well, if for no other reason than to reflect well on him.

A few minutes into the act, I went to the bag and got Paco, my pig puppet, who was wrapped in a blanket (get it?) and he joked about how scary it is for a pig in Georgia: "I am not a walking, talking sausage!" To close out my set and reenergize the crowd in the last few minutes, I sat down at a Baldwin grand piano and played some of my comedy song "hits." This included a parody of sexy soul songs called "Baby, Let's Abstain"—perfect for a small-college audience. Many in the crowd had grown up in the Christian church and "got" the irony (a sexy song about abstaining from sex: "Refrain with me, girl; cause some pain for me, girl; It's the kind of thing that makes a boy go insane. Oh, baby, baby, baby let's abstain!") Then I played a boogie to bring a rousing end to my little presentation.

Just as I finished, some kid from the balcony shouted, "Will you be in my band?"

The room exploded in applause and cheers.

So I took a bow.

I had done my hour (I walked off stage at 10:25 p.m.), keeping my act middle-of-the-road safe; it was nonpolitical and nonconfrontational and included nothing controversial. Comics of today are wary of the college market because the political correctness movement is so prevalent. I don't care. I knew what I was supposed to do, and I knew what I was *not* supposed to do. The director watched my entire presentation, standing in the wings to the side of the stage, his smile friendly and warm. "You still got it!" he shouted over the enthusiastic cheers from the student body as I came off. But now they were cheering for the woman who had introduced me over an hour before. She was back on stage holding court. She was really good—a natural.

A fleeting pang of envy.

The director walked me to my car. He talked about how the kids had changed over the years. ("Everything is political correctness now. I see you keep your act PC. Do you stay PC everywhere?" I shook my head "no.") He noted how much fun he was having. ("I still love the students and my job! But the administration is gonna make me retire in three years.") And he said he'd like to have me back ("if we can find a way to afford you"). He handed me a check as I opened the car door and threw the puppet bag in the back seat. We shook hands.

Then I gently took hold of his shoulders and said, "Hope to see you again soon!" I said it with all the sincerity I could muster, fighting the sheepishness since I couldn't remember the name. He smiled back and nodded.

"I hope so, too."

I backed out of the grassy area behind the auditorium and found the street to the main road. A few minutes later, I was retracing the drive in my rental car through the Georgia countryside underneath a moonless sky, passing those same little homes where now the windows were dark and the TVs were off. I drove back to my hotel room near the airport, where I would nap a couple of hours and catch my flight at 6:25 a.m. to Dallas.

It was 2015, but it might as well have been 1989. The college circuit had not changed all that much.

I would know. From the first college gigs I ever did through the beginning of the 2000s, my college booking agent and mentor Joey Edmonds booked me 150 college gigs a year. In doing these shows, my act grew in ways I could not have planned.

As the 1980s drew to a close, I began to pick up TV spots the same way many of my peers were doing. These would continue into the late-1990s and included Showtime, MTV, a very popular vehicle called Evening at the Improv and another called Caroline's Comedy Hour, and many more. Like most of the acts who were part of these different programs, I had honed my set for years. The difference was my background. I wasn't a typical comedy club act. I wasn't really a college act. Nor was I a corporate act or a theater act. Instead, I combined novelty skills (ventriloquism and music) with jokes. This allowed me to work for a broad spectrum of clients—clubs, colleges, corporate events, casinos, theaters, cruise ships, and Vegas and Atlantic City.

I haven't changed much. It's one of the reasons I've been able to have a career in showbiz without much visibility and a Q rating of 0. I always work, no matter what. There is no "bad time for comedians." There is no "good time for comedians." There is work. Sometimes you have to hustle for it, and if you don't, you won't get any.

I choose to work.

> Q RATING. A Q Rating (or Q Score) is a value or number that identifies the popularity or recognition of a brand, celebrity or product. It's based on a survey that asks respondents across the nation if they have heard the name of a performer or brand, and what their opinion of that brand, celebrity or product is. The actual score is calculated thru dividing the percentage of people who identify a product/celebrity as a favorite by the percentage of people who have heard of the product/celebrity in the first place. Drop the decimal point and that's the score.

One of the biggest advantages I had from the very beginning of my career, and especially in the college market, was ventriloquism. The fact that I used a puppet—or two or three or more—made me much more accessible to the age group and the demographics than a stand-up comic. Sometimes, I was the first live comedy performer that the eighteen- and nineteen-year-olds had ever seen. More than a few colleges opened shows to the community on a regular basis. So my audience was broad-based, with many backgrounds and ages and cultures present.

This made things perfect for what I was doing—a universal act that didn't care who was in the audience, because I was working for *all* of them.

There were so many stand-up comics and there were a lot of music acts, but there were precious few doing my hybrid of stand-up, music, and vent.

DEFINITION: vent. People in the business often refer to a ventriloquist as a "vent." It can also be a description: "She is a very good vent." I use it too. The word ventriloquist is so ponderous. Graceless. There is no perfect synonym for it. "Voice thrower?" Uh ... no.

Joey and I would put together tours and dates that maximized time and travel. There were a couple of times I woke up in New York, drove to Newark Airport, flew to the Midwest for a noon show at a college, and then flew back to Newark to dive into New York City and perform a late-night set of comedy at a club.

The success I'd had in the college market earned me a Showtime cable TV special called "Comedy on Campus." It was shot at Pepperdine University, a spectacularly beautiful college located in Malibu, California. Pepperdine sits on a mountain overlooking the Pacific Ocean and is as pristine and perfect a place to attend college as any in the United States, just based on its aesthetics. It is affiliated with the Church of Christ, good knowledge for a comedian performing for the students there. The other acts on the show included Rondell and an LA comic named Peter Gaulke.

Marsia came with me. Her career at MTV had morphed into a job with Nickelodeon, but she didn't really like it, so she had quit. We were going to start a family. A paid-for trip to the West Coast seemed like fun.

So she joined me. We were treated really well. I felt as if I was really starting to gain some mainstream viability in the world of comedy. My wife, of course, was accustomed to being around showbiz types. Her work at MTV meant occasional stars stopping by to see her boss, Les Garland. She had accompanied Madonna to the MTV Music Awards (Marsia was told she could not speak to, or look at, Mad-Girl ... even though they were sitting in the same limousine and in the same part of the car!). Marsia's professional life had been spent with two of the most famous showbiz entities in the country—the Second City Theater and MTV. She knew what was going on and who to hang with.

She spent most of the weekend around the crew and makeup people.

I don't remember much of the event itself. It was hosted by Ed Begley, Jr., star on a popular TV drama called *St. Elsewhere*. The head writer for the show was Kevin Rooney, friend to Jay Leno and all the big comedy stars. The week leading up to the shoot had been rehearsal time for Begley and Kevin, where they were to put together a monologue and bits to use as filler between the comedians who would be performing. That didn't happen for a few reasons. That turned out to be a bonus for me, because the producers gave more time to the performers.

I don't know what Rondell and Peter did on stage. I didn't watch their sets that night, and I've only watched myself three to four times over the years. I had what I thought was a strong performance. I was told to do ten to twelve minutes, but since Begley wasn't doing time, I did about eighteen minutes of my act. It included five minutes of stand-up comedy, tailoring most of it to the college crowd, and ten or more with my new vent partner Jake, mostly based on his "comedy club middle act persona." It all played well. I had been touring for three to four years at this point, and I felt very comfortable in the setting—a college.

> For "Comedy on Campus," I changed from the hard/wood/classic ventriloquist dummy JP to the soft puppet I named Jake. This new Muppet-like figure was blond and angular, with a much lighter body that allowed for more movement, more character, and more *life*. Jake lasted a couple of months and then became the dark-haired Romeo, who is still with me.

Watching it today, I think some of the material stands the test of time. I did a short "rap" as a college econ professor. I talked about sports and TV commercials—stuff that Middle America and a broad audience could relate to. It's clear I prepared material and a set, and the ventriloquism portion of the show got good laughs, based mostly on the jokes. There were lines ("I'm someone you can afford!") that I still use in my current performance! All in all, it was pretty decent.

I learned just how popular the "Comedy on Campus" Showtime special was a few months after the show aired, when I would show up at colleges for my gigs and the crowds would be full. "Taylor!" the audience would shout as soon as I walked on stage in the campus cafeteria or the student center theater. The activities directors would always say the same thing: "We usually don't get crowds this big. I guess they know you."

A few months later, I performed on the MTV *Half-Hour Comedy Hour*. It was a popular program on the network, and I got more recognition from that show than just about any other I've ever done. MTV was incredibly popular with the eighteen-to-twenty-four-year-old-crowd at the time. The shoot took place in New York City, and many of the staff, including the makeup team, was the same as I'd worked with out in Malibu for the Showtime program.

"Hey! I remember you!" said one of the women staffers with a big smile and a hug. "Where is your wife?"

There were two other women standing with her, smiling and nodding, making me feel very professional and accepted.

Wow! I thought to myself. *Now this is showbiz! I am on my way! The techs and the crew remember my work. I love this!*

I bathed in their positivity, shrugging and feigning humility, overpowered by my own aura, and so pleased with myself it was hard to contain my ego.

"Marsia didn't make it," I said. "She had to work late."

There came a noticeable change in the women's deportment. They took a collective step back and eyed me suspiciously. They looked at one another.

"She's not here?" asked one.

"Nah." I smiled. "She's over in Jersey."

The women turned together, almost as if they were a unit, and began walking away. One of them, who had hugged me and welcomed me moments before, turned and spoke over her shoulder: "Too bad. She's so *funny.*"

When 1990 popped up on the calendar, the United States entered into the centuries-old upheaval in the Middle East—a military operation called Desert Storm. The Furby, an odd little electronic toy that resembled an owl with ears, was born. A British computer scientist named Tim Berners-Lee put up the first ever website for the European Organization for Nuclear Research (CERN). A recession took hold of the United States, and the president doomed his reelection possibility by raising taxes, after promising he would not.

The year 1990 was a political anomaly. President Bush had ridden an unprecedented wave of popularity into office. An ex-military man, he wisely sold the importance and the strategy of a war in the Middle East to the public. So he was a popular president, and he led a popular war. But if a president lied in 1990, he paid for it by losing the office. Things have changed.

I was, as usual, out of sync. Stand-up comics would take over the 1990s. The highest-rated, most popular, and most influential

TV shows of the decade featured stand-up comics—*Seinfeld, Roseanne, Mad About You, Hangin' with Mr. Cooper,* and *Home Improvement* all featured household names who came from the world of comedy clubs. Even *The Simpsons* made use of stand-ups. (I'll throw in the seminal program *Friends* too—each one of those actors performed a sort of stand-up in character.)

How could I compete? Easy. I wasn't on television. I was performing live for a generation who enjoyed role-playing games, science-fiction movies, fantasy movies, and manga. This new demo didn't reject my ventriloquism outright. They had grown up on the Muppets! As the decade went on and the millennium approached, so did advances in technology. Home computing meant video games. A comedy act based on dream worlds and what would soon be known as virtual reality was not only acceptable, it played directly to what people wanted. My live act, where something inanimate "came to life," played to a demographic coming of age along with technology.

It wasn't just the colleges. I headlined comedy clubs. I took on more specialty and corporate shows.

Marsia and I had a baby.

The birth of our first child didn't really change the way I worked. We had saved some money, and with a little help from the in-laws, we bought a house in Verona, New Jersey. Marsia left her (successful) media career and became a full-time mom. Things got a little more hectic, but there was a certain normalcy living in the suburbs. Rascals Comedy Club was a five-minute drive from the house, and I played there regularly.

My weekly schedule: Fly somewhere in the states and do a couple of college gigs. Fly home and spend a day with the family before driving into New York for a showcase spot. Then a day or so later, spend a weekend in some city at a comedy club or doing a corporate gig somewhere. I was ambitious.

The frantic disorder of travel and family and showcases and auditions took its toll.

Unwittingly, I had some trouble with the law.

Chapter Seventeen
A Life of Crime

*Well I'm running / Police on my back / And
I'm hiding. Police on my back.*
—The Clash, "Police on My Back"

It was early 1991. I had flown into St Louis for a college tour that was to actually start at Quincy College in Quincy, Illinois, a couple of hours from St. Louis. My plane got in a little late on a muggy late summer night, and I drove like crazy through Missouri to a bridge across the Mississippi River that took me to the college, just a few miles north of Hannibal, Missouri. I got there on time and walked directly from the parking lot to the venue, an activities room in the basement, right before showtime. The kids were all sitting and waiting, and the harried director breathed an audible sigh of relief when I bounded down the stairs with my bag-o-puppets and a big smile.

"I can go on right away!" I said, shaking her hand and giving her as much positive vibe as I could.

She nodded and introduced me.

I was on an adrenalin rush, so I went up and did eighty minutes, got my check, and said thanks.

"Do you have a hotel for me?" I asked as I headed up the steps to my car.

"Yes. It's the Holiday Inn downtown," said the now happy woman, and she gave me directions. She didn't need to. Quincy is tiny. All the hotels are lined up on the same street just off the river, and I parked in the lot and walked into the lobby.

There were people milling around the front desk, and I waited until a young clean-cut kid, probably a little younger than me, said, "May I help you?"

"I want to check in," I said, handing him my credit card. "I have a reservation. Mason."

The clerk, wearing a silly Keebler Elf-like vest and short-sleeved shirt and tie, looked in the manifest for my reservation. He found it. "Oh, here you are. I'm sorry. Your room wasn't guaranteed, so I'm afraid we don't have your reservation any more. The hotel is booked up. Every room is taken. I'm sorry."

This was protocol actually. Hotels held a reservation until 6:00 p.m. If someone doesn't show, they give the room to a client who actually does show—unless, of course, the room is "guaranteed" with a credit card.

So, no room for Taylor. Not surprising. This kind of thing had happened before. The problem this night was that every hotel in that hot spot of big-time entertainment known as Quincy, Illinois, was booked. There was a festival going on just across the river in Hannibal, Missouri, celebrating Mark Twain—some kind of riverboat celebration. All the hotels in the area were full. Oh, well.

As was my custom at the time, I needed to do my six-mile run. It was unbearably hot and sticky, as if they were celebrating a Festival of Humidity, the kind of weather where you could take a shower, step out for ten seconds of cool comfort, and then be sweaty and clammy again.

I drove for a few minutes and parked the car at a gas station / minimart just north of town, right behind the one-story cinder block building. There were bright lights over the sign in front, and the lot was well lit, too, so I locked up the car, jogged into town, and crossed the bridge over to Missouri.

I did my full six miles, which took about forty-five minutes. And as I came back to the minimart, my evening completely fell apart.

The lights at the gas station were out. There were three to four police cars with lights flashing sitting right behind my rental car. Fully clad local officers were talking with a group of people. It was a residential neighborhood, houses surrounding the mart, at a point where Quincy stops and cornfields begin. As I came jogging up to my car the group—police and citizens—turned as one and looked at me with the kind of suspicion you see in TV crime movies.

"Uh ... that's my car," I stammered. I was wearing running shorts, socks, and shoes. My body sweat poured off my pudgy body, glistening in the colored lights of the police cars, and I was holding a set of car keys and nothing else.

One officer stepped up and said, "This minimart was robbed about thirty minutes ago. Where have you been?"

I explained, talking way too fast for an innocent man—parked the car, went for a jog. The hotel didn't have a room for me after my show at the college. There weren't any hotels. I thought I'd jog and then drive to my next gig (I didn't say where).

The cop looked at me as if I had confessed to a murder—as if I had said, "Yes, it was me. I broke in, stabbed the clerk, took all the Gatorade I could, and stashed the body in my trunk."

"Got any ID?" he asked.

An elderly man, tall and thin and quivery, came walking across the parking lot out of the darkness. He had stubble on his chin, and his eyes had that glazed, watery look of someone who drinks a lot.

"He didn't do it, Carl," said the old man to the police officer, pointing at me with a long bony finger. "I watched him from my front porch," and he waved toward the darkness behind him, "I wondered what any durned fool would be doing running this late at night in the heat. He may not be smart." He winked at me. "But he ain't your thief."

With that, he turned and slowly wavered back into the murky closeness of an Illinois early autumn night. I said nothing, because I was stunned. Because I was thankful. Because I was eternally grateful.

I said nothing because I can be incredibly obtuse and self-centered.

The cop laughed and shouted after the old guy, "Thanks, Del!"

He looked at me and repeated his question. "Got any ID?"

I opened the trunk, shuffled through the bags and puppets and clothes until I found my wallet, and turned to hand the officer my New York driver's license.

There were three police around me. They were staring into the trunk as if there was a body.

Oh, right!

I turned and looked into the trunk. One of the officers held up a flashlight that revealed the legs and shoes of a little boy sticking out of a big suitcase. It was the body of Romeo, my ventriloquist partner, but his stomach and arms were concealed. He was face down, the back of his head visible in the suitcase.

He looked like a small child sleeping—or worse, a small child stuffed into a bag in the trunk of a car.

I laughed the nervous laugh of some kind of sicko who has been caught, and I stammered, "Uh ... that's my ventriloquist figure."

Time stop.

I quickly pulled Romeo out so that the police could get a look at it. They did and then gave me the sympathetic oh-you're-one-of-*those* looks I had grown accustomed to.

Nobody said a word. I carefully packed Romeo in the big suitcase and handed my New York driver's license to the policeman.

He sat in his car and called in my name and number. I tried making small talk with the other police officers (they didn't oblige) and some onlookers from the neighborhood. One asked, "Can you do a puppet show for us?" I said, "Sorry. My puppet friends only work on stage." And that's the point where everything unraveled.

I knew from the way the officer was walking and holding my license that something was very wrong. It was a walk that said, *"You are guilty."*

"We don't hold you responsible for this," he said, "but your license has come up as expired or something."

"*What*!?" I grabbed it from the officer and looked at it.

"The date says it's good for two more years!"

The policeman nodded and looked at the ground. Another cop, this one a short heavy woman, walked up and said, "Look, it could be anything. You can work it out with the judge in the morning."

Oh, for cry-eye! She snatched my license right back and handed it back to the first officer.

"You can leave your car here. The judge gets in around eleven tomorrow morning. You can explain everything to him and figure out what's going on. But you aren't driving tonight."

They left me standing there. Guilty. Unworthy. A petty scoundrel. People walked back to their homes, and two of the police cars drove off. The policewoman who had been talking to me did some paperwork in her car as I sat on the trunk of mine, trying not to panic and thinking about what I could do.

The woman got out of the car and walked up to me. She pushed her cop's hat back on her head. She smiled. "Where are you going to stay?"

"Oh, I'll go back over to the college. The director said I could stay at her house if I needed to," I lied.

"Oh, Connie? She's great," said the woman.

Perfect, I thought. *She knows the activities director. I'm doomed.*

She smiled. "Look, here's your license. But you cannot drive, okay? We cannot take your car to the pound because it's on private property—state law. But you cannot drive. Understand?"

I said okay with all the sincerity of a cute puppy, my second lie to the police in ten minutes. And she got back in the patrol car with her partner. Then they sat there in the car.

It took a couple of minutes, but I finally figured out what was going on. They were waiting for me to leave. So I got some clothes out and jogged off toward the college, waving to my new friends in the police cruiser. I doubled back in the dark, staying behind trees and bushes, stealthily remaining out of sight. It was after 12:00 a.m. The police car was still sitting in the parking lot behind the minimart, maybe waiting for the criminal(s) who had broken into the building to come back, but probably waiting for me to attempt to drive off. Illegally.

I crouched behind some bushes, away from streetlights and houses, at the edge of a gravel road that headed north into the farmland of Illinois.

I was being eaten alive by mosquitoes. I was dripping wet, crouched behind bushes, holding a pair of blue jeans and a T-shirt and some underwear. Plus a toiletries kit. I was going to wait them out.

At 1:00 a.m., they pulled out, parked on the other side of the mart, and turned off their headlights and the dome light in the car.

They were still waiting for me.

An hour later, the car started up. The headlights came on, and they pulled out of the lot and onto the street and drove slowly into town. I waited, making sure they weren't going to double back. I was surprised by how calm I was, a criminal hiding in the bushes in western Illinois, about to leave the scene of a crime.

I broke for the car in a dead run, sprinting across the gravel, unlocking the door with my key. I started the engine. I didn't turn on the headlights but gunned the car, fishtailing onto the road heading north toward farmland that stretched out between me and Eureka, Illinois. I was cheering for myself, laughing at my audacity and good fortune. I flicked on the headlights. I jacked up the radio. I was so pleased with myself I barely noticed the patrol car going past me in the opposite direction just a half mile from the mart. It took a moment to realize those brake lights coming on in my rearview mirror meant my escape was far from over.

I'm from Illinois. I had accompanied my father on countless speaking engagements in little towns across the state, and I had taken a summer of flight class at the U of I. So I had my bearings. The Corn Belt is made up of one-mile square fields that stretch from the outskirts of Chicago to St. Louis. So I followed a plan I hoped would lose the police.

If they were following me.

I stayed on gravel roads—a mile north, a mile west, two miles north, two miles east, a mile north, a mile west, two miles north, and so on. It was a slow go, but I was on the lam.

I finally had to stop. I had run six miles just a few hours before. I had crouched in the bushes for who knows how long. I had driven another hour and a half. I was light-headed and feeling nauseous. I needed a drink. I rolled into a quiet, dark five-block-long little country town without a "welcome to" sign and pulled into a gas station. There was an outdoor vending machine, and I got a Coke. I downed it and bought another. I climbed back into the car, pulled onto the main street headed east, and cherry tops filled the night.

I hadn't seen the policeman, who pulled up behind me—a magician, he came out of nowhere! But I knew enough from my previous encounter just hours before: The police can't take your car if it's on private property. So I pulled into the parking lot of a Laundromat. The cop pulled in beside me. I got out of the car. I was still wearing nothing but running shorts and socks and shoes. I was exhausted, and I looked like a beaten dog.

"I saw you hit the Coke machine back there," he said. He was shorter than I, in full police uniform and hat, but not a state trooper. Local yokel. Friendly and courteous. "You okay?"

I smiled or tried to smile. "Yeah, long night," I said.

"Where you headed?"

No sense in lying. I told him, "I'm a comedian. I'm driving to do a show tomorrow at noon."

"You mean today," he said with a big smile. "I see. Well, let me take a look at your license, and you can be on your way."

I didn't move. I looked at him for a beat too long, trying to think of something to say. But my brain froze. I didn't say a word. I turned and went to the car, got my wallet, and gave him the license that had just been checked by his colleagues down in Quincy. I handed it to him and we both briefly tugged at it. Then he snatched it away and said, "Thanks."

He sat in his patrol car and called in my name and number. I opened the trunk and got a T-shirt out of my bag. I went to the passenger seat and got my toiletries, because, if I was going to jail, I wanted to at least be able to brush my teeth. I closed the car doors, locked them, and stood at the back of my car. I couldn't move. I just stood there, arms crossed, and waited to start my sentence.

It was a long wait. The cop was on his mike, loud static interrupting everything he said. He was talking to a female voice, who would give him information, and he'd nod and ask something else. Once he looked at me through his windshield and shrugged, as if to say, "Don't you hate when this happens?" He let the police lights flash, which made an annoying clicking sound in a staccato beat, joining the crickets in the muggy air.

I began to pour sweat from every pore of my body. Again.

Finally the lights went out on top of his white squad car. He turned off his engine. The crickets slowed their chirping. Even they knew it was all over.

He got out of the car, adjusted his belt, straightened his hat, and came walking toward me. He was holding my license between his left forefinger and thumb, and he flicked it a couple of times with his other hand.

"I think I know you," he said.

I stared. What? Knows me? From high school? U of I? Northwestern?

He was nodding. "Yeah, I know who you are. It fooled me at first—Franklin Mason. But then I seen your middle initial, T. And that got me to thinking." He was staring at the license, holding it up and reading it in the predawn light. He looked at me.

"T. For Taylor. You're Taylor Mason, right?"

He looked in the trunk.

"That Romeo?" He pointed at the arm and leg sticking out of the suitcase in the trunk.

Unbelievable. "Yes. My full name is Franklin Taylor Mason, but I've always gone by Taylor. And that is Romeo."

He was nodding, and he laughed out loud. "Yeah. I saw you on Showbox. The comedy show. You're funny."

Unreal. He called Showtime Showbox, but who was I to argue with a policeman?

"Thanks."

He flicked the license again. "Yeah, I seen that show about three times. It comes on late when I get off work on the weekends."

This was bizarre in every sense of the word. I was on the run. I was exhausted. I was going to jail. And this guy was talking about soon-to-be forgotten TV exposure.

He walked up to the bumper and stood just a few inches from me. "I love ventriloquism, man. Remember that guy on Soap?"

I nodded.

"Yeah, and I love it when comedians make fun of police," he said. "Cracks me up. Doughnut jokes, man! Do you do any?"

I didn't say anything. I was staring at him. I was starting to like the guy in some ways, but he was also annoying. I thought, *What the heck? Going to jail won't be so bad if I can just get away from this guy.*

He waited for me to tell a police-and-the-doughnuts joke. But when he realized I wasn't playing along, he nodded. "Okay, here's the deal. I'm gonna give you your license." He held it out for me to take, but then he pulled it away just before I could take it out of his hand. "But you have to promise me you'll start doing some police jokes in your act—especially if the jokes are about state troopers. Deal?"

"Yes! Yes I will!" I croaked, and I took the license.

He sauntered back to the squad car. "Drive safe!" he said. "Great to meet you."

He drove off.

I went right to the highway and drove to Eureka, Illinois, the small college there. I did my show that morning, a weird time for a comedy show, which just added to the surrealness of the whole thing. Afterward I headed for my next gig in Iowa, desperate to get out of Illinois before they put out an APB.

I got back home to the East Coast with a story to tell.

Marsia didn't laugh and wasn't impressed. "You have to talk to the State of Illinois and find out what the problem is!"

I said, "Okay."

So I completely forgot about the incident.

My criminal life was not over.

A few months later, we had moved from New York to New Jersey, but I was still using my New York license. I was in the middle of another college trip. I was driving north on I-55, headed for a job in Iowa, scooting past Lincoln, Illinois, when the police car lights came on. It was daylight, my show was hours away, and I had completely forgotten the night in Quincy some months before.

The policewoman who pulled me over looked like Angie Dickenson, except she was wearing aviators and her hair was black. She asked to see my insurance, registration, and license, in that order—the last being the moment I realized I was in trouble.

> Angie Dickinson was a major film and motion picture star starting in the 1950s. As a forty-three-year-old woman, she was cast as the star in a television series called *Police Woman*, breaking all kinds of cultural norms (particularly in Hollywood) and winning all kinds of awards. She was way ahead of her time. She was also married to Burt Bacharach, the songwriter, for a while.

No, no, no, no, no.

I wasn't speeding or driving dangerously. I know for a fact there were people doing those things, right on the expressway where she stood telling me why she'd pulled me over.

She had pulled me over for the new Illinois state law requiring all drivers to wear a seat belt. She went to her car, called all the information in, and came back to face me.

"We're going to have to tow your car and go to the station," she said, reprimanding me in a gentle, motherly way. "You have a driver's license issue."

"Why? What's wrong?" I squealed like a little boy. So embarrassing. I got the same story as before. I'd have to stay in Lincoln until the following day and see the judge. I looked at my watch. I had a little more than seven hours to get to western Illinois for my gig. I needed the money! I needed to have the rental car to get to the job!

I had to get out of this predicament.

I started thinking like a criminal. Let's face it—once you've evaded the law, you are, on some level, living like one. So what the hell?

"I have to do the show tonight!" I whined to the officer. "This is all I have! My wife and I have humongous bills. We have a baby. She might leave me if I don't start making a living, so this college tour is my last hope to show her I have a real career going!"

I was in the back seat, not wearing handcuffs but clearly a bad person, and I kept making eye contact with her in the rearview mirror.

Like most lawbreakers, I was lying. I was making up stories and babbling and martyring myself shamelessly.

There was something about the pitying look she gave me. It was the sad look people have when they say, "Aw, gee, look at that," to a wounded animal.

I kept doing my turn as fringe artist just trying to get by. "This is my dream! To be in showbiz! And the colleges that booked me. The shows are sold out! They're waiting for me! *This is all I have!*"

I thought she might give in as we drove into town and I kept up my pathetic story about show business and stardom and so on, but no. She seemed to be tuning me out. By the time we got to the station, she couldn't make eye contact with me any more.

At police headquarters, I was given a ticket. I watched the rental car get towed to the pound, and I was told I could get a hotel in town. She was almost apologetic, my arresting officer / Angie Dickenson wannabe. We were standing in the front room at the station house, where there was a bench and a pay phone. There was a desk with a window and double glass doors that led into the offices. There were scuffmarks on the white walls by a pay phone, where it looked as if something or someone had been dragged off as they clawed the wall.

"You can use the phone," she said, pointing at it.

I went to the pay phone and looked back at her, defeated. Depressed. Desperate.

I faked a phone call.

"Hello, Mrs. Stanton? Yes, it's me, Taylor Mason." I did a little "distant voice" ventriloquism, making it sound as if there was someone saying something—a barely audible sound coming from the phone earpiece—and I had a conversation with myself. Nothing I didn't do every night, so what the heck? "No, I'm afraid I'll have to cancel," I said to the imaginary person on the phone, the booking agent or director at the college I was performing at or whoever it was, whatever I could make it sound like. "There is no way I can make it. I've been arrested in Lincoln, Illinois." I made it sound as if someone were shouting at me on the phone - even held it away from my ear and looked at it, selling the whole show, pulling off one of the great performances of my life. "Please, Mrs. Stanton" (her name came to me out of nowhere), "don't do that! I'll do anything to make this up to you!" I went on, covering my face with one hand, pleading with the nonexistent Mrs. Stanton, and then I put the phone back.

Angie was staring at me. "What happened? That sounded bad."

I shrugged. "Well, it's my own fault. I should have cleared my license. I should have worn my seat belt. I've learned my lesson." I looked into her eyes and tried to make myself cry.

She looked away.

She put her hand on her holster, and she turned her back to me and put her head down. I thought I heard a sniffle. "Here," she said, her back to me, holding my license away from her body with her right arm. "Take your license. It won't do you any good as far as driving—your car has been impounded. But maybe you can get someone to forward you some money or something for the hotel."

I took my license. She walked away from me, a hand to her face, sighed sadly, and buzzed me out the double-paned doors into the sunlight.

I planned my escape.

Downtown Lincoln, Illinois, circa early 1990s was a ghost town. There was a barbershop, a hair and nails salon, and a restaurant. The storefronts remained, but the stores had moved to the mall.

There, in a corner building, calling to me, was a cab business—a dilapidated taxi stand in Lincoln, Illinois. On a bench out front sat a couple of grizzled old Midwesterners eyeing me as I strode down the street trying to act nonchalant.

"Hi, guys!" I said, cheerfully, walking up to the front door. I could smell alcohol. The two men on the bench grunted. The door was open. I walked in.

A makeshift counter was on the right, built up high so the man working behind it had to lean over to see me.

I smiled. "Hi there. How do? I need a cab to take me out to the pound!" I said. "Just got my license back, see?" I held it up with one hand for the man behind the counter.

One of the codgers outside snorted. The counter guy looked at the license, looked at me, and then picked up a giant walkie-talkie that looked like it had been pilfered from a WWII movie. "Billy," he said, "I got a fare for ya! Come on back to HQ."

There was loud static that apparently passed for a response, and moments later a beat-up red Buick appeared at the curb in front of the stand.

The car was rumbling and agitating, spasming with the sound of its muffler-less engine. It was loud. I couldn't tell if it was about to die out completely or peel out and leave me in the backwash of some kind of drag race. All the windows were open. The driver wore a white T-shirt under a faux black leather vest, and a cigarette hung on the edge of his lower lip. His dark hair was cut short, military style, and his black sunglasses gave him the air of someone who wasn't afraid of anything. When he saw I was the fare, he jerked his head in the direction of the back seat. I opened the door. It creaked. I climbed in.

He looked at me in the rearview mirror.

"Pound?" he asked.

"Yes." I nodded.

He jammed the gear into drive, and we shot through town, past the police station, and out into the cornfields.

After ten minutes on a blacktop, we veered off onto a gravel road, and kicked up dust and rock for another minute or two before he slowed the big car down. A farmhouse came into view. It was a classic Illinois farmhouse—two stories, a hundred feet off the road, big windows with lacy drapes fluttering in the afternoon breeze. We pulled into the drive, which was just an extension of the rock and gravel from the road, and stopped.

"Ten dollars," he said.

I gave him a twenty. "Keep the change!"

He didn't say thank you. Didn't wait for anyone to come out of the house. He backed out of the drive in a flurry of dust and rock and sound and gunned it back toward town.

I walked up the drive. It led to a large barn and formed a kind of circular parking / turning around area behind the house. There was a tractor and a pickup truck sitting by the back steps to the first floor. The barn door was closed. To the right of the barn, extending out into a field, were cars in varying states of decay and misuse. Some were missing tires or windows or engines. Some appeared to have been there for a very long time—like, maybe, decades.

Sitting by itself, between the house, the barn and the field of cars, was my rental. I briefly thought of checking for the keys and jumping in and driving off but didn't. Instead, I turned back toward the house and had started walking when I saw the porch, a screen door, and someone watching me from behind it. As I approached the stairs that led to that door, a voice spoke from behind the screen.

"What do you want?" It was a male. Young. Not nice.

"Uh ... that's my car," I said, pointing to the rental. "I want to reclaim it."

"You wanna what?" said the voice. He flung the screen door open with so much force it thwacked against the side of the house, and he caught it as it rebounded and then slammed it shut behind him as he walked down the steps to meet me on the gravel drive.

"I've come to get my car," I said, adding, "I'm happy to pay for a full day holding it. Thank you."

He was wearing a flannel shirt and blue jeans, heavy boots, and what I thought was a baseball bat. A weapon? He had long stringy black hair and stubble, missing teeth, and a scar on his cheek. He pushed past me and looked at the car. Then he looked at me.

"The cops just dropped it off," he said. "They told me you can't drive it. You got no license."

I nodded and smiled and held my arms out at my sides. "Yeah, well, there was a little mix-up," I said. "Big mistake. Not my fault! Uh ... nobody's fault! Just a clerical error or something." I produced the license from my wallet and showed it to him.

"Why'd they give this back to you? You're supposed to go to court in the morning!"

Who is this guy? And who ever heard of police telling everything to the junkyard man? "Right. Right. You're *so* right. Turns out there was some snafu or something between the State of Illinois and the State of New York with my license. All's well that ends well, though, huh? So what do I owe you? I'll get out of your hair. I'm sure you have important things to do."

"*Do not give him that car!*" came a woman's voice from inside the house. A baby started crying. "*He ain't tellin' the truth!*"

The man with the bat glared past me to the house. "Shut up, Corky! This is business. Got nothin' to do with you!"

He grabbed the license from my hand and studied it, the way someone who does not know how to read another language will stare at a page of words in an effort to understand them. I had the fleeting thought he might not be able to read at all.

"Okay," he said. "It's fifty dollars for holding your car. I'll get your keys."

He went into the barn, came out with the keys, and handed them to me. I gave him three twenties.

"Pleasure!" I said, a little too quickly and much too loudly, and I speed walked to the car.

I felt as if every endorphin in the known universe had been unleashed on my body. I shoved the key in the slot, slammed the car into drive, and made a wide turn in the circular drive behind the house in front of the barn. I gave the guy with the bat a macho flip of my head and burst out to the gravel road, heading back toward Lincoln.

A free man!

But being the worst criminal on the planet, I had made a fatal error in my haste to get back to the freeway, retracing the exact route the cabbie had taken to get me to the car. Now, as

I drove into town, past the tidy homes and the grade school and the park, I realized there was only one road—only one way to I-57, one path that would lead to my complete escape.

I had to drive past the police station.

I slowed to a crawl. No sense in taking any chances by going too fast and ruining everything by speeding. I tried to sink as low in the seat as I possibly could, so that just the top of my head and my eyes were peering over the passenger door, my hands at 10:15 on the steering wheel. I kept looking straight ahead. I crept past the parking lot between the station and the street, aware that the double glass doors were just off to my right, fighting the urge to look over. I told myself not to even make a cursory glance at the building. I tried not to think about it.

And then I looked.

She was there, coming out the doors. She saw the car. She recognized it immediately. We made eye contact.

I straightened up in my seat and slowly sped up to the official speed limit—thirty miles per hour. I was headed north. Applying the same technique I had used in my last brush with Illinois's finest, I made a beeline for the cornfields north of Lincoln. Then I took a gravel road to the west. Then I headed north for a couple of miles and then west. I heard no sirens. I kept looking for a helicopter to appear out of the sun, the feds chasing down a driver's license felon! But after a couple of hours, some sixty miles north and west of Lincoln, I got back on a freeway and headed to my gig.

I flew through my show at a college in the Quad Cities of western Illinois, where I acted as if everything was peachy and got my check. I put my props back in the car—and a girl from the college asked for a picture. I sat JP in the driver's seat on top of a suitcase, and I got in the passenger's seat, so when she snapped a shot of us, it appeared that my vent dummy was driving the car. She was pleased.

Let's go! I shoved JP over to the passenger seat, where he sat like an inanimate passenger, and I drove off, headed for a show in Iowa.

I needed to get out of Illinois as quickly as I could. I was driving on I-80, the interstate that connects the east and west coasts of the United States, and as I got close to the Iowa state line, I saw red taillights in the dark about a mile in front of me weaving crazily back and forth across the highway. The vehicle veered off into the median that separated eastbound and westbound traffic, disappearing into the grass and trees and pitch blackness. I slowed down, got into the left lane, and pulled over onto the shoulder. I saw the red taillights again. In the dark I could pick out a pickup truck that had just crashed in the middle of the median between some trees and bushes. It didn't appear life-threatening.

I put my car in park, turned on my flashers, and got out. I had walked a few feet when the driver appeared, stumbling around his truck, kicking the tires and cursing. He was alone. He saw my headlights and waved at me.

"Man, am I glad to see you!" he shouted. "I gotta get outta here!"

I sized him up—swerving truck, crash, the too-cheerful demeanor (considering he had just *crashed*).

"Are you all right? Are you hurt?" I took some tentative steps toward him. My only concern was that he might need medical attention.

"Nah!" He laughed. "Can you give me a ride over to Davenport?" He was walking toward me.

I started walking backward toward my car. "Nope!" I shouted. "I'm in a hurry. I'll stop at the next gas station and call a tow truck!"

From behind the man and his truck came the flashing lights of a police car that pulled over on the eastbound side of the expressway. A policeman got out of his car and shined a bright flashlight beam on the crashed truck and then on the driver.

He shouted, "Are you okay?"

Now the man was running and stumbling after me, pleading. "Come on! We gotta stick together on this, man! Have a heart!"

I shouted to the cop, "He's okay, officer!" I turned and ran to my car, the driver of the crashed pickup coming up behind me. I opened the car door. The overhead lights came on.

The driver was just a few feet behind. I opened the car door and turned around to face the driver. I was going to say something—something like, "Please leave me alone."

He looked at me with a goofy smile.

Then he looked in the car.

He screamed the bloodcurdling scream of an actress in a gory horror movie being captured by the most evil of all evil evildoers.

I followed his eyes to the passenger seat of my car. There, spotlighted by the interior car lights, sitting at a disturbing, inhuman angle, was my ventriloquist partner Romeo. His mouth was open in an unearthly smile, and he was staring directly at the driver who'd crashed. It was a horror movie come to life.

The man screamed again.

I didn't think. I moved. I got in the car. I put the key in the ignition and turned the engine over. I did not look at the driver or the officer. I just eased back onto the expressway and headed west. Ten minutes later, I drove across the state line.

Yes!

I finally did call the State of Illinois office for motor vehicles a week later. The problem was resolved within about two minutes. I had never changed my address. That was the entire problem.

What an idiot.

good.

It always seems like I get some new great material, and then I'm off to some unheard-of place at the end of the world... next week? Kansas + Missouri.

Too many magazines out there. I read ME. Me magazine. It's all about me. What I did, where I did it, who I did it with... also, You magazine and Them magazine. And We Magazine. On sale at newstands everywhere.

FROM TAYLOR MASON'S PERSONAL DIARY.

Chapter Eighteen
The Dance

There is something profoundly blind about this dance. There is an enormous question being carried about by all these creatures moving before our eyes. It is no way distinct from themselves. They carry it about with them without understanding it, like an animal that turns in its cage and never tires of butting its head against the bars.
—Jacques Rivière, French writer, reviewing the Stravinsky/Nijinsky ballet *The Rite of Spring* in Paris, 1913 (the ballet itself caused a riot)

Life and work. Work and life. Gigs, auditions, travel, and an occasional career-enhancing moment, followed by long stretches of introspection and self-evaluation, asking, "What am I doing?" I had become a road warrior. I would take a week in a comedy club, come home to my wife and children and spend time with them, followed by a week of college gigs and then maybe a local booking or two so I could be home while keeping all of it in some sort of balance. It was ambitious. But it wasn't impossible.

I had been running in five directions since getting out of college. Keeping with that lifestyle, we sold the house in New Jersey and moved to Southern California.

Show business is risk.

Risk it all.

I signed on with a personal manager, someone to keep the bookings coming, a "player" who could get me some big-time exposure and maybe land me a big TV or film job. Rick Rogers would work his butt off for me, and I will be forever sheepish I didn't make a bigger splash. Joey still handled the colleges, but Rick got me on a number of television programs. He got me interviews with the Disney Corporation (they rejected me) and auditions for major motion pictures (I was never cast). And he never stopped hustling.

The television program *Star Search* was inflicted on the public sometime in the 1980s and gained a significant following from the start. It was the first of the reality/talent shows that are as common as TV commercials now, a fast-moving montage of music, dance, comedy, and surreal weirdness. (For a couple of seasons, there was an "acting" competition, where people would perform a theatrical "scene" and get judged on their abilities to emote—in two minutes!) The list of winners is long forgotten. The list of people who lost, especially in the comedy portion of the program, is pretty impressive.

The first winners in comedy were Brad Garrett and John Kassir, both of whom went on to successful careers in Hollywood. The single artist who really put *Star Search* on the map and made it a household name for many years was a singer, Sam Harris, whose "Over the Rainbow" performance was so captivating it made the program viable over night.

> This has always struck me as odd—often the winners of talent shows like *Star Search*, *America's Got Talent*, *The Voice*, *American Idol*, and the like—never top that moment. Look up the finalists, and you'll find most have (like me) worked in relative obscurity for entire careers.

By the time I was cast, the show was a proven commodity, and it had it's own vibe. The talent competitions included comedy, bands, singers, child singers, dancers, and … spokesmodels!? It was my eighth or ninth audition for the show over the course of six to seven years. When I finally got it I wasn't so much excited as I was relieved. *Everyone* in the comedy community had done the show. Most of the comics had great fun with it, win or lose, and they were always making fun of the whole concept. You'd get two minutes, the live audience who attended the taping would vote via some kind of handheld device, and an act would either get to perform on the next show or go home. The voting was done with stars, 4 being the highest grade, 1 being the lowest.

I don't remember everyone I worked with in the ten to eleven sets I taped, but I won every week. And the more I won, the more comfortable with the program I became. Rick Rogers was incredibly helpful and had sage advice from having booked acts on the show and being around it for years. "Don't worry about the clock; just keep doing your act until you're done," he said.

We came up with a simple battle plan: The more jokes I could pack into two minutes, the better. So, if we could get a punch line in every fifteen seconds, that meant I could get up to nine jokes in my little presentation, even if it meant going over my time by a few seconds. Sometimes the act I was competing with would do a solid performance, but he or she'd have three to four big laughs in his entire performance. Even if I missed on half of mine, I'd win by attrition, getting five big laughs out of my nine jokes, as compared to my competitor's three or four. The concept worked from the start, so we stayed with it.

We also committed to doing Romeo every show. Ventriloquism was just starting to become acceptable in the zeitgeist as an entertainment "art." Comedy clubs were using ventriloquists on a regular basis, particularly Jeff Dunham, Dan Horn, Pete Michaels, and the ever-present Jay Johnson. Rick felt a ventriloquist was the perfect act for this TV vehicle. The show appealed to a large swath of the United States, which included all ages, since it aired in much of the country during prime time.

The subject matter for the show had to be universal as well. So we zeroed in on things that everyone knew, regardless of race, education, background, age, and so on. Those premises included jobs, school, cars/planes/travel, and clothes—the kind of things everyone understood.

Sometimes we'd tape two shows in one day, which was fine with me. After winning a couple of times, I got used to the scene. I knew staffers and production people. I was comfortable with the set and stage. And the process became less intimidating. In turn, the audience became friendlier with each episode.

The Hollywood TV audience, as an entity for live performances is—to this day—its own subculture. A given TV program will bus in all manner of people of all backgrounds just to fill the seats for a live taping. That means high school students and senior citizens, tour groups and visiting college kids, people on vacation and fans of the show, and any other breathing body who will sit and clap their hands when the *applause* sign comes on. As a live entertainer, you perform for a cross section of America, which played perfectly to the act I'd been doing all over the United States for seven or eight years.

My favorite of all tapings came when I competed with a stand-up from New York, a very funny act I'd worked with many times. Jim David is an incredibly talented and funny comic, one of the funniest people playing the rooms in Manhattan, and we'd done a ton of shows together at Stand Up New York. Jim told me one night, "I'm doing *Star Search* next week. Are you still on the show?"

Together we hatched a plan for our tête-à-tête.

The concept for *Star Search* was simple: Two performers (singers, comics, dancers, whatever) were introduced. One would perform. The audience would vote. The next act would perform. Again the audience would vote. Then host Ed McMahon would bring the two different acts together, and scores would be announced for each, via stars that appeared under their names on the TV screen. Whoever got the most stars moved on. Usually the acts would shake hands, the winners would wave to the audience, and the losers would walk off. At the end of the show, the winners would all come back on stage and stand together, congratulated by Ed, and that was an episode.

David and I planned something different. We did our sets, his was really strong and very funny, and I went up and did my tight nine laughs in 135 seconds. Romeo did his thing, we finished strong to applause and laughter and then came back to be judged. Ed stood between us, the votes were totaled, and the stars were given. I won.

Instead of shaking hands (accepted format), Jim stepped in front of Mr. McMahon and walked right up to Romeo, ignoring me. There was a moment of eye contact. And then Jim, feigning anger and insult—as in, *I cannot believe I lost to this idiotic puppet!*—hauled off and slapped Romeo across the face. He stormed off the set. It was great TV, and for years afterward people would ask me, "That guy was so angry at you and Romeo! I bet there was a scene backstage, huh?" I always have played along, saying, "Oh, yeah. He's never forgiven me. We used to be such good friends."

By the time we got to the last rounds of the show, I was surprised. I had been rejected in the audition process so much that just getting on the show was a big deal. Actually winning a couple of times was inconceivable. Making it to the final rounds was a pipe dream, and here I was. By now, I knew every act I was competing against. Some of the people I "beat"—I say that with tongue firmly in cheek because the whole thing was such a crapshoot. Who knows why/how I got to be selected every week?

> Some of the comedians I "beat" on *Star Search* have used that experience as fodder. More than one comic out there spent a few years doing a whole routine based on, "I lost on *Star Search* to a puppet."

My semifinal round was a tough test. Torian Hughes, who today is an accomplished comedy writer as well as a stellar stand-up, was my foe. I had worked with him many times, often at Zanies in Nashville, Tennessee. It's hard to build up any animosity for people you know and like and admire, so it became sort of a personal test. I wasn't so much trying to defeat anyone. I was just pushing myself to do the best I knew how. I was competing with myself. It was a lot like emceeing the college conferences. I wasn't so much trying to show up the other acts. I wanted all of them to have stellar performances. I just wanted to do my best work and let the chips fall.

I don't have to be the best comedian here tonight. I just had to be the best when I was performing.

Torian rocked the room, and I was nervous when I hit the stage. Marsia had come to Los Angeles to be part of the finale, if I could make it that far. Our baby was with my mother-in-law, "Vovie," back in New Jersey. I was emotional. There was money, prestige, my ability, and my career on the line. I barely won that round, maybe by a half star or something. And I'm sure if I were to watch our performances today it would be hard to say I did "better" than my friend Torian Hughes.

DEFINITION: My mother-in-law is Brazilian. Vovie (pronounced vaw-vee) is a loving term given to my mother-in-law by her children, which is an Americanized version of the Portuguese word for grandmother: Vova. Her real name is Marisa, but I called her Vovie - as did my wife and our children - from the time I met her.

The *Star Search* championship taping was as good as it gets in Hollywood. There were celebrity judges (Bud Friedman from the Improv was one of them) for the show and a certain buzz backstage before the big night. My competition was another comedy act I knew, Geechy Guy.

Geechy had a great rep on the West Coast. He knew everyone, and all the comics knew him. He was one of those offbeat, unforgettable, totally unique, and hysterically funny people who naturally gravitate to comedy as a career. I always loved working with him. His act a combination of "geek" and "smart"—the "idiot savant" who endears himself to every audience. Before the show that night, he introduced me to his mother, who had flown in from where she lived in the Midwest.

Again, it was hard for me to think of myself "competing" against someone I knew. Rick and I put together a set, a total of ten punch lines. One of the producers of *Star Search* came into my dressing room before the taping began and said, "You've been pushing the clock. You need to keep it down to two minutes. Okay?"

I lied to his face, "Yes, sir!" I knew full well I was going to go over, that I wanted an extra punch line in the set, and that I was going to try and win the prize. If that meant "cheating" a little bit, so be it.

It was really no different than playing football against the odds in college. No different than competing with the way-above-average-intelligence men and women at Northwestern University. No different than putting my butt on the line everywhere I went, for gigs with leaders and stars and the makers and shakers from all walks of life. If success meant pushing the clock or adding an extra punch line, so be it. We weren't talking about life and death. This was show business. Let's be honest; the whole thing is a parlor trick. At its core showbiz can be sleazy and narcissistic and sometimes crooked. I "do what I have to do" the way that everyone does in a lot of businesses.

Making a living and having success in the business of comedy is all about risk. I've lived so long out on a limb that taking risks and living with risk is like breathing. I do it without thinking.

I won *Star Search*. Geechy was brilliant, which meant I had to nail my set. And I did. But it easily could have been Geechy. Or Torian. Or Jim David. Or any one of a number of other great comedy acts. I had a picture of our newborn son Hank in my pocket, and as Ed McMahon read off the names of the winners,

I squeezed it so hard I might have rubbed the image off the paper. When my name echoed through the soundstage and out into the audience, I looked at my wife. We both were laughing. And then I shook Ed's hand, and I moved on with my career.

The show ended about six or seven in the evening. It was a weekend, so we went over to our Chicago friend Claire Berger's house, where she was having a party with a few Chicago expats and theater types who were hanging out and enjoying the night. I don't think we even told people I had won the show. We were happy to have earned what we did, happy to be a small part of the TV community.

I picked up my check a couple of weeks later. It came to just under $100,000. I paid some bills, and we put some in savings, and I think we might have purchased a car. For the next couple of years I toured clubs and colleges, introduced as "*Star Search* Grand Champion Taylor Mason," and a certain viability came with that intro. I'm proud of the work I did on the show, and I'm one of the very few people who still use *Star Search* as a credit when I make public appearances.

When Rick Rogers called, he was always even-tempered, calm, and matter-of-fact. It was business as usual regardless of the event. But one day his call—his typical behavior—was different. There was drama in his voice, a telltale inflection that meant excitement.

"You're working Igby's Friday night, and Jack Rollins is coming to see you."

It was 1993. Marsia and I had a house out in the Santa Monica Mountains, out past the valley in Thousand Oaks, and she was pregnant with Everett, our youngest. I had been pounding the boards for more than a decade. I had a résumé that made me at least somewhat viable (on paper). And I was always a little frantic about making something happen.

"I'm ready for my close-up, Mr. DeMille."

Rick had been handling my career as a personal manager for a couple of years. He was a fighter and a doer when it came to the acts he handled. I considered him a friend. He had big-name clients (Bill Engvall to name-drop one). (And by now you should know that I will name-drop anyone I've ever worked with or met, whether they remember me or not!) He had signed on with Lorimar Productions in Hollywood. Rick was always trying to push my career into the next level, whatever that might have been.

Somehow, he got Jack Rollins to come see me at an LA comedy club.

Jack Rollins. Of Rollins-Joffe. Charles Joffe. The duo that produced Woody Allen. Just saying the name "Rollins" raised eyebrows in the company of showbiz types during the '80s and '90s. Rollins-Joffe managed none other than David Letterman (yep, him) and brought the kind of cachet that you literally could not buy.

And Rick got Jack Rollins to come see me.

My performance would take place at Igby's.

Igby's was a long-gone comedy club that was a true joy to play. Just off Sepulveda Boulevard in a friendly part of Los Angeles, it offered consistently great shows and all the name comedy acts of the day, at a lower price than the Improvs or the Comedy Store. It was run by Jan, a really nice guy who always treated me with respect and sincerity and gave me more stage time than I deserved.

That night's thirty-minute performance for the typically energetic and responsive Igby's crowd featured just about everything I had in my arsenal—ventriloquism, music, and stand-up, all bound tightly in a cohesive set. I performed "Meet the Flintstones" as Elton John and Billy Joel and Prince and Sir Mix-a-lot. I did some politics. ("The presidents of my lifetime—Carter, Reagan, Bush, and Clinton—they're like the anti–Mount Rushmore!") And I closed with a tight ventriloquist presentation, where Romeo talked to an audience member, and the person talked back, which allows me to do some improvisation and show off both my ability as a vent and my ability to think on my feet—all while keeping it funny!

A decade of one-nighters and clubs and colleges and corporate shows, of TV spots and gigs in church basements and in concert halls—all of that fast-forwarded into a mash-up blur to coincide with a little "showcase" in a now-forgotten comedy club for the biggest comedy *player* on the planet.

Then we met, Mr. Rollins and I, on the little porch right outside the front door of Igby's as the show went on inside, the laughter washing over us every time people opened the door and walked in or out of the club. He shook my hand. He shook his head. He got right to the point. His words echo through the years, and I can hear them as if he were standing next to me as I write.

"You'll never make much money," he said. "You're smart. But the audience doesn't like smart. Smart is boring. You don't have to be smart. Drop the puppets. Drop the music. You need to concentrate on doing more stand-up comedy."

He wasn't mean. He wasn't insulting. He had a lifetime of experience and knowledge and an "eye" for talent and what worked and what didn't work, and he gave me advice. He tried to find positive things to say. He was not interested in how I approached my job. He didn't care about the moment or the audience reaction, because he was interested in something else. He was *looking* for something else.

Or maybe someone else. Let's be honest. There were then, and there are now, a lot of talented, funny, interesting, and dynamic comedy acts in the world. Jack Rollins just did not "get" the man with the puppets and the music and the "too smart" takes on current events.

Now it's a few lifetimes later. Rick Rogers moved to Dallas and is quite successful in his new life. Bill Engvall went on to fame and fortune with the Blue Collar Comedy Tour. Igby's is gone but not forgotten. Jack Rollins (and his longtime partner Charles Joffe) have passed away.

Me? I was not deterred by Rollins's dismissal. I wish I could meet him face-to-face for a moment now. Just in passing. Two old souls crossing paths in some kind of comedy space-time vortex. I'd approach him with a smile and an outstretched hand. "Mr. Rollins? You won't remember me. You came and saw me a long time ago, and you told me I'd never have much of a career. You were wrong. No hard feelings."

Rick did end up getting me a two-year deal with a Denver, Colorado, electronics company called Soundtrack. Romeo and I did a bunch of thirty-second radio and TV spots for them. This got me my Screen Actors Guild (SAG) and American Federation of Television and Radio Artists (AFTRA) union membership, important because the health insurance they offered was excellent, just what the doctor ordered for a young family.

Chapter Nineteen
Romeo

"Romeo, oh Romeo, wherefore art thou Romeo?"
—from Romeo and Juliette by William Shakespeare

I had rejected the hard woodenheaded puppet, JP, from my act after meeting a woman named Verna Finley. A brilliant creator of ventriloquist and puppet characters, Verna had come to New Jersey while we were still living there and taught a class for ten to fifteen people on how to build ventriloquist puppets. Included in the class, sitting behind me for most of the lectures, was a young ventriloquist named Jeff Dunham. I was familiar with him because we played the same comedy clubs, we played the same colleges, and we got calls for the same corporate shows and specialty shows and so forth. When we met, Jeff said hello to me using a "distant voice," making it sound as if someone underneath his seat was saying hi.

Some fifteen years after this meeting, he would become a household name in the Unite States.

> People in the comedy business often say this to me, backstage or at a dinner meeting or in rehearsal: "You must hate Jeff Dunham." I understand. He's had the kind of success that very, very few people enjoy. Jealous much? No. I don't hate him. There are people in showbiz who transcend talent, hard work, and luck. Whatever that thing is that makes someone a superstar—and I have no idea what it is—Mr. Dunham owns that. To his credit, he has not wasted it. He's one of those black swans you gotta love about the business: You can't quantify special. And, to be honest, I have probably benefitted as much as anyone due to Jeff Dunham's success. He made ventriloquism "hip"—which many people told me was impossible. So thank you, Jeff Dunham.

DEFINITION: black swan. Something that deviates beyond what is normally expected in a given situation and would be extremely difficult to predict. A ventriloquist becoming the biggest-selling live comedy act in the world, for example (Dunham did it), is a black swan. The phrase was popularized by Nassim Nicholas Taleb's book *The Black Swan: The Impact of the Highly Improbable."* Mr. Taleb is a finance professor and former Wall Street trader.

Verna reminded me of my grandmother Mildred Mason, the same woman who had helped me with my sock puppet as a child. I was immediately taken with Verna's style and grace. During her class, she revealed the same kinds of techniques Mildred would have used. She incorporated everyday things. A coat hanger with pipe cleaner became eyebrows. Cut out an ear from a piece of foam, cover it in terry cloth, and sew it on the foam head of your puppet. "When in doubt, sew!" said Verna. She cut a Ping-Pong ball in half, and it became a puppet's eye. The entire process and workload was low-tech and accessible.

I loved it.

> Verna Finley always took my phone calls and treated me with more respect than I deserve. I kind of merged her with my grandmother in my live performances, where I explained how Romeo, my main muse, came to be. Note: Mary Ann Taylor and her puppet builder daughter treat me the same way these days.

Verna would retire soon after this class, but she would lead me to Mary Ann Taylor, another genius puppet builder who I have worked with for the past twenty-five years.

Irreversible

> I have worked with other puppet builders as well—Barry Gordemer, Folkmanis, the late great Ray Guyll, and Steve Axtell. They're all amazing.

I began using soft puppets exclusively. My own Muppet-like puppets—starting with the blond boy figure I named Jake, who morphed later into the dark-haired puppet I use today, Romeo, made travel much easier. These soft characters seemed less frightening and more in tune with the times, where the hard wood-carved figures connoted horror movies and seemed dated.

> Today's "hard" figures are mostly fiberglass and composites. They look great.

In Romeo I had a character—a completely unique, different, totally opposite of me character—which endeared me to the many disparate audiences I played for then and play for today.

Romeo is an amalgamation of a lot of different things. In truth, he doesn't know what he is or who he is. And why would he? He's a fictional character whose personality is based on whatever is current. He lives only for the moment. He is selfish, narcissistic, and a little bit greedy. He's incredibly vain and poorly educated, mostly because he doesn't apply himself. He's a frustrated lothario who has never, for all his machismo in live performance, spent more than a couple of minutes talking to any female.

At the same time, this makes Romeo kind of an every man. He's great for kids' shows, because he constantly mocks authority (me), and he can make children laugh just by his outrageous body movements. He's good for corporate and specialty shows, because he's wonderful comic relief from the business at hand or the reading of notes and lectures. He can win over the boozy, partying late-night comedy club crowd, and he's funny enough to please jaded, experienced comedy aficionados. There have been nights that I have finished a second show Friday in some rowdy saloon, the crowd has laughed for an hour, and I'll get this underhanded compliment: "The puppet saved you."

Romeo can relate to every audience. Since I am not profane, and I don't spend my act in the bedroom or the bathroom, I need a common denominator for those crowds who want some "edge." Romeo gives me that edge.

We moved west after *Star Search* and lived for three years in Thousand Oaks, California, up in the Santa Monica Mountains near California Lutheran University. The United States had elected a dynamic President Clinton, who oversaw an economy that grew dynamically and geometrically for almost a decade. Grunge music took over the airwaves. (It sounded a lot like Neil Young from my childhood, but who's complaining?) There were wars in Europe, the Serbia/Croatia/Bosnia war emblematic of issues to come. Terrorism struck in Oklahoma City while we were living in California, and we were there for the Rodney King riots that happened just a few miles from us.

We had our second child in California. The constant craziness of my schedule had become routine, and every once in a while, Marsia and I would take a break. For example, we drove to the Northridge Fashion Mall on January 16, 1994, to see a movie. Later that night—actually the morning of the January 17—an earthquake with a magnitude of 6.7 struck the exact spot we had been the night before. We were home in bed when the ground under our house began to shake.

I knew immediately it was an earthquake. I had been working at the Hilton in Guam just five months before when a 7.8 magnitude quake rocked that little island. So I recognized the feel of helplessness and fear that grips your central nervous system when the *planet* begins to ripple. I told Marsia to get Hank. I grabbed our one-year-old, Everett. And we ran downstairs to huddle underneath a ceiling beam separating the living room from the dining room in our house in Thousand Oaks. It wasn't just scary. It was life-changing.

It was over quickly. Minutes. The ground stopped acting as if it were waves on the ocean, and the household objects that had been shaking and falling off tables and crashing to the floor all steadied and stayed.

Marsia is a Jersey girl. She looked at me and said, "We have to move."

I didn't argue. She was raising two children. Her best friends, her family, her comfort zone was back east.

> Our three years in California included fires, riots, and torrential rain and accompanying mudslides, not to mention corrupt politicians and a major earthquake. We didn't just deal with a disaster. Somehow, we had signed up for a monthly subscription to disasters.

Our time in California was chaotic. I was auditioning and performing and flying around the country. The nation seemed to be in an uproar. Marsia asked me more than once, "What kind of world did we bring our children into?"

I went to Rick Rogers and told him I was leaving LA and Hollywood and his mentorship. He explained that I was giving up on so much progress we had forged and opportunities that might lie ahead. "You're making a mistake," he said. "It will be very difficult to keep yourself vital if you discard everything we've built here." He was right, and I knew it.

We shook hands and parted ways. It was one of the hardest things I've ever had to do as a professional.

The home computer was becoming essential in our everyday lives, already defining culture, society, politics, and finance. The internet and the World Wide Web took hold of the national psyche, and the '90s experienced an economic boom. I bought into the computer concept from the start, and I think I benefitted. It kept my bookings, banking, travel schedule, and creative output easily accessible.

Computing helped because I was busy. I toured incessantly. I auditioned for just about every kind of television program you can name. I took acting classes. I was a working comedy act, and I had sacrificed much to get to the point where the bills were paid and my family had a "normal" life at home.

As if on cue, I met another very hardworking personal manager based in New York named Stan Bernstein. We met in a comedy club in Manhattan, shook hands on a manager/client relationship, and he went right to work. Like Joey Edmonds and Rick Rogers, Stan hustled and did everything he could to make Taylor Mason a star. He cut a deal with the Improv Comedy Club in Arlington, Texas, where I would perform with musical impressionist Mark McCollum doing a wild two-man comedy presentation for a three-month run. Stan booked me with the Gatlin Brothers in Myrtle Beach at their beautiful theater for a summer run. He put me in Branson, Missouri, for another summer, working on the *Branson Belle* riverboat. But his biggest coup, or what should have been his biggest coup, was landing a TV deal that was my biggest justification for leaving the West Coast and moving to New Jersey.

Working on the *Branson Belle* is a poignant memory. We stayed in Branson for the summer, my children joining me every day on the boat. I closed some of those shows singing "That's the Glory of Love" to them with my ventriloquist partner Romeo. I can still see both kids, sitting above me in the balcony, their little heads over the banister watching Dad do his act. It always makes me smile to think of them up there, following my every move. Years later, I asked both of them, "Do you remember those shows on the *Branson Belle,* you coming to see me every day and I sang to you?" Both kids looked at me with blank looks of amnesia. They shook their heads. "What are you talking about, Dad?"

Stan hooked me up with a man named Marvin who had been a successful sitcom writer and television comedy producer. We had a meeting at a TV studio in Secaucus, New Jersey. I proposed an idea for a segment on this new network, a short daily comedy/puppet act.

I would be the voice and the puppeteer for Buddy, a Labrador retriever who looked exactly like the Clinton family pet dog in the White House. My idea made Buddy an "inside reporter," who would give daily updates as to what was really going on with the president of the United States.

Marvin, a short salt-and-pepper-bearded man with a friendly smile and easy laugh bought it right away. And *boom*! I had a real job!

I called Joey Edmonds, canceled a bunch of college gigs, canceled comedy club appearances, and got a chocolate Labrador retriever puppet that looked a little bit like Buddy, the Clinton's dog. I actually made the puppet myself, modifying a stuffed animal I found in a toy store in Greenwich Village. The station made a dog bed that was a replica of the presidential seal, and we started recording on a Monday.

I did the voice, a panting, excitable little boy voice with a "gee willikers" attitude, and I knew from the start the concept and the bit was good. "You wouldn't believe what's going on here today!" I'd have Buddy talking as a "reporter" from just outside the Oval Office.

The techs would often laugh out loud, and we'd have to start the taping over. There was a scandal going on in Washington, DC, centered on a rumored affair the president was having with an intern.

The new TV network? It was to be called Fox News.

I hired Paul Seaburn, a comedy writer I met in Houston during a weekend run at a club. "I haven't been paid yet," I told Paul, "but when I get my first check you'll get a check too."

Buddy's riffs included the inside dope on meetings the president was scheduling. "He even had a meeting to discuss having a meeting about a meeting!" He talked about foreign policy. "Then there were these two men in the round room, which is perfect for the president, because everything around here is going in circles anyway. One guy was agreeing with everything and kept saying, 'Yes, sir.' Then he insulted him, calling him fat. 'Yes, sir, Arafat."

I probably did two weeks of taping altogether, maybe twenty total videos and final scripts. Marvin didn't question anything. He'd just have the techs set things up, and we'd start shooting. By the second week, I didn't even tell him what the subject matter was or what I had written for the day's shoot. We'd just go to the set and let the camera roll. Fine by me!

DEFINITION: Yasser Arafat. Arafat was a political leader from Palestine in the Middle East. He was the head of the Palestinian Liberation Organization (PLO) and the Fatah political party, which he founded. President Clinton worked tirelessly but in vain to forge a peace agreement between Israel and Palestine, even having Arafat come to the White House.

At the end of the first week, some cracks began to show. One of the lighting guys said, "This is a waste of time. I mean, you're funny and all. But this is supposed to be a news channel. I don't know what we're doing here!"

Another tech told me, "I haven't been paid for last week. I'm getting a bad feeling about this."

It was not what I needed to hear. I hadn't signed a contract. I didn't have anything "official" as far as documentation. So I called Marvin. I got his machine.

I called him repeatedly.

He finally left me one message: "Please stop calling me."

And that was the end of my job with Fox News.

I had moved my little family from the West Coast to the East Coast, the TV job being the carrot. "Hey, I have work back east! This is perfect!"

I had rejected a hardworking agent and manager in Hollywood, I had blown off all my contacts in television out west, and now I was broke and jobless in New Jersey.

I would have to start over.

Chapter Twenty
The Gym

Trust me, if you do an honest 20 rep program, at some point Jesus will talk to you. On the last day of the program, he asked me if he could work in.
—Mark Rippetoe, strength training coach

I hate the gym. I hated it the first time football coaches at Hinsdale Central High School taught me how to bench-press and squat and curl. I hated it at the University of Illinois where I spent five years building muscle mass in my legs and chest so I could compete with men who were naturally bigger and stronger than I would ever be. I hated it most when I started having to pay to do something I hate (go to the gym) when I was in my twenties. And I hate it now.

I go to the gym every day.

It's my addiction, and like most addictions, I wish I could stop. Unlike most addictions, it is not making my life worse. There is a direct correlation between my (admittedly modest) accomplishments and the fact that I have kept myself "in shape." Going to the gym essentially comes down to this—working out and keeping fit is a necessary evil that allows me to keep what absolutely qualifies as a ridiculous travel schedule. I spend much of my year traveling through time zones and date lines, going without sleep and working in environments that can be emotionally and bodily taxing. My peace of mind and my physical well-being are dependent on feeling comfortable regardless of whatever is swirling around me personally, professionally, or logistically. So I train every day (and twice a day on the Disney ships). And *the workout* hangs over my head like a cloud from the time I wake up until it's done.

I belong to multiple gyms so that, no matter where I go in the United States and around the world, I can find a gym (er …

"fitness center" in the current lingo). I swipe a fob or use an app on my phone that gains me admission and get my workout in. I know how this sounds. It's beyond being health-conscious, beyond an obsession. I'm a slave to the weights, the machines, the cardio equipment, and the exercise.

I am fully aware that it's possible to get a great session in without going to a members-only club or gym. But I need the equipment, I need the routine, I need the mindless familiarity. I'm a workout snob. Most hotels have their own "fitness centers," and I've used many. But that's usually a last resort—which is fine. I have certain needs for my workouts, so I use the gym. The barbells, the bicep machine, and an abs bench are requirements.

I don't need the mirrors, which only show me how quickly I age, how little I've accomplished physically in the past how-many-decades of workouts, and how much more work I need to do. I laugh out loud at myself and at the other meatheads sometimes. "What are we doing here?"

> For some people, a major part of the fitness club experience is not just the weights, the machines, the cardio equipment, and the exercise classes. Just as important are the hundreds of floor-to-ceiling mirrors where people admire themselves.

Some of these men and women have attained their ultimate body mass. There is nothing more they can do. They have 0 percent body fat and rock hard physiques with definition and cut muscles on top of muscles on top of muscles. They look like cartoon superheroes in their Lycra and skintight shirts and pants. They move as if they're posing and presenting at a bodybuilding event. "Did you drop your towel?" they'll ask and then go into an elaborate pose and pirouette to pick it up, flexing their pectorals and displaying their abs, even when I say, "Uh, that's not mine." I see them grimacing at themselves in the mirror, doing one-armed curls with a 120-pound barbell, their entire being bulging with each rep. "Excuse me," I want to say, "but you're done. Really. Even if you've been named Mr. or Mrs. Universe, you are not a universe. You cannot expand indefinitely. You are finite as a human being. You cannot possibly add more muscle—unless you're trying to attain mass with your head. And if you are, that's just gross."

My hatred for the weight room started in college, where I found myself lifting with people who could bench-press a small car. The weight room under the stadium at the University of Illinois was filled with people who were chiseled like sculptures in European museums. Six-packs were common. I felt like the "before" picture in every weight loss / fitness commercial ever made.

> Perhaps most important to people is the way they dress for the gym, choosing their fitness outfits and designer clothing. When I see someone on an elliptical machine wearing sweatpants with the word "Pink" printed over their glutes, next to someone wearing sweats with the word "Juicy" printed over the same body part, my first thought is not fitness related. My first thought is—they should do a mash-up and make the word "grapefruit."

Most depressing was my fifth year there, my last season as a player, having spent half a decade pumping iron. In came some freshmen, some of them five years younger than me. They were just kids who had *never touched a dumbbell, and they were already much stronger than me*!

At age twenty-three, I was able to join "the 1,300 pound club" at Illinois. The strength and conditioning coach, Lloyd Carr, instituted a program for the players, and the goal was to lift 1500 pounds on four different lifts—deadlift, military press, bench-press, and squat. I made the 1300-pound level, and he gave me a T-shirt. That was all I got out of the weight training I did all those years.

Irreversible

> Lloyd Carr would go on to be the very successful head coach at the University of Michigan, where he would win a national championship in 1997. His quarterback for much of 1998 and 1999 was someone named Tom Brady.

> Nobody told me that, when a young person between the ages of eighteen and twenty-three concentrates 30 percent of his or her life to weight training, *said young person is obligated to keep that regimen up for the rest of his or her life! Otherwise, that muscle turns to fat.*

There are very few athletic people in my immediate family. I had a couple of uncles who bowled and played tennis or golf. I had an uncle who played high school football and another who played small college ball. But nobody related to me has what could be called an "athlete's body." Most of us are not so inclined. I will never look like a "jock."

> Even after all this effort, my body shape is not what anyone would mistake for "athletic." In fact, some of the major fitness apparel companies, like Under Armour, Nike, Reebok, and Adidas have threatened me with lawsuits for defamation if I wear anything with their logo in public.

There is one redeeming factor to daily workouts. It keeps you mentally focused.

Here is what I'm currently focused on, mentally—I hate working out.

That's the gym. I suppose it keeps you looking fit. And there is no doubt that exercise is probably better for most people than doing nothing. But it's as much about the mind as it is about the body.

Chapter Twenty-One
Moorestown

Money magazine today released its list of 100 Best Places to Live. Topping the list is Moorestown, NJ.
—Business Wire, July 11, 2005

My mother-in-law, Marisa, owned a board-and-bred horse farm / operation in Mt. Laurel, New Jersey. It was beautiful, a few acres of farmland tucked in among quiet suburbs across the river from Philadelphia. We were married on that farm. And when Marsia and I decided to move back to the East Coast from Cali we made the decision to look for something nearby. We wanted something close to her, close to a part of planet earth that wouldn't start shaking in the middle of a night after you went to see a movie and the kids were safely tucked into bed and the lights were turned off and the last thing you were thinking about when you kissed your spouse and drifted off is where to go and what to do when *the ground begins twerking as if it's auditioning for a Niki Minaj video.*

> My wife's name is Marsia. My mother-in-law's name is Marisa. The reverse of letters "i" and "s" in the spelling might be confusing.

> I don't believe in coincidence or irony—except as theatrical devices—so the fact that my family history is agriculture and my marriage took place on a farm was, in my opinion, preordained. Horses, farms, and family stuff—sounds old school to me.

> Just a personal note. Whenever I hear or use the term "old school" it occurs to me that no matter what's being referenced, just drop the word "school." RIght?

> My father was kept out of WW II for a physical ailment. He had broken his left foot and ankle while "breaking" a horse (remember, no irony!) and was denied enlistment in the armed forces. Think Jimmy Stewart in *It's a Wonderful Life*.

To find us a new place to live, I got a weekend job playing a New Jersey comedy club sometime after the earthquake in LA. It was a snowy March day, and I drove to the farmhouse. I picked up my wife's mom, and the two of us went looking for houses. The realtor was a personal friend of Marisa's, and we looked at a couple of nice little bungalows. But my in-law said no without getting out of the car. After a few more no's, we finally came to a split-level home in Moorestown. The three of us—Marisa, the realtor, and myself—walked in the front door.

"We'll take it," said my mother-in-law.

The realtor's eyebrows raised, as in *I can't believe it!* She looked at me. "Don't you want to see the whole house?"

She was being helpful, professional, and sincere. That would make sense, right? We should check the bathrooms, look for mold or damage, whatever.

Nope.

My mother-in-law said, "We don't have to see any more. This is the one we want."

There was an uncomfortable pause.

The realtor said, "Okay, well let's go to the office, and we can discuss."

Marisa shook her head. "No, we don't need to." Turning to me, she said, "Pay her, Tay."

With that, we ended up in the sleepy little Quaker village of Moorestown, New Jersey, just a five-minute ride from Marsia's mother and about fifteen minutes from where my wife grew up.

Our children would enjoy some benefit. We started them in private school but soon learned that Moorestown had incredibly good public schools, which as where they went. We had access to lots of activities for kids, including sports and theater and music and the Mason favorite pastime—reading. New York City as close enough that you could drive in, see a museum or a show, and drive home. Philadelphia was right next door, offering its own cultural events and institutions, not to mention professional sports and theater.

Three of Marsia's childhood friends lived close by, and she would end up working as a substitute teacher while our kids were in school, another huge benefit. We soon moved in town to a house on a cul-de-sac and lived there more than twenty years by a big field that served as a ginormous backyard. It was a great place to hang out or jog the track and walk the dogs.

In all, it was not a bad way to raise a family. I was there for the birthday parties and the high school musicals. I attended the dive meets and parent-teacher nights and coached Little League. I helped with piano lessons and homework. I saw the high school football games and the concerts and fall plays and graduations.

That's nothing to be proud of. It's what parents do.

The problem, of course, was my job. Ventriloquist/comedian/musician in South Jersey?

Huh?

Start with buying that first house in Moorestown.

Getting home loans as a nameless comedy act was problematic. Throw in the word "ventriloquist" at a local bank or lending institution, and you might as well be asking strangers on the street for access to their bank accounts. It's so far out of the realm of what is acceptable that I am always, to this day, amazed when I "qualify" for a loan.

Irreversible

"What is your profession?" a banker will ask.

"Ha ha ha. That's a good one!" they respond when I say, with all the sincerity I can muster, "I am a professional ventriloquist."

I've had loan officers sitting at their desk, head down and pen in hand, ask me, "What do you do for a living, Mr. Mason?"

"I'm a ventriloquist by trade," I'll say.

The loan officer stops. Hardens. Full on rigor mortis. He's alive, but time stands still as he is sitting there at his desk, pen in hand, held steady in place just above the paperwork. Like a statue or a wax figure at Madame Tussauds, he's frozen. This isn't a pause. It's not a moment.

This is a long, exaggerated, wait-did-this-guy-say-he's-a-ventriloquist? time blockage, where I can see the computerized pinwheel of death spinning inside the guy's brain.

For a couple of decades, I was the only (living) comedian in Moorestown. To make everything work, I had to take on the jobs that most people in comedy will never do—bar mitzvahs, bat mitzvahs, auctions, fundraisers, Fairs and festivals, and anniversaries and birthday parties. I played church basements. I played prisons. I not only booked college gigs all over the nation, but also added institutions for troubled youth, correctional facilities, and prep schools.

> The former Miss New Jersey and hysterically funny Deanna Blizzard moved to Moorestown a few years ago, making me the second comedian to live in town. I defer to Ms. Blizzard as Moorestown's "first" comedian. She's funny, she's beautiful, she's talented, and she has a wonderful family. She is capable enough to work live in person and on the radio and as a warm-up act for TV shows in Manhattan. Yeah, yeah, she's perfect. But is she happy?

You might not believe this, but southern New Jersey is not a comedy hotbed. I was stunned to find there aren't any showcases for TV and film in Moorestown or even next door in the spectacular city of Palmyra. I worked locally when I could, particularly in the back room of a pizza joint called Casa Carollo that seated maybe 110 people.

Mostly I drove or flew around the United States of America, in search of an audience.

Here's an example. I would pick the kids up from middle school and drop them off at a violin lesson or baseball practice. Then I'd drive six hours to a gig. I'd perform for my client—might be a college or a corporate group or a philanthropy just outside of Pittsburgh, say. Then I'd drive six hours home. It would be 5:00 a.m. when I walked in the door through the garage to our house. I'd take the dogs for a walk. By the time I got back in the house, the kids would be up, and I'd give them breakfast.

They might not even know I had been gone all night.

I went from doing ten TV appearances a year to an occasional spot on *Nashville Now*, a talk show that had a few viewers on cable. Getting booked wasn't a problem. For one thing, they didn't pay, not even the SAG/AFTRA minimum. So I would call and say, "Can I do the show on Wednesday?" I was never told no. I would book my own airline ticket, fly to Music City, drive a rental car over, and do my six-minute spot. Then I'd turn right around and fly home that night. Why? It was my only link to television.

I was so far off the grid of viability and respectability in my chosen field I had to find some way to make what little I had better. There is always one area that any person in showbiz can work on—even if he or she isn't in New York or Hollywood.

That's what I did. I worked on my act.

I get paid by the laugh. I'm booked to make people laugh, really hard, for X number of minutes. The cost for that varies. It might be $10,000. It might be $10. It might be a handshake. I know what I'm worth. But when someone books me, we're just talking about the price. And the price of laughter, in this world, can sustain a ventriloquist in the United States.

The way for unknown comedy acts to get work is through word of mouth and successful shows. To have a successful show means getting big laughs for most, if not all, of your time on stage. To do that requires a lot of practice.

I write jokes all the time. I write and edit and reedit, and re-re-reedit almost every waking hour. It's one of my little obsessions.

I'm not bragging.

I applied all the background and tools I have been given by teachers and mentors and other comedians over however many years it is. I used Northwestern University Professor Don Schultz's concept, which is basically "get to the punch word using as few words as possible." The hours working at Second City taught me to be in the moment; find the opportunity for humor; and, most important, always take the positive when you're improvising comedy. Zanies taught me how to work a crowd. Miss Fennessey at Ottawa High School taught me how to walk on stage and deliver a line. Joey Edmonds and Rick Rogers and Stan Bernstein all guided me to putting a set together and delivering the appropriate material to a given audience. The Sigma Chi fraternity gave me incredible confidence and the best support a newbie can get—unconditional encouragement. Working with the great comedy writer Paul Seaburn on Taylor's Attic - not to mention Marc Andre our musical director - taught me that no matter how much you think you know about writing jokes and/or songs, there are always new things to learn (and talented people to learn from).

I'm not even mentioning the techs and theater staff and stage managers who've made me better than I am. And then there are the puppet builders and the sound engineers and so many others.

These days, Tim Grable handles my "business," while combining the best of many of the people I mentioned above.

But for all those years that I worked without notoriety, a peculiarity in a rich man's town, I would sit in my office on the second floor of that house in Moorestown and write. These were wonderful years. Being unknown has never bothered me. Celebrity really does bother me. And I have always enjoyed writing.

The Joke
To write a joke, pick a topic. Try and keep things simple, universal, and easily accessible for any audience.

For example, take cars.

It's such a broad subject that I start by writing down as much information as I can think of—foreign, domestic, make, model, engine parts (carburetor just *sounds* funny), seat belts, speeding, whatever I can think of.

After writing down as much info as I can (and this is where personal computing has made a big difference, and gets more efficient every year, because there are word search tools and cross-referencing and a thesaurus at your fingertips), I start making connections and finding what might get laughter.

To begin writing, I look for the smallest idea, the most mundane, the one that might be most obvious.

Start small. Literally. In this case, what is the smallest car? The Smart Car. So I start there, writing jokes and ideas mostly based on the word "smart" with car. Here are the lines I wrote in a couple of minutes:
- What is a Smart Car? You get in, you punch the address for a destination in the GPS, but being a "smart car" it automatically drives to the library (or the college or the law school or some other such place).
- I picked up a Smart Car today. I thought it was a stroller (because the Smart Car is small).
- I was at the grocery and saw this bottled water called Smart Water. I put it in the gas tank of my Smart Car. It worked. When I turned on the radio, it began teaching me the history of the Ottoman Empire and then taught

a course on the French Revolution and finally explained basic theories of quantum physics.
- Smart Car? If my Smart Car is so smart, how come I feel so stupid when I'm driving it in the left lane on any expressway in the country?
- I was able to sell my Smart Car. Yes, thirty-three out-of-work clowns pooled their money and purchased my glorified skateboard. I thought, *Come on. They can't all fit in there.* But sure enough. They opened the door, and they all fit inside. Unfortunately, the Barnum & Bailey Circus is out of business. So when they typed "circus" as a destination into the GPS, it directed them to Washington, DC.

> As a comedy writing rule of thumb, I try to "work to the top of my intelligence." This is a tip I learned at the Second City. It's another way of saying, "Give the audience the benefit of the doubt." So when I mention the Ottoman Empire and the French Revolution in a joke, I do it with the knowledge that not everyone knows what I'm talking about. Quantum physics might not be part of everyone's base of reference. It's what I know. And my IQ is what? Eight?

Five jokes. I'm not saying these are funny. I think at least one might be, but I won't know until I put them in a semblance of order and stick them in my act hoping one will work. I usually put new material in at the beginning of the act because I want to see what really gets laughter. Sometimes if I wait until I've done twenty to thirty minutes and then put my new jokes in, the audience laughs just because they're enjoying my work.

If the joke doesn't work as a stand-up routine, I use it with one of the ventriloquist puppets. Sometimes a joke has more oomph with ventriloquism.

And as I change from writing stand-up to ventriloquist bits, the jokes morph into something else.

I write out the dialogue for Romeo and myself in script form. This helps me memorize it.

> Romeo. I got a job as a crash test dummy in a Smart Car.
> Taylor. Great! So you can drive and improve your IQ!
> Romeo. Shut up, Taylor. I had to quit.
> Taylor. Why? That sounds like a great job!
> Romeo. I did what I was hired to do. I crashed the car. The inflatable air bag came out.
> Taylor. So?
> (*Numerous punch lines came to mind here and I wrote the first three down.*)
> Romeo (1). The airbag turned out to be an old girlfriend—and she's still an airhead.
> Romeo (2). The airbag turned out to be my mother, and she started criticizing the way I drive right away.
> (*and*)
> Romeo (3). The airbags on both the driver and passenger side came out. It's a Smart Car, so they're pretty small. I made some balloon animals out of them.

If a joke doesn't work for stand-up or ventriloquism, I try and use it in a song.

This might morph into a completely different idea as well.

After struggling with the lyrics of "The Smart Car Song," I added "self-driving" to the premise. In turn, it became a self-driving car song—which ended up as a country song about a self-driving truck: "My girl left me, my beer bottle was empty, and my self-driving truck drove herself away."

> There is such a thing as "getting laughs on character." Jokes are the basics for any live comedy performance, but there are comedy performers whose act is derived from their very personalities. Their personas are so funny that it's not so much *what they say,* it's *how they say it.* Go to a Woody Allen film festival in New York City, and the audience laughs the moment Allen walks into a scene—before he says anything. For ventriloquists, watch Jeff Dunham's old man character Walter, where the audience is laughing and applauding before Jeff puts words in the old guy's mouth.

For the latter part of the 1990s and into the new millennium, I kept creating material and staying current, which meant my schedule stayed full. President Clinton, who had seen an economic boom led by the tech industry, was suffering through impeachment hearings. I had started the decade doing lots of political stuff, but by 1999 I had stopped. Everyone was making fun of the Clinton/Lewinsky affair. I concentrated on everything *but* that. The iMac was introduced, and I became an Apple user. The student activities chairmen and women would offer me a "mixtape" when I played their school, which is how I discovered Eminem and something called "Thong Song" by Sisqó.

I had an office on the second floor of our home, above the garage. Marsia lined the dormer with pegs sticking out of the walls where I could hang my menagerie of puppets. She posted a brass sign above it that read "Puppet Alley." I had a computerized music studio and some of the soundtrack for *Taylor's Attic*, the children's TV show, was edited there. The room was spacious and bright, with big windows overlooking the field out back. But it was always in a state of total disarray. It was my writing room, my practice room, my workroom, and my escape.

The year 2000 approached, and I was still rocking comedy clubs, the Stardome in Birmingham, Alabama, being one example. It's a great room to this day, where the staff is amazing and the audiences are incredible. It was around this time that, after one night of a four-night run, a young man came up to me and asked, "Do you sell tapes?" The VHS tape was still the universally accepted comedy calling card, serving as a promo and (for some of us) a way to earn a few extra dollars.

He would send that video to a man named Danny de Armas, who would book me on a tour of arenas in big cities across the United States. They are another couple of people to whom I am forever indebted.

Chapter Twenty-Two
On Tour

I always say, you gotta play a dive bar like you play an arena, and you play an arena like you play a dive bar.
—Lady Gaga

My mother suffered a debilitating injury right after Marsia and I had packed up the kids and the dog and our lives and moved back to New Jersey. On the advice of my Aunt Gloria ("Taylor, you have to grow up now and do the right thing for your mother," she said), I moved Mom from southern Illinois to live near us in an "adult community" ten minutes from our new house. I would often stop in and play piano to entertain the senior citizens on weekday afternoons after flying back from some one-nighter, before picking up the kids from school or coaching a Little League practice. The seniors—some of whom were in their nineties but still spry, would gather around the piano leaning on canes or bouncing in their wheelchairs, a grateful, responsive, wonderful audience. It was a real scene. I wasn't getting paid. There were no other showbiz people around. So there was absolutely no pressure.

Well, no pressure except I had to keep up with their demands. Since these weren't planned events, everything was a little disorganized. I'd come in the door, check in at the front desk, and ask, "Where's Mom?" I never really needed to do this, as she was in the same place every day—the library. I'd go find her sitting in a chair with a book. I'd say hi, ask if she needed anything, ask if she wanted to listen to her son play piano, and we'd go to the big all-purpose room together. I'd find her a chair, and then I'd sit down at the piano and start. Men and women from age sixty-five to the beginning of time would shuffle in when they heard the sound of live music. They were not shy about calling out, "Play some Elvis," or, "Do Ray

Charles," or requesting their favorite Broadway show tunes. Ten minutes after starting, I'd have close to a hundred senior citizens gathered around me deharmonizing "King of the Road." Sometimes I'd bring Romeo and perform, getting big laughs and making my mother smile.

Those impromptu shows for senior citizens turned out to be great practice for a part of my career I could not have predicted, which happened right after 9/11.

Obviously there was a change in everything after that. I have no idea what was happening in the comedy world for a few years because I was out of the loop. My kids were growing up. Marsia planned family vacations and outings and was substitute teaching at the kids' school. The four of us watched *Family Guy* and *American Idol*. We went to the hit movies like *Lord of the Rings* and *Pirates of the Caribbean*. The United States of America went through a short period of "togetherness," followed by the fracturing of an already fragmented populous.

Me?

I went on tour.

I got an offer to join The Homecoming Artists, which I accepted and then traveled the country for three years. It was incredible. I worked for a genius named Bill Gaither and performed my ventriloquist-comedy act in twenty thousand-seat hockey and basketball arenas coast to coast as the "comedy relief" during a four-hour music concert. The audience, primarily age fifty and up, gave such sincere attention and support to the performers that it felt like a family reunion. Every night. No matter where we went, the venues sold out, meaning even those seats up by the roof were filled, and even the folks who filled those seats were able to enjoy my performance. Whether sitting in Row 1 by the front of the stage or way up in the rafters, regardless of age, everyone could see what was happening. The tour used state-of-the-art sound and lighting, with giant TV screens that brought everyone right on stage with the performers. It felt just like working at the adult community where Mom was living, only on a bigger platform, with much better tech.

There were many nights I walked on and watched myself perform, the fuzzy image of my head reflected back at me from rows and rows of people reacting and responding to my routine. I had to play big, engaging a room with thousands of seats, and I would watch a giant mural of my face now made up of their faces. It was a living pointillist painting, so my jokes and their laughter and applause created a magical duality between us, as if the audience was no longer just viewing my act but had now become a physical part of me, completely in sync, comedy nirvana. It was magnificent and breathtaking and exhilarating, a spiritually intoxicating experience I'll never duplicate.

> Bill Gaither is bona fide. He's one of those people who can hold two to three thoughts in his head while conversing about a completely different subject and keep all the data compartmentalized. He's worth googling.

The brilliant and talented artists I worked with on tour treated me with more dignity than I deserve. I performed in some of the most famous venues on the planet—the Red Rocks Amphitheater in Colorado, the Sydney Opera House in Australia, Carnegie Hall in New York City. A decade and a half later, I still get booked for shows based on that tour.

I slept between concerts on a tour bus, hanging out with the staff whose job it was to set up and take down the sales kiosks around the arena before and after every performance. They also took me in as one of their own, and we spent a lot of nights sitting in the big Winnebago laughing, telling stories, and eating a lot of pizza. That forty-month period of my life was its own story, another book that I'll need to write, if I can piece together everything that happened. I enjoyed my run immensely. But the memories are oddly vivid and disjointed now, coming back to me in bits and pieces like a dream you were enjoying before you woke up, and now you can't remember the exact and most important details.

I loved doing my job. I loved all the people on the tour and the people we worked for. I tried very hard to adopt the protocol of an arena tour, a lifestyle that means a different city and a different venue and a different time zone on a day-to-day basis. I adapted.

But I never got used to it.

A tour like that means you live on a big bus. It's the most effective and efficient way for an entourage of musicians and tech and staff to travel, no doubt, and I understand the logic and logistics of music-tour-travel. I just could not get comfortable. I would knock my head against the roof of my bunk every morning when I woke up in some city hundreds of miles from where we had played the night before. Finding a gym was a daily inconvenience, requiring the exasperating issue of getting local staff to give me a ride to and from a fitness center, sometimes miles from the arena. The rest of the day was spent on location with occasional meals, daily rehearsals, and showers and preshow prep all taking place in the bowels of some sports stadium.

I couldn't get accustomed to the life. I was spoiled. My showbiz roots were airplanes, rental cars and hotels. A tour like this meant you slept on the bus, you ate on the bus, and you hang out on the bus. And *you can never be late for the bus.*

Chapter Twenty-Three
Get a Gig, Get There, Get Paid

Punch line. The final phrase or sentence of a joke or story, providing the humor or some other crucial element.
—Oxford Dictionary definition

Punch line. The last word or words of a joke, which is followed by a paycheck.
—Taylor Mason's definition

If you could boil show business down to its essential elements, what you'd be left with is—getting a gig, getting to the gig, and getting paid for the gig.

That's it. Easy enough.

Or not.

Television and major media appearances are what drive most careers, mine included. And I still get those opportunities, but on ever more rare occasions.

No matter, because the landscape has changed with the internet, social media, and the constant availability online, where people who are interested in booking Taylor Mason can do so. Parlaying that exposure into a paying job requires constant networking. I've had long, positive, and fruitful associations with some wonderful agents, bookers. and personal managers over the years. Somehow they've always found a job for me so I could earn a few dollars and keep this career moving along.

My current manager-agent-consultant is Tim Grable. We've been together for some fifteen years. He's the fourth manager who's handled my bookings since the mid-1980s, and that's the way I like it. One reason I stay loyal to people like Tim is because consistency means people know who to call in order to solicit my services.

Another reason is because Tim is much like the others I've worked with—accomplished, knowledgeable, and focused—good people.

> Comedians are considered isolated, singular performers who live in a bubble. That goes double for ventriloquists. I could never describe myself as a "loner." There are too many people who help me. The managers and agents and bookers for one thing, not to mention the thousands of techs I've worked with, all make it impossible to call myself "a one-man band." I've worked with wonderful writers and musicians and directors. More to the point, comedy is dependent upon its audience, which has to be engaged, responsive, and intensely focused. I'm lucky mine is attentive, appreciative, and amenable.

Celebrity acts with major television credits never have to worry about "getting the next job" (since they're always in demand).

Not me.

I rely on a variety of people to find me employment. And that comes not from appearing on popular television shows or YouTube videos or Netflix specials. I depend on word of mouth and networking. Every performance is an audition.

Giving every ounce of available energy whenever you walk out in front of an audience and present your material is gratifying and a sort of validation. But it's also an advertisement for my service. It's why I do so many fundraisers and benefits. It's why I still play little hole-in-the-wall comedy clubs and take the jobs some of my peers wouldn't touch. I meet people who, after seeing me, are interested in having me perform for them in all kinds of situations. I get a lot of work based on people having seen me do a show.

For that to happen, I have to get to the venue, on time and ready to do a job. "Getting there" is the operative, often aggravating and infuriating, part of every showbiz person's life. Grable, longtime manager and spiritual guru, puts it this way: "We work for free. Nobody has to pay us for the show we give them. What they have to pay for is the insane travel we put up with ten times a month."

He's right.

Ten thousand hours on stages all over the planet has meant traveling to every kind of destination, unpacking and sound checking, taking a cursory glance at my notes just before presenting, and then breaking down and repeating that same exercise night after night, week after week, and year after year. And it's made me adept at getting from Point A to Point Z in every forum or location there is.

I have performed in basketball and hockey arenas in every major US city, wandering the underground tunnels and locker rooms until I was called up on stage in the bright lights of modern showbiz. I've done shows for children in church basements, and I've played beer-soaked roadhouses, snarky saloons, and makeshift comedy clubs in every state. I've come to know TV soundstages and big production houses, as well as outdoor arenas that feature open-air seating and all the weather-related issues that come with that kind of locale. Synagogues? Convention centers? Theme parks? Check, check, and check. I've done shows in high school auditoriums and college classrooms and middle school gymnasiums and hotel conference rooms. I haven't seen it all, but ... Wait. You know what? Yes I have.

I have seen it all.

Thirty-some-odd years into my career, everything has become automatic.

Maybe I'm walking through the hustle and bustle of a crowded kitchen in some luxury hotel in London on my way to a stage, barely avoiding busy waitstaff as if I'm part of a live video game: *"Puppet boy in London!"* The object of this game is to get the ventriloquist with his big hockey bag-o-puppets past the waiters and the angry chefs as they work their food prep areas. Extra points for picking up a roll and eating it just before going on stage!

Or maybe I'm dragging my keyboard from the parking lot into a joint in some city, two minutes before showtime, bumping into the backs of chairs and apologizing to the seated audience, hurriedly plugging in all the connections and doing a five-second sound check: "Is it on? Can you hear it? Yes? Okay, let's do this!"

I'm chronically "barely on time," rolling my giant bag of puppets and props into a show room or theater. It doesn't matter where I am, who I'm working for. or what the physical building might be. I follow the exact same routine at a five-star hotel on Maui or a comedy club in Chicago as I do at a kids show in a library in suburban New Jersey.

I've reached the point where nothing intimidates me. Once you get the vibe and gain complete understanding of protocol and presence, you know where to go and how to get there—no matter what the situation is, no surprises.

> Show business access is similar to access in major governmental jobs, federal or local, or in the military. An act can usually get him or herself to the venue, the stage, the theater, or the set by carrying something important (a notebook, a bag of props, or just some documents) and walking with intent, all while not making eye contact with people. It's critical to adopt a certain vibe: *I am important. I am in a hurry. Do not bother me.*

I've walked into jam-packed establishments at the last minute, out of the wind and rain and directly into the show room just as the emcee is finishing my introduction: "So please welcome one of our favorites, Taylor Mason!" I've put my props together in public bathroom toilet stalls, while men no doubt wonder about the goings-on when they see what looks like children's toys and shoes and pants scattered around and what appears to be a little kid getting jammed into an athletic bag on the floor.

My puppets, for all their wonderful qualities in performance, are problematic. Depending on the client, the show, the audience, and the expectations of the people who booked me—or those who paid to see me—I might need two large cases filled with props. When I bring my own piano keyboard, it adds to the mayhem.

Because of late flights, bad weather, traffic tie-ups, and occasional itinerary miscommunication, I sometimes arrive minutes before showtime, panicking the on-site personnel and leaving him or her emotionally scarred for life. (*What will we do if Taylor doesn't show? Aaaahhhhhh!*) When I arrive, I take a minute to size up where I'll be working, where the audience is sitting, what the parameters are, and how I can maximize things to my benefit.

I have pared the prep time down to practically nothing, throwing puppets and props and stage gear together in minutes and then hearing my introduction just as I put the last shoe on Romeo! "Let's have a big welcome for Taylor Manson" or "Mason Tabor" or "this next guy!"

Clearly the life of a comedian-ventriloquist-musician is harried. It's nonstop preparation and planning and packing and unpacking. It's editing on the run when a promoter says, just before you walk on stage, "Please don't do any puppets. Our crowd finds them clichéd and ignorant. Okay? Thanks." It's being flexible when you're told, "Uh ... sorry to tell you, but the mike doesn't work. Can you just talk loudly?" There are acoustic pianos where "only the black keys play"; there are jobs in tents by the pool at a Las Vegas resort in the middle of the day in 100-degree heat; there are venues where the lighting illuminates the audience but leaves you, the performer, literally and figuratively in the dark.

I once did a show on New Year's Eve where the power went out in the hotel, and the ballroom I was working went dark.

The emergency lights came on, lighting the wall behind a table where a party of four sat. I moved their table five feet from the wall, stood in the makeshift "spotlight," and did my hour set—until the stroke of midnight—in that one spot where the light was directed.

I got my check, and then I drove home.

No doubt travel—especially air travel—is *the* definitive headache for my act. Obviously there is the ever-present fear of damaged ventriloquist figures after flights, no matter how much careful packing, padding, and protecting I've done. Transportation Security Association (TSA) personnel have accidentally broken a wire or technical aspect to one of the characters on a couple of occasions. And I cannot be angry; their job is to protect fliers. But it is so hard to hang with.

> In my world, TSA stands for "Taylor Searched Aggressively."

The only time I'm not fighting to be punctual is on a cruise ship or for corporate clients. They're paying a lot more than some of the other work I do, and part of the deal is to be early, gain the trust of the tech crews, and deliver a strong comedy set to that audience.

The world gets very small when you work for every kind of audience in any and every kind of venue around the globe.

As for getting paid …

Paychecks come in several packages. Some are not monetary.

There have been jobs I did for "free," but I needed the meal or the airplane ticket or the hotel room for a night.

Irreversible

> I long ago stopped doing jobs for "exposure." It's better for all parties concerned if we agree that, if I'm working pro bono, I am happy to do so, for whatever the reason. (The reason has to be *perfect*.)

In the current financial climate, it's more and more often I get a check wirelessly transferred directly to my bank account. There are, of course, traditional paychecks handed to me in envelopes or inside large folders with tax documents attached. I've had people hand me wads of rolled up hundred-dollar bills or five times-folded personal checks, where the ink is smudged beyond readability. I have been given corporate checks, traveler's checks, certified checks, and money orders. I have also been handed brown paper bags filled with single dollar bills, pocket change, food stamps, and sincere IOUs.

But I have always been paid.

Well, except for that one time in Omaha ... and the one in Seattle ... and Boston. But the start was in Vermont.

I did a short summer tour of resorts and restaurants in the Northeast the summer of 1990. I was working with a Boston comic, a very funny guy and someone who made an impression on me. We had done a great show in a bar somewhere, and the bar manager refused to pay us.

"I work twice as hard as you, and I don't make this much money." He pointed at the envelope he held in his hand, standing in defiance behind the bar as waitstaff cleared tables and cleaned up.

The comic on tour with me laughed in his face. "Well then maybe you should get a different job. Be a comedian. I don't care. *Give us our money!*"

We got our cash.

Creighton University is in Omaha, Nebraska, an excellent college with wonderful students and a very good administration.

At the time I was booked to perform there, the school had a student activities director who thought he could blow off my paycheck.

I got to the school theater in plenty of time for the show and looked around for my contact person. There was nobody around—no tech, no director, no house manager, nobody.

There was just one student sitting in the theater.

"The director is really mad because we had a speaker here last night and nobody came. So he said he's not paying you tonight."

The kid was there on my behalf, basically there to support *me*. He explained that his boss, the activities director, had canceled my performance that morning—without telling me or my agent, Joey Edmonds!

I went back to the school the following day. I barged into the office, and the director nonchalantly looked up at me from his desk. He was drinking a coffee and eating a donut, and with an annoying aplomb said, "Oh, hi, Taylor. I'm never gonna pay you. Bye."

I made this a vendetta. I was going to get paid no matter what.

Joey Edmonds, a truly decent person and a great personal friend and agent, had to make all kinds of threats and ultimatums on my behalf before we finally got a check (and an apology) from the university. That student activities director? Who cares?

Seattle is a great American city for the arts. On a given day, it's absolutely spectacular, with the water, the bays, the islands, and the surrounding—breathtaking—ecosystem of trees and mountains. There is a certain *future world-ness* to it—that surreal Space Needle right out of *War of the Worlds*, for example; lots of hipsters; an omnipresent vibe that some kind of new Microsoft program or hardware is about to drop and revolutionize life as we know it in the next minute. When I'm there, it feels a little like I've become a character in that iconic 1960s cartoon show *The Jetsons*.

Irreversible

> The cartoon dog in the Jetsons was named Astro, later to become the name of the Houston Major League Baseball team. It took the franchise almost forty years to overcome that unfortunate team name.

That mix of organic beauty, an eight-month rainy season, plus a cosmopolitan mentality provides a perfect petri dish for artists—music, graphics, comedy, theater, all of it. I began playing the great Northwest during my college tour years and then worked the Seattle Improv Comedy Club when it opened sometime in the early 1990s.

Now *that* was a gorgeous venue. Once a showcase for big bands and dancing, it had fallen into disrepair. The Improv took over the space, rehabilitated it, and turned it into a spectacular gig, with good lighting and perfect sound. In addition to the show room, there was a bar with tables and a big-screen TV, where people could enjoy a drink and finger food and wait for the next performance. Or just hang out. The place defined hip.

By the middle of the decade, I was headlining the club, but the name had been changed to the Music Box or something. Soon after that, the entire operation went into a swift decline to once-upon-a-time land.

I had moved back to Jersey when my then manager and business partner Stan Bernstein booked me at the club for a Thursday through Saturday run. I showed up for the first show, expecting that giant room with the beautiful stage and theatrical effects.

It was gone. Instead, the owners had moved the entire operation into the little bar area, with seating for maybe a hundred people They had kept the technical aspects of the theater, so there was pristine sound and lighting, but it was nothing like what I was used to. The energy, the joy, the thrill of playing this job had been eliminated.

Not only was the physical plant depressing; so was the staff. When I walked into the bar to do a sound check, the assistant manager was on the phone. I listened in on the conversation as I set up my keyboard. "Yeah, we have a show tonight. A little song, a little dance, you know, a good time." I was thinking, *Cool! A song and dance duo for my opening act? Perfect!*

It took a couple of minutes before I realized he was describing me.

"A little song? A little dance? That's how you tell ticket buyers about my act?" I challenged him.

He was a big-boned blond guy wearing a ZZ Top T-shirt, blue jeans, and a leather necklace with what looked like a claw pendant. "Yeah. Song and dance. You do puppets right? Music? So? That's song and dance in my book. And the caller? They didn't buy any tickets. Nobody ever buys tickets. We'll have maybe twenty-five people tonight. I hope." He gave me the obligatory once-over; looked me in the eye; and said, with some hostility, "I guess you're not a draw."

We did five shows over the next three nights, all in the bar, none drawing more than fifty people. I busted my butt, mostly because I had looked forward to the date, and I felt like I owed the room—*that spectacular room!*—my best. I had been the opening act for the great comic Monica Piper the first time I played here. She sold out six shows during that week. Now, some five to six years later, the place was on its last legs. I felt bad. So I gave everything I had at every show.

Saturday came. I rocked the two smallish crowds that night and collected my gear. I went to get paid. The big blond guy was in an office with a woman. She was in her midthirties and wearing a dark woman's business jacket and dress. They ignored me as I stood at the door.

I knocked lightly.

No response.

"Uh, can I get my check?"

It was uncomfortable. Something was wrong. They ignored me, talking to each other, pretending I didn't exist.

I don't leave without getting paid, remember?

Finally the big guy spoke. "Look, we talked to your manager. The act he booked in here last week drank all our Courvoisier. So we took that out of your check. See ya." With a not-so-gentle push, he closed the door in my face.

I was infuriated. I remember exactly what I was thinking, almost from the moment the door shut in my face. And that was twenty years ago: *I'm gonna come back here and get my money.*

I talked to Stan, my agent, and asked him to try and get my week's salary. He was noncommittal: "Look, I'll try. But it's not gonna happen soon. These club people, you know ... blah, blah, blah."

A month later, I was booked at Harvey's, another premier comedy club, but one that lasted a lot longer than the Seattle Improv. Located in downtown Portland, Oregon, Harvey's was a blast. Similar to Seattle, the city was progressive and young and picturesque. The club had a strong repeat clientele, was always full, and was a joy to play. Like Seattle, I looked forward to it.

It was a Wednesday through Saturday run, so I flew in. I did the first night, and on Thursday morning, I got up and drove to Seattle. It only takes about an hour and a half, the perfect amount of time to formulate a plan. I got to the Music Box or whatever it was called, at 11:00 a.m., walked in the open door on the street, and bounced up the stairs to the bar.

The place had that haphazard we-don't-care atmosphere you might find in a college drinking establishment—or one that would soon go out of business. I had the feeling they never really locked up. I walked in. A staffer was picking up glasses and wiping down tables. He was a young guy, early twenties, just a working kid with a job at a bar. We nodded to one another.

"Your boss around?" I asked.

He pointed toward the office. "She's not here," he said. "She comes in on Thursdays at 5:00 p.m."

I nodded again. "Well, I don't have until then." I walked over to the control board and the amplifier and began unplugging it.

"You the sound guy?" asked the kid, some nervousness in his voice. He stopped cleaning the tabletop. He might have been young, but he wasn't stupid.

"Nah," I said, pulling cords from the back of the board. "I worked here a month ago, and they didn't pay me. So I'm taking all the tech. I'll be done in an hour." And I started unplugging speakers.

Fifteen minutes later, wearing the exact same jacket-and-skirt combo she'd worn thirty days prior, the woman came into the bar. I had the preamp, the control board, one of the four speakers, and the microphones sitting on the floor, waiting to be taken to my car.

She pointed at the equipment and looked at me. "What do you think you're doing?" There was some trepidation in her voice, a little giveaway that she knew things had already reached crisis stage and there wasn't room for negotiation.

"You didn't pay me, so I'm taking your sound system," I said. "It won't cover what you owe, but I'll get something for it."

The blond-headed guy who had pushed me out of the office in our previous meeting strode purposefully into the room, trying hard to give me the tough guy persona he'd used before.

He looked at the woman and then glared at me. "What do you think you're doing?"

"I'm getting paid. You thought you could cheat me out of my money. I'm gonna get my check somehow. Your tech isn't worth anything, but maybe I can trade it for new props."

He walked up to me and did that macho a macho guy thing, putting his ugly mug really close to mine and said, "You're f——ing with the wrong people."

Irreversible

I stared back at him, smiling, *daring* him to do something. We stood face-to-face for maybe twenty seconds. He put his finger in my chest. I swiped it away.

The woman grabbed his right arm and pulled big boy away. They stood shoulder to shoulder, and she whispered something into his ear. She crossed her arms and posed for me. "I'll call the police."

I laughed. "Go ahead. You call the police. I'm not leaving here without something. You either pay me, or you don't have sound."

The two of them turned and walked into her office. I continued gathering "my" equipment.

The kid was standing behind the wooden bar, pretending to clean while he watched the proceedings. "Man!" he said. "I've never seen anyone stand up to them! That was excellent!"

Minutes later, she appeared. She handed me a check. "Okay, here's your money." She held it in front of her, teasingly, far enough away that I would have to reach and take it.

"*No.*" I didn't move. I stared into her eyes—heavy on the blue eye shadow, matching her suit but overdone. I felt pity. She wasn't even calling the shots, just doing what some jerk somewhere was telling her to do.

I said it again, "*No.* Cash or the sound system. You guys decide."

From the office, the big blond baby bull shouted, "Told ya! Lemme f—— him up!"

She spun on her heels and clomped into the office, slamming the door. She walked out a minute later and announced, "Okay! Let's go!"

I followed her to their bank and followed her inside to the teller where she took out my full payment in cash. I made her count it right there, in the lobby, in front of customers depositing paychecks and applying for home loans and bank tellers staring wide-eyed as if there was a crime taking place.

I made her count it twice—slowly. It was right. I took the dollars, said thank you, and drove back to Portland.

I called Stan. "I got my money, Stan."

As he started to reply, saying, "Good for you! Listen, as far as my commission—" I hung up the phone.

I had two other moments where people tried to stiff me. That's a total of four on this nonstop, workaday, no-end-in-sight tour.

Which is pretty good.

I was working with the comedy trio Mary Wong in Boston. Mary Wong was not an Asian female comic. Mary Wong was a three-person improv comedy group from Chicago. I knew them from working there back in the day, and we had done a college tour together.

Mary Wong was made up of three African American men—Ali, Lance, and Tim—all of whom went on to pretty decent careers in comedy.

But the gig we did together, at a dying disco in South Boston in the late 1980s, was fraught with all the racism and hatred you might imagine. The crowd was hostile, loud, and belligerent.

The bar manager and owner were worse.

Those two—the manager and owner—literally hid (*hid*!) from us after the show. Mary Wong, all three guys, said, "Let's just go."

But I was driving. I have a code, and I was as angry for them as I was about not getting paid myself.

"We're gonna get paid," I said. "You cannot work and not get paid. I don't care how uncomfortable this gets." And I hunted down the bar manager, who I found hiding in an office upstairs away from the crowded bar.

"What do you want?" he asked.

"I want my money, and I want you to give me Mary Wong's money."

He laughed in my face. He used some racial epithets. He was sickening. "No. I'm not paying you. You were all terrible. Worst mistake I ever made hiring you."

I did a Seattle. I went into the disco, went into the deejay booth, and began unplugging equipment.

I got paid within ten minutes.

Typical Travel Day

When I'm preparing for a four-day run with Disney or headed to a venue that requires me to bring my own keyboard, it's an ambitious, complex ordeal. It's time-consuming. Fitting my clothing, puppets, music, the odd magic trick and toiletries into my travel bags is a little bit like playing Tetris. Everything has to fit, or we start all over. *Aaaaaahhhh!*

The truth is there is no checklist. There isn't a plan. The routine is total mayhem.

For big trips, I'm packing three bags. The first is a keyboard, really a synthesizer, my musical accompaniment. I've tried everything to pack these pianos safely, starting with the giant steel-ribbed hard cases that come with lifetime guarantees. Those last about ninety days before the steel ribbing says, "Fine. This is insane. Nobody travels like this. We give up. Please recycle us or let us die in peace. *You travel too much.*"

I've had to come up with my own keyboard travel system. I buy an extra large soft musical instrument bag. I get a huge roll of bubble wrap. I went online and bought a tractor tire-size roll of bubble wrap, bubbles the size of a human head. And I wrap the piano. This has served me well over the years. The damage to the bag itself is severe, and it has to be replaced on a regular basis, but the piano inside is no longer damaged.

The other two large bags take less effort but as much time. I use hockey bags because I've found they are durable, they're large, and you can get a hockey bag with straps so it becomes a giant backpack! I enjoy walking through airports with this humongous thing on my back. People shout, "Are you a hockey player?" I shake my head and answer, "No, I'm not a hockey player! I packed my kids in here. Right kids?" And using my ventriloquism, I throw my voice into the bag: "Help! Let us out!"

One bag is for the puppets. Currently I have a large penguin and a space alien, plus the space ship for the alien (which is really just two big dog dishes bolted together with Christmas tree lights glued on it). I have a homemade thing made from fur that has some moving parts and then some backups and giveaways that always come in handy.

> This troupe of comedy props and puppets is always subject to change. So by the time you read this, one or more of these may no longer be with my traveling medicine show of puppets and music and comedy.

The puppets get wrapped individually. I know, you're thinking, *Oh my gosh, he's nuts! He wraps them individually? He's psycho.*

Yes, each puppet gets put in primary layer of coverage, usually a plastic wrap or a cloth protector, and then gets put in a large laundry bag.

The biggest reason I use the soft-headed, Muppet-like, foam and terry cloth puppets are due to travel.

Here's the story.

There was a mom-and-pop bar/restaurant on the South Side of Chicago back when I was just starting out. The place had weekend comedy shows, and all the local acts did the room. I can't remember what it was called, but I didn't have a car at the time. I was in grad school; living up in Evanston, Illinois; and using Chicago's public transportation system.

I was using JP then, my woodenheaded graduation gift / ventriloquist figure, and I traveled in the classic ventriloquist manner: The big puppet was secured in a beat-up suitcase, covered with a soft bath towel, easily accessible and stage-ready.

The trip from the northern suburbs of Chicago to the south end of the city took more than an hour. I grabbed the "L," took it as far as possible, caught a bus, and then walked the last half mile to the joint.

One night, it rained—a cold, depressing Chicago-style hard rain that made me consider just walking back to the bus and going home. The thought kept going through my head, *You must really want to do this, Taylor, because this is stupid.* But there is something romantic about that, too—this young guy with an act who will do whatever it takes to get on stage wherever it is, for whoever might be there. So I trudged on through the downpour, a guy and his suitcase on a mission.

I was late. I got to the club, and the husband and wife were waiting. "You need to go right on!"

So I did. They introduced me. I walked up to the mike and apologize for being so wet. "You would think I had just walked through the rain to get here!" (Laughter.) "But that's wrong. I took a shower in the back but had to rush right on stage. Anybody have an extra towel?"

I picked up my suitcase and set it on a stool on stage. "I don't work alone," I say, launching into my set. "I used to have an imaginary friend. But he's turned into this!" I opened the case. The inside was soaked. JP was waterlogged. He was literally lying in a swimming pool. The cheap suitcase hadn't protected my prop at all.

"You'll have to excuse us, but my partner is taking a bath." I was trying to get my wits about me, worrying about the condition of the figure, wondering how I was going to complete my performance when I dumped a little water out of the suitcase on the stage. I remember a woman gasped. "I'm serious!" I said. "He took a bath!"

I pulled the puppet out of the case, water spraying everywhere. People in the first tables next to the stage got spritzed.

JP was dripping wet. I put my hand into his back entrance and grabbed the lever, ever so slowly turning his head to look at me—the universal puppetry move indicating frustration or anger. There was some laughter, people were clapping their hands, and it felt like I was going to luck out and get through the set.

"Well, JP, looks like you got as wet as I did."

I pulled the mouth lever. I couldn't. I was squeezing as hard as I could, but it was stuck. Rather, the mouth was stuck. The slot-jaw wooden mouth was immovable, tragically warped due to the rain and the water.

It could not move.

And I had just started my performance.

There should be a guide that comes with all classic hard, wood or fiberglass ventriloquist dummies when the maker sends it to the buyer: "What to Do When the Mouth String Breaks."

I pulled down on the mouth lever a couple of times, trying to get the spring that connected to the mouth to make it open. Nada. JP just sat there, his mouth tightly clenched. I took my left hand and pulled the mouth down, opening it manually by holding his chin. And with more than a little effort, I finally was able to drag the lower portion down to the open position.

I had him scream, "Wah!"

Laughter from the crowd.

The mouth stayed open. The moisture had corrupted the wood and the paint to the extent that it couldn't move. JP's mouth was motionless, staring at the audience with his mouth wide open, and I laughed out loud. It was ridiculous.

"JP? Is there a problem?"

With his mouth stuck open I had him nod and grunt, "Uh-huh."

People laughed.

I said, "Oh, wait! You're made of wood!"

JP. Uh-huh.

Me. "You're soaking wet, and you're made of wood, and your mouth is warped and is stuck open!"

JP (*nodding*), Uh-huh.

(The audience was laughing pretty hard. I kept this going as long as I could.)

Me. How can we do our act if you can't talk?

I had JP mumble something close to, "I don't know."

That was the night I decided I would switch to using only socks and soft puppets in my act, which I've done for decades except on very rare occasions. There are a different set of care rules for these Muppet-like creatures, and I wrap them individually. Plus, as you might guess, hockey bags are waterproof—the players are around ice all the time, ice melts, so the cases are waterproof! *Perfect*!

The second hockey bag contains my wardrobe. This includes jeans and a T-shirt for a club job, a couple of pressed shirts and slacks for corporate shows, another pair of jeans or dress pants, and a "showbiz shirt"—something I'd never wear except on stage. Also included are shoes for the show (as opposed to the shoes I'll wear on planes and for travel and the gym); electronics for my keyboard and the laptop (including a microphone, extra cable in case the venue doesn't have it, and any special extras for sound); my toiletries; and workout gear.

I travel with two carry-on bags. One is a backpack with my laptop, my iPad, and some writing material (notebook and pens). The other is a big carry-on with my "Fab Four" essential ventriloquist sidekicks—Romeo, Paco, Ramon, and Paquito. These are essentials for most performances, so having them with me on the plane ensures I have a set when my checked bags get sent to Uzbekistan.

Packing is a two-hour ordeal. When I get out on the road working, it unloads and repacks quickly—sometimes in as little as fifteen minutes—if I've done a good job at home preparing for the trip.

Many times, when I'm out for just one or two nights, I manage to do the entire trip with just two carry-ons. When I'm doing the big gigs, it's the full monty of gear.

I've always wondered what the TSA (Taylor Searched Aggressively) men and women and customs officials think when they unzip the bags and find all my puppets, individually wrapped and carefully bagged.

Sometimes the airlines demand that Romeo and Paco are "gate checked." I pack these two essential vent partners in a carry-on bag, so if my luggage is lost I still have an act. But even then I've had two experiences where an airline lost those and I had to scramble to build puppets, *last-second,* backstage as the audience was being seated in the venue!

> I see losing a ventriloquist's bag-o-puppets as akin to stealing a blind person's seeing-eye dog. How low can you go?

There are good things about having the puppets on the plane. Crying children or unruly children can be calmed and entertained—for a while, anyway—by puppets.

I have been charged thousands of dollars by air carriers around the planet for my "oversize" and "overweight" bags (an insult to the puppets, by the way, none of whom are fat, save my sumo wrestler). And I foresee that issue getting worse and worse.

> I have successfully combatted the airline baggage fees this way—I pay children who are on my flight $25. All they have to do is hold my puppets and tell the flight attendants, "This is my toy!"

Chapter Twenty-Four
A Bronx Tale

The saddest thing in life is wasted talent, and the choices that you make will shape your life forever. But you can ask anybody from my neighborhood, and they'll just tell you this is just another Bronx tale.
—Callogero 'C' Anello in *A Bronx Tale*

For all those years living in New Jersey, while I maintained a career off the grid of big-time show business in secluded Moorestown, I worked at the cross streets of the United States of America. My gigs had no common denominator. I went wherever I could get someone to pay me to perform my act, and I became a comfortable fish out of water, accepting whatever I got. My audience had no communality, so I had to find them, regardless where that might have been. My schedule was a mash-up of cultures and demographics, a schizophrenic ever-changing sea of faces reflecting what I consider is real America, where urban meets rural meets suburban.

My blessing of "skills" (music, comedy, ventriloquism) was also a curse. As TV and movies skewed more toward *Jackass* and *Jersey Shore*, I stuck to my ethic, which took me to some wild places.

I had a booking on Long Island, New York, at one of the thousands of weekend (Friday to Saturday) clubs that dotted the country during the "comedy boom" (they've all been replaced today by Starbucks, Subway sandwich shops, and vapor bars). It was actually in "the Hamptons," that world-famous summer getaway for the rich and famous. Plus the hotel had a tennis court, so Marsia came with me. It turned out the money wasn't great and the accommodations were pathetic. But what they heck? We played some tennis, and we mingled with the well-to-do!

True to form, the club was basically a bad country song: "Don't Put on a Swimsuit Momma, It Ain't That Kind of a Dive." It was dark, dank, dingy, and small; the smell of beer emanated from the walls. But no matter! It was the hip place to be any given weekend twenty-five years ago, so they sold every seat, every show. And, quite frankly, that's the ideal room for comedy—small and tight so that laughs ricochet off the walls and the floor and the ceiling and the comic rides that vibe for his or her entire set.

There's a standard rule in the comedy club world: The toughest audiences are the late Friday crowd, which is usually tired from the work week in addition to being drunk. But the Hampton second show Friday was fun—a rowdy, loud, happy audience that was attentive and responsive. Hey! It was gonna be an easy gig!

Saturday's first show was packed, but there was something odd about the people when I arrived some ten minutes before showtime. There was a buzz, that preshow glad-to-be-here-let's-have-fun excitement you get at any live performance, but it was a little off. Something wasn't right. It wasn't a negative energy, and it certainly wasn't threatening. It was just weird and un-comedy-like. It was as if the crowd was there to see something other than a comedy show. I was uneasy as the announcement came over the crackling loudspeakers hanging from the ceiling: "It's showtime, ladies and gentlemen! Please keep table talk to a minimum! And now please welcome your host for the evening!"

True to my instinct, things started out badly. There was a table in the front (why do they *always* seat the worst audience members right by the stage in these joints?) that was loud and obnoxious. On top of that nobody from the club—not the manager or a bartender or a bouncer—said a word to them. In fact, their waitress kept bringing them drinks, bantering with them as she took orders and served food and acted as if their behavior was perfectly normal!

That group is etched in my mind. There were seven to eight people sitting around two smallish wooden tables pressed together. Four to five were stunningly attractive women in their early twenties dressed like music video models. A couple of them were young men wearing open-collared designer shirts. And there was a gentleman in the middle who wore a sport coat and an expensive watch. He was quite a bit older than the group at his table and much older than anyone else in the place. But he commanded attention. The focus, from the moment the emcee walked into the hot spotlight on stage, was clearly on him.

They weren't heckling the acts so much as they were kind of putting on their own show, mostly starring the older guy. My opening act, who was quickly followed by the middle act, had exactly the kind of performance you would expect—awful. The show format was typical for the time. The emcee warmed up the crowd for fifteen minutes; the middle act does thirty minutes, and then the emcee did a quick three to five before bringing up the headliner, who did forty-five to fifty. Both men who preceded me baled on their sets after just a couple of minutes, failing to gain any attention span from the audience. The table in front of the stage was getting louder and more confident with each failure on stage, and now I was introduced.

I can honestly say that nobody who was there remembers my name.

I walked on to nothing. No applause. No acknowledgement. No respect. (I wish I could say that was my last experience like that, but it still happens. I still don't care.)

I stood behind the mike for at least a minute or two—just watching this old guy with these young people telling inside jokes and passing finger food around. They finally responded.

"Go ahead," said the old man. "We'll let you do your show!"

I smiled—a difficult thing to pull off for a live performer because, in a situation like this, your mouth has gone dry, and the flop sweat is ignoring your hope it will stop forming on your hairline But I held as big a smile as I could for a couple of beats before I said, "I'm sorry ... you'll *let* me do my show? How about I let you stay and watch?" I hit the big (fake, but they don't know that) smile again.

The entire audience—and I mean everyone in the place—gave an "ooooooooooh," sound, which I liked. It meant I had taken the focus.

The old man laughed.

So I laughed too. "What are you even doing here?" I asked. "The limo got lost on your way to the mansion?"

He laughed. He clapped his hands. "I came here to have fun!" he shouted.

"Great," I said, "me too."

One of the young guys at the table said, "When does the show start?"

I beat him to the laughter by saying, "The show started when you people walked in here and sat up front. How much can I pay you to leave?"

I sat down on a big stool, the only prop on the stage, which prompted the old guy to say, "Why are you sitting down? I thought this was stand-up comedy!"

I answered, "Because every time I sit down when I'm dealing with hecklers, I haven't been shot."

This, apparently, was the funniest line the old guy had ever heard. He doubled over with laughter.

He wasn't the only one. The whole room was laughing. The waitress was laughing. Hell, I was laughing.

"Who are you people?" I asked.

The room went dead silent. As loud as it had been a moment before, that's how quiet it was now. Then, from the back of the room, someone shouted, "That's Mr. Trump!"

The place went up for grabs. He waved to everyone. It was Donald Trump, Sr.

And for the next forty-five minutes, I told every joke I could think of about real estate and corporations and New York and his kid (including some comments about Marla Maples—google her if you don't know the name). I got through the night.

The show was over. I was standing by the bar nursing a cold bottle of water, and here came the man himself, his posse following him. He walked right up to me. "Son, you could sell real estate. How about it?"

I looked him in the eye. I gave him the appropriate response. "Excuse me?"

He smiled and said, "I'm offering you a job. I think you could be very successful."

I nodded and smiled and looked right back at him. "Thanks, but I have a job." We shook hands.

I met Donald Trump, Sr. He wasn't a bad guy. He had a good sense of humor. No, I'm not endorsing his son, the president. No, I'm not telling you who I voted for. I'm telling you a story about a small-time comedian who, some years ago, performed in a long since gone comedy club out on Long Island and the commitment that comedian made and continues to make in what can only loosely be called a "career."

I get all the spaced-out-gigs.

There is a certain class of working magicians—talented professionals doing card tricks, illusions, mentalism, and audience-participation bits for birthday parties and business conferences and so on—who call themselves "40 milers." The name defines the radius from their home base they're willing to travel. It's an unwritten rule, and they do this for a number of reasons: They might have an act that is as good as the game, and they could easily get bookings all over the place, but they like sleeping in their own bed. They might want to avoid stepping on a fellow magician's territory and taking away his or her gigs. Some have day jobs, so magic is a moneymaking hobby.

I'm not a magician, but I love the concept. "I only take gigs within forty miles of my front door!" I would be home every night! My travel costs would plummet! I would never have to fight through lines and mayhem and the surreal obstacle course of airline travel ever again! It's enough to make me grab the thirteen-volume *Tarbell Course in Magic* off the shelf in my office and start learning a few tricks.

But I'm a comedian. Make that an unknown comedian. Make that an unknown but working comedian. As such, I take jobs wherever and whenever I can—emphasis on *wherever.*

It comes with the territory. I wanted a career in comedy, and I got it. Yes, yes, I thought I by now I'd be mugging for the camera on soundstages in Los Angeles or tapping away at a computer keyboard in a writer's room on the thirty-second floor of a building in Manhattan, and I sometimes still allow myself that pipe dream. The truth is that my career has taken me to the kind of strange, offbeat places that every bottom-feeder uses to earn a living and stay "in the business."

Hey, it's a living.

If there is a periodic table of elements in showbiz, you can find me wedged between juggler, clown, and the one-man-band. You know the one-man-band? He's got the harmonica attachment around his neck, cymbals on his knees, bells on his shoes, a kazoo in his mouth. and a squeeze-ball horn attached to the fret of the guitar. He doesn't get any respect, but I've always wondered why. He's a multitalented musician, playing four to five instruments at once. Give it up for the one-man-band!

Usually these odd gigs are fun. These crazy gigs are ones I remember most, the places where live comedy was never meant to be performed, for audiences that are just as confused as I am when I begin presenting my "art."

I'm not talking about "hell gigs" and hecklers. That's run-of-the-mill type stuff. This is different. These are *insane* jobs, the ones a very few of us agree to do. Maybe we need the money.

Irreversible

Or we owe a favor to a booker or friend. Or, as is most often the case, we had no idea what we were booked for until we arrive at the scene. So these are the experiences tattooed on my brain and the ones I most love talking about.

And let me bare my soul a little more. Trust me on this—sharing show business nightmares with friends or family over dinner or in a green room at some theater is nothing more than braggadocio.

My Uncle Ben Miesenhelder used to travel the world, taking an old-fashioned 8 mm camera with him. He showed his movies to us whenever our family visited his home. He had artifacts and collectibles from all over the planet, which was no mean feat in the 1970s. He had been "behind the wall" in East Berlin and into Russia. He had explored Africa. He and my Aunt Marcelyn would sit in their living room, packed with memorabilia from their excursions around the earth. I'd sit with my family and listen, transfixed, as this little old white-haired man would tell us how he had escaped the police in Burma.

Like him, I love recounting stories as a way to remember where I've been and what I've done.

There is a theater at Hershey Park, Pennsylvania, where a train would run directly over the stage every ten minutes. I timed my jokes to coincide with the train.

I did a trade show in Denver where the contract for the job read like this: "Talent will do anything and everything that will get passersby to come into our booth." I was the "talent." To fulfill my agreement, I sometimes grabbed people by the arm and dragged them into a little tent staffed by a small internet start-up company that was trying to get people interested in their future. (True story—the police came and escorted me off the premises.)

I had a show one time where I was separated from my audience by the Tennessee River in Chattanooga. It was during a music festival, and my face was shown on a giant big-screen that could be seen from Mars.

I did a bar mitzvah in the vestibule of a millionaire brain surgeon's home, a spectacular mansion that looked out over the Pacific Ocean in Santa Cruz, California.

I did a show in a barn, on a hay wagon, and the entire audience was *Amish*. Yes, I said Amish. The folks who wear black and say "ye" and still travel by horse-drawn carriage. (Great crowd, by the way.)

I have a wealth of honest-to-God showbiz experiences that are so far off the beaten path that I ate Hansel and Gretel's breadcrumbs. I have not only met the Wicked Witch, I did thirty minutes of stand-up for her and her friends. (They loved my cauldron joke: "How does a witch know when the bubbling brew is done? Just keep stirring until the ingredients stop resisting!")

But none of these stories are so fun to tell and relive than a show I did one night in the Bronx, New York.

Rich Ramirez would call me every eight to nine months with an offer for a one-nighter. He was a wonderful comic, a gentleman, and an excellent businessman. His crowds were blue collar, hardworking men and women in the Bronx, most of whom were Puerto Rican and Cuban. He had a stable of acts that he would call upon, and he always paid on time, in cash, a little more than what you got from everyone else for these kinds of dates. Richie had figured the angles. His shows were presold total sellouts, and he wanted every one to be better than the last. If he sensed the audience was not completely impressed by the end of the evening, he would go onstage himself (always getting a standing ovation as he took the mike) and proceed to do whatever he felt was necessary to please his crowd. He told personal stories, new unproven jokes, old jokes, bad jokes, off-color jokes. Look, he would even retell *your* jokes and get a better response from the crowd, even though they had heard you do the same exact line an hour before!

Rich Ramirez might have had professional aspirations beyond making money and pleasing the people who paid for his evenings of entertainment. He never told me. He knew, or seemed to know, every single one of his paying customers by name. He would ask about their families and their jobs and their new babies and so on. He might as well have been a politician. I'd have voted for him, campaigned for him, written speeches for him. He was special, and I'm sorry I never asked him what his goals were or what he wanted out of comedy. I'll never know because he passed away a few years ago.

The problem for Richie was a venue. He didn't have one. There were no comedy clubs in the Bronx to speak of. If he did the shows in a bar or a restaurant, he had to split the take with the manager of the joint, which was not part of the business plan as far as I can tell. He didn't have the kind of money to buy a place and probably would not have done that even if he had the cash on hand.

Richie Ramirez had a different strategy.

He waited until a building was going to be empty for whatever reason, and he'd rent it for the night. Maybe it was about to be razed and had been vacated or was fire damaged and declared "contaminated" and "off-limits." Whatever, his business plan seemed to work thus: Scope out the joint, figure out what he needed, and put together a sort of plan for a dinner/show with comedy or music and entertainment. He would promote the date with flyers and phone calls and text messages when that technology kicked in. He often had to turn patrons away.

Rich Ramirez had it going on.

Most of the comics he used were New York City acts, and they worked blue. This was Da Bronx, after all. Their biggest laughs came from slice-of-life observations about being a minority, dealing with authority, and life in New York. And lots of them spoke Spanish. Some spewed profanity-laced diatribes and rants and personal opinions that were anti–white guy. You won't believe it, but I never felt threatened or singled out. I always closed the shows, even though I work clean and kept my sets pretty universal. I had picked up some Spanish just hanging around New York, and it came in handy when I worked for Mr. Ramirez.

On an icy February Thursday night in the late 1990s, I drove up Gun Hill Road to a Richie Ramirez gig in the Bronx. It would be my last-ever show for him, as our paths veered off in different directions. I was driving a minivan, a husband and father now, living in the suburbs with two kids under the age of ten, car seats and plastic cups and toys scattered all over the floor. This was the perfect auto to drive into one of the toughest boroughs in the city, where carjacking was a part of daily life. I was confident nobody would come after my dirty family man van, with the scratches and dimples on the sides.

And I was right.

It was a really, really cold night, so I had the heat blasting in my face. I moved with traffic past the boarded-up, chained buildings and past the fires in garbage cans on the corners, concentrating on the streets and checking the map Richie had coached me to follow on the phone earlier that day. "It's gonna be cool," he told me. "When you get to Golden Avenue, turn right. You'll see our place on your left. It's the only building on the block." He laughed.

I knew I had found the venue right away. I could see red taillights of cars stopping in the middle of the street, letting people out. There was no place to park, and I was fifteen minutes early. The building was a three-story structure, painted white in the front but brick and stone on the sides, standing alone and stark in the night, a survivor of abandonment or fire or city planning. People were walking past me, in the middle of the street, bundled up and huddled together against the cold. I drove past the crowd that spilled out of the front of the joint onto the curb, finally parking three blocks away by a restaurant that had an "Open 24 Hours" sign on it. I grabbed my prop bag, locked up the van, and quickly walked back to the venue.

As I got closer, the music started, coming from inside, loud and upbeat, salsa or mambo or something. A large group of people piled through the gaping hole that served as the front door. Just outside stood a massive young man wearing a windbreaker and a skullcap. He took tickets and greeted people as they rushed to get in out of the cold. It felt as if the entire building was bouncing to the vibe coming from within, as if it was redeemed for one last evening until the wrecking ball came. The doorman recognized me and said something in Spanish. I smiled and said, "Yo," the universal "hello, thank you, what's up, it's all good" that can fool some of the people some of the time. I was pushed past him by another large group of partiers right behind me, and I was a little surprised by how dark it was inside.

There was light coming through a doorway to the left, and I moved with everyone in that direction, which led to a staircase down to an underground room. The event was taking place down there, so I headed down, the music getting louder with each step, the light getting brighter, voices shouting and people laughing. And all of a sudden I was in the Movie In My Head, the minivan and my suburban home lost to another time and space. I was surrounded by strangers in a huge underground hall that must have taken up at least half the block. There was a long table on the wall to my right where people were helping themselves to food. The bar was behind me, people waiting for drinks in two lines that extended into the middle of the room, where dancers had already started. At the far end was a stage, about head high, and a Puerto Rican band was putting on a show. I counted twelve musicians in all, including a horn section, background singers, a bass and guitar, and drums and a pianist. I was smiling so hard my face hurt. Behind the band was a big metallic arch that stretched from one end of the stage to the other, the highest point right in the middle, just above the drummer's head. I was being jostled and bumped by people who apologized and smiled and offered me some of their food or their drink as they passed. But I was oblivious, overwhelmed by the circumstances, completely swept away with the drama.

Richie appeared. He put his arm around me. "This will be a great night!" he shouted over the music. "Do you know the Valdejas Brothers?"

I shook my head. I wasn't going to try and outshout a twelve-piece Puerto Rican band. And what did it matter who else was on the show? I was thrilled to be a part of the bash, and even if these guys were the greatest performers in the world, I wasn't worried. This crowd was ready for a good time. Richie shouted something else I couldn't make out, and then he morphed into the melee of dancers and late-arriving guests, heading toward the stage. I went back to the bar, found a little space where I got my props together, and then went back to the middle of the room to watch.

There were some chairs and tables on the wall to my left, but it was clear that most patrons on this night would be standing, which didn't seem to matter because that kind of energy was contagious. Who wanted to sit on a night like this? There was some sort of dance contest, run by Richie. The crowd got into it, the winners getting serenaded by the band and given a bottle of champagne. There was applause and cheering and more shouting and laughter, and then it was quiet.

Every person in the room surged toward the stage. I had no idea what was going on. A local celebrity? Maybe a professional athlete had walked in the room? Had someone gotten hurt?

I was looking around, hoping for a clue in the faces of people near me. Then I looked at the band, who talked among themselves for a few minutes. They moved and took places upstage, under that big arch. The audience was attentive and quiet. I looked for Richie, thinking he might be bringing me up any minute, and tried to edge my way to the front of the room.

There was an explosion of applause and cheering. I was now in the center of the room, packed into my spot by bodies pressing all around me and looking up at the stage as the band kicked into a sort of mambo/fanfare. Someone grabbed me from behind and firmly moved me to the left. It was the bodyguard from the front door.

"Yo," he said.

He was making an aisle, a pathway for three 300-pound Puerto Rican men, dressed in bright yellow shirts, red bandanas, loose-fitting blue jeans, and bright red Converse high-tops. The crowd was going bonkers, giving them high fives and touching them as they made their way through the room. When they reached the stage, audience members cheerfully helped them up, one at a time. The lead singer for the band shouted, "The Valdejas Brothers!" And the five hundred-person audience screamed an orgasmic cheer of expectation.

With that the Valdejas Brothers began dancing all over the place, doing all kinds of athletic moves that should be impossible for 300-pound men. They shook their fat, and they moved their muscle, and they ran in place, and they boogied down. They did some kind of break-dancing thing where one would get down on his back and the other two would twirl him around. They did a kind of synchronized rolling-and-jumping-over-each-other routine that drew ever-louder shouts of encouragement from their fans. They did slapstick-type body slams and pretended to be knocked unconscious. Then they would jump up and do some new body shape-defying trick, taking bows and blowing kisses at the end of each song. I was transfixed. I was stunned. It was the greatest show on earth, and I was there to see it! I was cheering along with everyone else, laughing when they did a belly dance, screaming when they did the splits, applauding their ability to defy nature and their own physicality with ballet moves. They brought a girl up from the crowd, and the three of them merengued with her and made her a star for the night. They were fun and funny and hugely entertaining. I had forgotten where I was, who I was, and what I was doing. And who cared anyway?

The band stopped. The brothers stopped and held their arms up over their heads. In turn, everyone in the audience did the same thing. Someone began singing, "Ooh-ooh-ooh." Soon, the entire basement was singing in unison, "Ooh-ooh-ooh," louder and louder. The band kicked in, playing a raucous version of a song called "It's Raining Men."

The Valdejas Brothers went to the back of the stage, in between the band members, and returned to the front, each holding a small trampoline, about the same circumference as a floor rug. There was pandemonium all around me, as if the crowd had been stuck with some kind of energy prod. The brothers put the trampolines down on the stage, lined up from left to right. The crowd had lost it. They were out of control, clapping and singing and exhorting the brothers.

One skipped across the stage in time to the music and then turned and ran toward a trampoline. He leaped into the air, came down hard on the trampoline, and jettisoned himself out over the crowd, which parted in a circle as he came down with a loud thud where the people had made a landing spot for him, about ten feet from me, in perfect unison with the chorus, "It's raining men!" I realized he was holding a wireless microphone, and *he was singing*! "It's raining men! Hallelujah! It's raining men!"

I could not believe what I was seeing. The audience helped him back to the stage. Another brother was skipping in the path of the first one, and he now turned toward his trampoline. On the chorus, he bounced out into the crowd, and once again the crowd parted. He landed on his two humongous feet, shout singing, "It's raining men! Hallelujah!" into his mike.

It was the most unbelievable thing I had ever seen. I was screaming. I was crying. The crowd was jumping and cheering as they lifted the second brother back.

And here came the third one, making a lazy half circle across the stage and then sprinting to the trampoline. He took a perfectly timed jump and then caromed out into the mob, which happily parted so that he could land safely, sing the chorus, and be helped back to the stage.

The band was pounding out the beat, raising the enthusiasm, and giving definition to "raising the roof." It was complete, total joy of being alive. It was everything. My hands hurt from clapping. I could not hear my voice. I was soaked in sweat. The room temperature had to be ninety degrees. The brothers were hugging one another and wiping their faces with towels. The band vamped. The brothers looked at the crowd. We cheered and screamed as loud as humanly possible, dwarfed by the nine hundred pounds of talent in front of us.

Every great act has a closer, the thing that brings the house down—a hit single. It's a comedy routine everyone loves—something that sets the act apart and says, "The show is over. Thanks for coming. Drive safely." The Valdejas Brothers had absolutely blown me away. Bouncing ten feet into the air, landing in the crowd, and singing a song cannot be topped. That is the definition of closer. They had the best I had ever seen.

As the band vamped, the audience began clapping in unison, and chanting, "Ooh-ooh-ooh." The Brothers Valdejas pretended to pick up their trampolines and then looked at all of us. We pleaded for one more thrilling explosion of trampoline-ism.

They each held up a finger. "Uno mas?" they asked into their microphones.

We in the audience held up one of our fingers back to them and agreed: *"Uno mas!"*

And the brothers grabbed the edges of their trampolines. They pulled the outer strings tighter, for maximum bounce-a-bility. They put their trampolines down in the same places on stage. Then one turned to the left, and the other two turned to the right. They walked to the respective edges of stage left and right, and then they began to climb the arch.

Yes. There were steps on the arch. The Valdejas Brothers slowly and unsteadily climbed to the top. I could feel my heart pounding through my chest. The band was crescendoing, and the three brothers stood facing us. They held hands. The crowd hushed. On the chorus they jumped as one, each hitting his trampoline dead center, and they careened out into the audience like giant human pinballs. The audience parted, and each brother hit the floor on both feet as he sang, "It's raining men!"

The room went nuclear. Pandemonium. Bedlam. Girls were kissing the Valdejas boys. Men pounded them on the back. The three of them limped back to the front of the stage and waved. I couldn't hear the band anymore, even though I could see the drummer hitting his kit. Someone shouted "Valdejas!" and something else in Spanish that I couldn't make out. And for fifteen minutes the crowd cheered the three men, chanting their name. They struggled to a back exit and left.

Richie Ramirez appeared at my side—all smiles and laughter.

"You're on," he said.

Chapter Twenty-Five
Mickey Mouse Operation

*This is a Mickey Mouse operation
compared to Lyons or Paris.*
—Jack Higgins, author

> When people call something a "Mickey Mouse operation," they're insulting something or someone. Or they're being sarcastic. I don't get it. I suppose you could make the case that Mickey is always in a crisis situation and has to accomplish the impossible to make everything work out. But the Walt Disney Company is worth almost $150 billion! Would that I could be a Mickey Mouse operation.

After three years touring arenas from coast to coast, I left and went back to my own solo career around 2004. The world was in an uproar. Wars were being fought on at least four continents. The attacks on 9/11 and the following fallout would divide the citizenry of the United States along political and social lines that have become even starker in the years since.

> I'm not sure what the correct lexicon is, but I personally refer to the years 2000 through 2009 as the 00s (sounds like "ooze").

I was in a unique position to get a feel for the pulse of our nation as I rode a bus from city to city, giving me a firsthand look at our country from New York to LA and from Seattle to Miami. I met people from all walks of life. The comedy premises for my performances, particularly ventriloquism, took on the subjects that became more and more important to people during the first decade of the new millennium—travel; safety; jobs; and what would become a difficult situation for many Americans, a devastating recession.

> Ventriloquism's "golden age" is said to be the 1930s, during the Great Depression. I see no irony that, during the Great Recession of 2007 to 2011, ventriloquism became very popular again. Hmmm.

A fledgling TV network based in Columbus, Ohio, booked me to perform a set of my comedy act for a video release. They let me do a forty-five-minute cable special type act—puppets, music, and stand-up. It taped in a legit comedy club—the Funny Bone. The program was called "Bananas Comedy," and it got me a lot of air time. They had me shoot another (different) forty-five-minute set, and my "Bananas II" also did well.

Those comedy shows led to a great opportunity.

I had signed on with Tim Grable, who was based in Nashville, Tennessee. He negotiated a deal for a TV series produced by the same company that made "Bananas."

We would film two seasons of *Taylor's Attic*, a children's TV show that took place in (you guessed it!) the attic of a middle-class house somewhere in the middle of the United States in the middle of the 00s. The premise is simple—a middle-aged man spends much of his waking hours in the attic with his imaginary friends.

> Social media became part of the national discourse as Facebook injected itself into our lives in 2004, eclipsing MySpace. And what ventriloquist could not relate? What are Twitter, Facebook, Instagram, Snapchat, LinkedIn, and all the rest other than one person having thousands of "imaginary friends"? It's a ventriloquist's dream!

I hired Paul Seaburn as the head writer, and we had a great couple of years, filming twenty-six episodes that included a lot of music and comedy. I voiced all the characters (there were as many as nine altogether) and wrote most of the songs with Paul and a wonderful music producer named Marc Andre, who also served as the sound engineer for the entire project.

The experience was not without the craziness that has been the earmark of my career. The set for *Taylor's Attic* was built in an old barn thirty miles east of Columbus, Ohio, just off Route 70. That was our production studio. We weren't shooting in Hollywood or New York or even Columbus. We filmed and recorded in a barn next to the highway.

I loved it!

The set builders would win a regional Emmy Award because they created an amazing work of art—a real attic with strategically located holes and openings so that arms could fit through and operate a puppet without being seen by the camera. They built a "roof" so we could shoot scenes "outside" looking up at the stars or the clouds (we did a lot with green screen). The barn was drafty and cold in the winter and hot in the spring when we did most of the shoots, but nobody complained. There was a grand piano off to the side, where Paul, Marc, and I wrote most of the songs for season 1— usually at the last minute and always under a lot of pressure. We often had to have a song done in forty-five minutes! That included writing it, recording it, mixing it and having it ready for a shoot the same afternoon! For the second season we took a few months and wrote the songs and musical score in my living room in New Jersey. People who love "Taylors Attic" often tell me their favorite parts of all the episodes are the songs.

DEFINITION: green screen. A "green screen" is used for film, television, and video. The process is known as "chromakey." A moving/talking subject is filmed in front of a green (or blue) background, which allows a separately filmed background to

be added to the final image. Thus, for *Taylor's Attic,* we shot the show in a barn. But there are "rooftop" scenes that look as if we're outside looking at "stars."

Paul, Marc, and me: "Sure."

I'm forever blessed to have worked with everyone involved, and I'm regretful if not outright embarrassed we couldn't make it work for more than two seasons. I don't know all the parameters around the cancelation of *Taylor's Attic*. But as the person whose name is on the title, I feel guilty we couldn't make it work for a few more years.

I loved doing it, and I loved the cast and crew. I owed Paul Seaburn then, and I owe him now.

Paul and I arrived at the studio one Monday morning, after our thirty-minute drive over from the hotel in Columbus, to find one of the puppeteers holding "his" character close to his body and off to the side.

We looked at each other, and said, "Uh-oh." Something was wrong.

I went over to the talent. He was crying. I put my hand on his shoulder.

"What's wrong?" I asked, with all the honesty and love that I could muster. These were hardworking people, and I understood they could become attached to their … uh … partners.

"You know darn well what's wrong!" he said between sobs.

"No, I really don't." I wanted to keep an open mind.

He looked up at me, eyes red, mouth quivering, squeezing his puppet to his chest. "You're writing us out of the show."

I stared at him. "What are you talking about?"

"You're writing us out of the show!" he shouted. "Two weeks ago, we were the stars. The whole episode was about us! Then last week, we only had a few lines. And this week, we hardly have any dialogue at all. It's like we're extras! We've become ghosts! *We want more lines*! You're writing us out of the show!"

He went back to crying, holding his character the way a parent might hold a child who had been cut from the travel soccer team.

I looked at Paul who gave me an I-don't-have-time-for-this-and-besides-I'm-not-getting-paid-enough-to-work-as-a-therapist look. He turned and went back to his office—er, back to the stall in the barn that had been made into an office.

You can look at this any way you want to. I prefer to think of it this way: Our cast—the people who took on these puppeteer jobs—took our little show seriously. They worked under stressful conditions, and they brought these puppets/roles to life. I will always maintain the real show, the true story that needs to be told, is not what you can still see by finding an old *Taylor's Attic* DVD or a YouTube video. The show that will never be seen and the one that should be told happened behind the camera. This show stars the cast and crew and staff that made up *Taylor's Attic*.

Our puppeteers were folks looking for a job at the time—a window cleaner, a divorcée who had operated puppets at her church, a college graduate who couldn't find something in his field. There were a couple of heavy metal musicians who needed a day job to keep the band going. The office staff and production assistants were forced into manipulating a puppet on a regular basis because someone called in sick or had a dentist appointment or got stuck in a snowstorm.

They were all professional, and they all deserved better.

These staff members and the puppeteers did incredible work. This is especially truly when you consider that most of the folks who worked as the talent on the show—who brought to life characters like a slacker roach named Rocco, a smart pig named Paco, and a whiny creature made of dust on the attic floor (aptly named "Dusty")—had *never* worked with puppets before, much less performed for a TV show!

Jonathan Bock, who as of this writing, works in Hollywood. A former comedy writer and now a producer and promoter and player, he had a vision for a comedy series starring acts that stayed away from the bedroom, the bathroom, and the profane. He titled his comedy series "Thou Shalt Laugh." Over a six-year period, he lured some big names to host his five comedy videos. Patricia Heaton, Tim Conway, Sinbad, John Tesh, and Christian comedy superstar Chonda Pierce all did the honors as emcees (and big-time names) on his video series. I was honored to be part of all five of the shoots. Each one was a thrill.

While all these shows were being taped and distributed, I began working for Disney Cruise Line.

Since the middle of the early 2000s, I spend some seventy plus days every year on one of the cruise ships that make up the DCL fleet. It has been a successful partnership, me performing four shows in the Walt Disney Theater or on a nightclub stage over the course of four nights. In return I get paid. It's not really a career move, but it's not something to scoff at either. I'm working for the biggest show business entity on the planet.

I'm of a certain age, a forgotten segment of American society that grew up when "color television" was a novelty. On Sunday nights when I was a boy, *Walt Disney's Wonderful World of Color* aired on NBC. It was my introduction to Mr. Disney himself, and I never take for granted that it is a dream come true that—some forty years later—I would be working for his company.

It's a privilege to work for Disney Cruise Line, and not just because the name is so familiar. The time I spend on the ship is an immersion into some of the greatest talent in music, comedy, theater, film, and writing in history. The live shows feature young, energetic, talented and focused singers, actors, and dancers from around the world. Just as important and just as meaningful as the oh-so-recognizable characters, songs, and movies is the emphasis on customer service. It cannot be duplicated. It is brilliant, it is state of the art, and it is quintessential.

I am always humbled by the cast members on the Disney ships, the room hosts, the servers in the dining rooms, and the stagehands and techs. All are some of the best people and most sincere service industry professionals I'll ever work with.

One of my wife's childhood friends from South Jersey had a daughter who married a firefighter/EMT who lost his life to cancer, a result of his being a first a first-responder on 9/11. The couple had two little girls, twins as a matter of fact. Marsia and I conspired to take them on a Disney Cruise. On a hot August Monday about a year after his passing, they boarded the spectacular *Disney Dream*.

The day was also the twin's birthday. When they walked into their stateroom, they walked into the beginning of an unforgettable, unbelievably fun week that exploded into their lives in ways only a Disney cruise could do. Their room was overdecorated with banners, balloons, greetings, and treats. It was a surprise for the two unsuspecting children and their mother but only the start.

We wanted something special for the three of them. The little girl's grandmother and my wife had grown up across the street from one another. They were, in every sense of the word, *family*. And there is no industry on the planet that takes a situation like this, and the word "family"—in all its incantations—more seriously and with more attention to detail than Disney Cruise Line.

Each day began with a new adventure. The girls were treated like princesses. The Disney Cruise Line officers, particularly Cruise Director Jimmy Lynett and Assistant Cruise Director Lesley Dallas, could not have been more gracious, caring, and attentive. There are too many moments to recount here, including the incredible meals, the fireworks at sea, the original and mesmerizing live shows in the theater, and the heartfelt send-off on the final night.

But it's not just about these two girls and their mom! The way all the cast members work so diligently on the boat, seeing to it that *every* passenger is having an incredible experience, is what makes DCL the singular entity it is. I am blessed and fortunate beyond belief that I got to witness the magic, the wonder, the fantasy, and the dreams come true that Disney can afford its passengers—through the eyes of two little girls and their mom.

Chapter Twenty-Six
Synergy

Remember everything that I told you / And I'm telling you again that it's true / When you're alone and afraid / And completely amazed / To find there's nothing anybody can do / Keep on believing
—Jim Steinman, "Rock and Roll Dreams Come Through"

Show business is as much about the "business" part as the "show" part. The sooner people in the creative arts figure that out, the sooner they seem to become successful.

Comedian Tommy Blaze is a good example. He's defined "successful stand-up comic" for some thirty plus years, delivering heat-seeking punch lines across the United States and appearing on a myriad of television programs and in major motion pictures. He's now overseeing an online comedy show called *The Comedy All-Stars*, a vision he shares with Chris DiPetta (longtime comedy mover, shaker, and booker) and the folks at Pure Flix who produce it.

> Pure Flix is most well known for its hit movie *God's Not Dead*.

I got to be a part of this brainchild. It was a throwback and, at the same time, a look into the future. And it really worked.

There were some fourteen comedy acts on the first evening of video that took place at the gorgeous Clayton Center in Clayton, North Carolina. Hosting these segments was Sinbad, whom I've worked with before. Sinbad is a singular icon in entertainment and, like Blaze, a successful/killer live performer. He drew an amazingly diverse audience, matched only by the multiracial, multigenerational comics who performed on stage. That bucket list of talent included Mary Ellen Hooper, Dwight Slade, and Dale Jones. They are three of the funniest and most seasoned people in comedy. All of them deserve their own sitcom or movie or platform because they're brilliant.

Some of the younger performers, Mia Jackson, Terri Moore, and Chase Anthony, looked like they'd been born on stage. Each brought down the house, making me think, "I'm sure glad I don't have to follow them."

Karen Rontowski, Jamie Bendall, and Jamar Haynes Lee were not known to me when we met. But as often happens in the biz I am a fan now. Kevin Downey, Jr., fresh from an appearance on TV's now-defunct *Red Eye*, closed the evening with his off-the-grid, insanity-meets-reality style, which was a perfect way to end a long evening. (Our audience stayed attentive and responsive and strong for the entire night! That was a tribute to Sinbad's style and the quality of the above-named comedy all-stars.)

My particular episode included two pals from the business:
- Horace H B Sanders and I have done some TV/video work together, and he is always hilarious. It was great to work with his energetic flow and his dynamic persona.
- Patty Vasquez, who hosts a radio show of her own on WGN in Chicago (yay! My dad's old employer!) has shared the stage with me for a few gigs as well. Her takes on marriage and motherhood are timeless.

There were two more tapings over the weekend, hosted by my old Chicago pal Jeff Allen who is a comedy lifer with the kind of resume most of us would die for. His career has taken an upward trajectory over the past ten to fifteen years, due in large part to his work ethic and attention to detail. He is a mesmerizing live act, whose humor has all sorts of edges to it, and to see his success is inspirational and admirable. The last evening featured one of the funniest and most endearing people in all entertainment—Louie Anderson.

There is a feeling I get, still as vibrant and vital today as it was when I first began working, that rocks me just before every live appearance. I'm guessing that everyone who makes a living in front of a crowd gets it in some form or another. It's a combination of excitement and energy, an overwhelming jolt of stimuli that puts all my senses on alert, as if every endorphin in the universe has been released into my bloodstream, and I can barely maintain composure.

It doesn't matter where I'm working or who the audience is or how many people are watching. I might be driving up to a comedy club when I see my name on the marquis and a line of ticket buyers waiting to get inside to catch my show. That jump-starts the whole thing, my heart pumping, and my mind begins a race with reality. Maybe I'm running up on a big outdoor stage in front of a fun-loving festival crowd, or maybe I'm only doing a little presentation for small kids and even toddlers in the children's section of a library. It doesn't matter; the vibe is the same. It's such a positive reinforcement that I don't think I will ever stop working.

> I have this recurring self-manufactured daydream where I'm working a small theater in Manhattan. It's off-Broadway. The title—"An Evening with Taylor Mason and Friends"—glows in bright lights from the sign over the front door. There is a long line of men wearing ankle-length beige businessman's coats with lots of buttons and flaps, women in fluffy designer jackets and high heels, all standing arm in arm for a city block, waiting to pick up their tickets at will call. Taxis are dropping more show-goers off at the curb. Somewhere in a hotel across town there is a man sitting at the edge of a bed in a suite, wearing a newly pressed white shirt and black tie, sport coat across his knees, talking to the bathroom door. "Honey, can we please hurry? If we don't leave right away we're gonna miss Taylor's opening, and I hear that's one of the best parts of the whole show!"

The truth is that reality is not far from my fantasy. I'm not sure if that's luck or fate or just the way things are supposed to be.

It was late winter just a short time ago. I was working at the Comedy Cabaret in Doylestown, Pennsylvania, for a weekend. It has been kind of my "home club" for the past X number of years since moving to New Jersey, even though it's thirty-five miles and at least an hour away. I'm here four to eight times a year, depending on my schedule. The staff—at least for the couple of nights we work together—are my friends." I know many of them by name. Pete and Lisa have become more than acquaintances. So have many of the waitstaff. I look forward to seeing them.

It's an idiosyncrasy of show business. Maybe it's true in other industries, like insurance or construction or health care; I don't know. But in the world of performance art, the people you work with on any given project or in any venue become your friends. Since work takes you all over the place—for me, that's all over the world—lasting friendships are hard to come by. It's practically impossible.

I'm traveling. A lot.

So the folks who work the gig with me are, by happenstance, my friends.

With a TV program, commercial shoot, or film, the techs, actors, producers, and staff are your pals— at least for the duration of the taping. In a theater, it's the stagehands and manager. And for a weekend run at a comedy club, you befriend the bartender, the waitstaff, and the whomever. These events put you together for a period of time, and then it's a new job, a different situation, and a fresh set of connections. For me, it's a new place to work; for them, it's a new face on the stage. *Next*!

For this job, I left Moorestown, New Jersey, after dinner with Marsia. We ate downtown at a glorified pizza joint we've been frequenting forever, talking about the kids and the new house and the trivia that makes up our days. The neighbor wanted to sell us a bicycle. I got a great job working for a week in Southern California, and maybe she'd join me for that run. Mick, our dog, needed to see the vet. We were comfortable with all of it. The kids have asked more than once how I knew Marsia was "the one," and I still don't have a good answer. I don't have a story of romantic courtship. I married her because I'd have followed her wherever she went, regardless. It was just easier to be with her than not. Life was *better* with her than not. Some would call it a choice, but it really wasn't a choice then, and it isn't now. We are *together.* So after dinner we came home. I took a shower and dressed. We kissed goodbye.

I drove through Philadelphia, barely cognizant of the Saturday evening traffic. I was going over the lines I wanted to try out. (Some hostile country said they had an ICBM that can reach Los Angeles. So what? I know that town, and it's not easy to be "the bomb." Sure, anyone can get to Hollywood. But you need a hip PR firm, a good agent, and some clout before Universal or Warner Bros will even take your call! Sure, the missile might have a unique *headshot*, but come on.) It was a preperformance preparation routine—the meal with Marsia, the shower, the drive.

Just past the city start the tony suburbs of Bucks County, and I followed the steady traffic north on Easton Road. The mom-and-pop diners, the franchise restaurants, and the occasional four- and five-star eatery parking lots were full. So were the strip malls and movie complexes. I took this as a good sign. There was a certain vibe on this late-winter Saturday, some snow from the previous week's storm still on the ground. Maybe winter was over. I took it all to be a good sign.

It was.

I got to Doylestown about forty minutes before showtime. I drove right up the main drag, past the chic boutiques of designer clothing now closing up shop and past the bistros and bars where upscale hipsters milled around on the sidewalk; a couple of them jogged across the street in front of me. I passed the county courthouse and the centuries-old homes, that preshow rush just about to hit my frontal cortex. The club itself, on the northern edge of town, took up the second floor of Poco's, a Mexican American restaurant. I'd only eaten there once in all those years. It was very good. You got the feeling that Poco's was always busy. The establishment had attained "local attraction" status long ago. Everyone was a "regular."

Poco's and the Comedy Cabaret were part of a complex actually. There was a Days Inn Hotel connected around the back, and I parked in front of a "hotel guest parking only, violators will be towed" sign. I had spent a lot of years parking right here, in front of that warning, behind the restaurant kitchen door by some steps that led to a long row of hotel rooms. Those steps also led to the back door of the comedy club, which I braced open with a broom and carried my keyboard to the stage.

The room was really an attic with a postage stamp for a stage, a red curtain beginning to fade after decades of theatrical lighting and a long bar in the back. It could seat up to 225, maybe 250 people. Tonight felt like about 500 human beings were packed into the chairs and stools that surround small tabletops. There was a video playing on a pull-down screen on stage. The soundtrack blared through the speakers. But the crowd was competing quite well, thank you, talking and laughing and shouting to one another—preshow positivity. If it sounds tight, cramped, and small, it was.

It was perfect. The room was usually pretty full when I was here. (I'm not bragging; I'm guessing it was always like this.) And the closeness of everything—the walls, the people, the ceiling—meant that laughter pinballed through the space and doubled back on the performer. It was electric. Terrific. Dramatic.

"Buffalo Stance," Neneh Cherry's incredible 1988 single was pumping out of the big speakers as I snaked my way through people who had paid to see me, taking care not to nail someone with the sharp edge of my Roland piano.

As I was placing it on the stand, a man came over and grabbed my arm. "We were here last time you were, and I brought fifteen people to see you!" he said. He had a wild look in his eye and exuded a definitive positive vibe. He was so up for the evening that it was hard not to laugh.

"Thanks for coming!" I shouted, trying to plug the keys in and set the cables. "We'll have a blast!"

He nodded, waved, patted me on the back, and disappeared into the mayhem of waiters and audience.

The man that booked the club, Andy, was there. Sitting on stools at a tall table were his wife and one of his twentysomething kids and a friend. We all said hi. We briefly talked over the surrounding sounds. "How's business?" "How is the family?" "Have a great show!"

I headed for the green room and closed the door. It was tiny—a couch, a bookcase, and a mirror. There was a small table with a notebook on it, notes for one of the other acts. I was just setting my bag down when Pete, the manager, came in. "Do whatever you want," he says, referring to my time on stage.

I was scheduled for forty to forty-five minutes, and I told him I'd do all of that.

I ended up doing closer to fifty-five, which was too long, but no excuses.

Andy, who owned the Comedy Cabaret franchise and booked the comics, actually had his own act, and tonight he served as emcee. He warmed up the crowd, read them very well, and brought up the first act.

Marsia and I have always been impressed by the number of talented people there are in this world. We've met and worked with a lot of them. Writers. Actors. Musicians. Singers and painters and dancers and comedians. It is astounding. Especially young people. Every single one I work with is so gifted, so innate, so far ahead of where we were at the same age.

The "opening act" that night was a Middle Eastern man who was in his twenties. He played off his look, his heritage, and the sociopolitical ramifications of being who he was in the United States of America in the twenty-tens. The Cabaret crowd, mostly upscale and white, was responsive, attentive, and giving. "My uncle is Egyptian," he said. "He lived through two civil wars and all kinds of violent upheaval. But he says he's scared to death to drive through Kensington" (a tough neighborhood of Philadelphia). The audience erupted. The comic's name was Fady—pronounced "Faddy." He did twelve minutes, and he could have done thirty—easy.

He was followed by Tracy Locke, whose edgy energy and frenetic pace synched in time with the general vibe in the room. She was a short blond wearing a blue dress, and she worked the crowd, like a musician vamping with a band, only the microphone was her instrument and the laughter was the beat. She became everyone's BFF in the first thirty seconds she's on stage, and for a half an hour, she held court. She was what my dad would have called "a personality kid"—impossible not to like. Her takes on dating, sex, the melting pot of East Coast cultures, men, and sports played right to the heart of the crowd. Her observational humor and one-liners had women shrieking and applauding. The men were shrieking and applauding. Hell, I was shrieking and applauding.

Andy came back to the green room. "Selfie!"

We talked for a few minutes while Ms. Locke was blowing the roof off the building. He got an introduction from me - I told him that I would appear on Pure Flix Comedy All-Stars with Sinbad - so that's what he used for my intro.

I was on.

The first show of the weekend was Friday, the night before, and that crowd was rowdy and more than a little crazy, even for a comedy club. It was the usual big crowd, but boozy and unruly, cheering and pounding the tables and shouting out comments during everyone's performances. Don't get the wrong impression; the crowd wasn't angry or mean. These folks were "happy drinkers," people out to forget their troubles and have a good time. Just before I went on, I got insightful data from Lisa at the bar. "Welcome to hillbilly heaven!" she shouted over the din.

I had a blast.

I spent much of that evening's stage time acting like an agitated schoolteacher or, better yet, a camp counselor. I played a role that I gave myself for this particular performance, pretending I was someone given a position of authority over a group that cannot be contained. It was raucous and wild and fun. And funny. Some friends, Bev and Lou, came, and I know they enjoyed the different kind of presentation they got outta me. They'd been following me for years, and we'd met in places all over the world. Wait. Maybe I'd been following *them*.

This Saturday night crowd was just as energized as the night before, but they were more attentive, more in tune with the proceedings. They were relaxed. Saturday night in any live venue is universally the best night to perform because the audience is fresh. Most people didn't work all day before coming to the show. There is no urgency. There was no specific age group for this performance, just a broad range from early twenties to early sixties. So I did kind of a "greatest hits" of my comedy career, the way a popular 1980s band might do all the top 40 songs from their best-selling albums. I had a wealth of material to fall back on, plus the ever-growing catalog of new stuff, so there was never an issue about what to do.

Brian Dorfmann, my friend who runs Zanies Comedy Club in Nashville, Tennessee, once told me my act was like a jam band show—there isn't a "set list," the band just picks a song, and they riff until they don't want to riff it any more.

I threw in a couple of new lines. ("I love Disney, and tried to do a *home version* of Disney World at our house. It starts with a scary ride I took with my wife. I call it *marriage*.") It felt like a condensed version of my life in show biz. I was put in the right place at the right time, given an opportunity, and if things weren't absolutely perfect, at least things were good. I did just under an hour, probably a little too long, but that fits the narrative, huh? "Always leave 'em wanting more ... unless they've already left."

Pete handed me a check as I was packing up. There were lots of congratulatory handshakes and pats on the back from this group of strangers and club regulars and fans who had come out. "You did a completely different show than last time!" shouted the man who brought fifteen people. His wife said, "We love you!"

I can live on a good compliment for about three months, so this pretty much had me covered until then. I packed up the gear—the puppets and bag, the Roland and the cords and foot pedal. I said my goodbyes. I tried to be as cordial and sincere as I could. "Great working with you," was my comment to the waitstaff, because I felt as if we were all in this service business together. They served food and drink. I served the entertainment. It was synergetic, at least to me.

There was a time where the "high" from a successful performance would stick with me for hours. I'd replay the evening over and over until morning. I still record my performances, but I don't listen to the playback over and over, analyzing every syllable these days. I find the points that need work—pronunciation of certain words as a ventriloquist, why a joke didn't get the usual response, the water break I took at the forty-minute mark that worked beautifully. I make a mental note. Next.

The postshow recovery has evened out over time. The high is more intense while I'm on stage now, the moments of explosive laughter and applause more acute, more precious. I don't take anything for granted.

But now, when it's over, it's over. I am happy to shake hands and talk with folks after a job, but I'm also happy to get everything in the car and head home.

My bank has a location right next to Poco's, so I went to the ATM and cashed some of my check—Marsia's money for the week. I drove home on a different route, through a forgotten part of industrial Philadelphia along the river. Traffic was sparse. There were few streetlights here. It was quiet and dark, and I maneuvered around the endless potholes listening to blues on the car stereo. I took the Tacony-Palmyra Bridge over to Jersey, and I quietly rolled into our driveway.

Home. Marsia had left a light on in the dining room. I climbed the stairs. Mick came out of the bedroom to greet me with a tail wag, and I gave him a scratch behind the ears. I took off the T-shirt and jeans I wore for "work" and slipped into bed.

Marsia rolled over. "How was the show?" she mumbled in her sleep.

"Great."

I gave her a kiss. She rolled over and pulled the covers up tight.

I'd be there in the morning when she woke up.

Chapter Twenty-Seven
False Ending

Dr. Eleven. What was it like for you at the end?
Captain Lonagan. It was exactly like waking up from a dream.
— Emily St. John Manuel, *Station Eleven*

A couple of days ago, I got a call from Tim saying there was an "opportunity." He was skeptical, but I was still doing the hustle, so there I was.

Another audition.

I was ready.

It was a cliché, a cattle call of performers. So I was in a cavernous big city convention center surrounded by all kinds of acts—singers, jugglers, magicians, dancers, comedians, balloon animal makers, and dog trainers, along with musicians and clowns and children and a couple of really, *really* old people who were holding tubas. You get the picture.

I was enjoying the scene. I didn't feel out of place, and I certainly didn't feel superior—or inferior—to the people around me. There was a teen-aged dance troop wearing sparkly purple outfits and being videotaped by a TV crew. Everyone stopped to watch them. A team of jump rope artists (is there a name for jump rope artists?)—twelve young people wearing matching white tees and brown slacks—tried to compete with the dancers by "rehearsing" just to the side. Right behind all of them was a group of Asian gymnasts climbing on top of one another until they formed a ceiling-high totem pole of humanity.

I loved this kind of stuff.

It was a "talent show," and I have prepared a short six-minute music/comedy/ventriloquism set in hopes that I'd be chosen.

I could use the exposure.

I could use the viability.

I could use a shot, just one more shot, at something—anything.

Tim told me this morning that I had been rejected by a talk/variety show on a cable channel that had offered to book me. The offer had been rescinded.

No complaints, just stating it: I could really use one more shot.

My name was called.

Actually my number was called: "Is 5246 here?"

I raised my hand, 5246 matching the flimsy paper tag safety pinned to my fave blue shirt with the paisley design. I hurriedly picked up my nylon bag of props and half-jogged to the person shouting for me, a young woman wearing skinny jeans, a white T-shirt, and a pink headband. She didn't wait or make eye contact, just pointed behind her and started walking that direction. I followed.

We came to a room just off the giant hall about two hundred feet removed from where all the other acts were preparing or waiting. She opened the door, strolled in, and left it open. I leaned around the corner and looked inside. There were three people sitting at a long folding table in an airy, bright room with big open windows that afforded the view of another brick-and-glass city building. These three had to be my interviewers. Each one had some notes in front of him or her. There was a high-def camera on a stand right behind the person in the middle, a woman, probably in her early forties with black hair. She wore a loose-fitting white button-down shirt and no jewelry, except a high-tech watch. To her right was a well-manicured man in a brown suit, a white shirt, and a red tie. He had a stack of papers—a lot more than the others—in front of him. He was young, maybe in his mid-thirties?

At the far end, on the left of the woman in the middle, was another woman. She wore a gray low-neck sweater over a light blue T-shirt. She was older. Or maybe she'd just lived a harder life. She had muddy blond hair, parted down the middle, and she wore way too much lipstick. She was talking to the other two as I walked in. The woman who'd brought me sat with a loud whump in a folding chair in the corner, pulled out her iPhone X, and began doing the cell phone prayer, using her thumbs to tap out data or pictures or angry texts about how much she hated her job.

The camera operator, a young man wearing a bandana and baggy jeans, stepped behind the lens.

I walked to the middle of the room. There was a chair facing the camera and my three gatekeepers. I sat down.

I knew what was coming. I knew what to do.

I placed my prop bag on the floor next to me—hands on knees, big smile.

I was "*on*."

"Hello! My name is Taylor Mason. I am a comedian, and I am here today to earn myself a booking on your program."

The woman in the middle put her elbows on the table, folded her hands together forming a sort of tripod, and rested her chin on her fingers. The woman on the end leaned back, a pen in her mouth, which she took out and waved when she laughed—a gesture that was loud and obnoxious and lots of fun. The man smiled a big smile and nodded his head for my entire presentation.

I started off with the exact material I had rehearsed. "I know you've seen a lot of ventriloquists." And the man said, "We're looking for the best one!" The three of them nodded and gave me the kind of attention I rarely enjoyed in situations like this. Even the man behind the camera was responding with muffled laughter as I worked. My patter started with how I started—the socks rolled up so it looked as if they were little creatures smiling up at me—and things kept getting better.

I took Romeo out of the bag, and we did a routine about jobs. ("Do you know why the TV golf announcers whisper? They don't want to wake the people who are watching at home!")

The three of them allowed me some extra time and I knew it, so I didn't waste it. They asked some sincere questions. They talked among themselves for a minute.

The woman in the middle turned to me and flashed a bittersweet smile. "We really like you. You're very talented. And I'm sure you'd do very well on the show. But there are a lot of things working against you for this season."

I turned her off at this point. I didn't need to know that they were going in a different direction or that they had another ventriloquist (or two or three or four) or that I don't fit the demo (I was too old) and so on. I got it. I wasn't mad or spiteful or even a little upset. This was show business. They knew their show, they knew their audience, and they knew what they wanted—and what they didn't want.

They didn't want me and I was okay with that.

I put Romeo back in the bag. (I did have him make a comment to the woman who'd brought me to the interview, sitting by herself in the corner: "You! Texting with your phone! Listen! There is a really good app that can give you guidance as to when it is and isn't appropriate to use your phone in public or in private. Check it out." My three interviewers and the camera operator laughed and look over their shoulders at the woman, who ignored all of us.)

I zipped up the bag.

Romeo gave a muffled, "I didn't even get to do my Drake impression," from inside the bag.

I was packed and halfway to the door when the blond woman said, "Wait! I love your name!"

I stopped. I didn't turn around. I was talking to the door. "Thanks."

I took hold of the doorknob. She said, "I mean I really love your name! It's like two last names! Or two first names! Taylor. Mason. Mason. Taylor. See? It works frontward and backward!"

I turned the knob.

"No."

I was headed out the door. I was doing the Movie In My Head, watching myself leave the audition. I had a drive home and then I was taking Marsia to dinner. I wanted to call both kids, and I needed to do some writing. I would like to practice piano, maybe work on a song for Romeo. And I left in forty-eight hours for San Diego, which made tomorrow a pack-the-bags-and-get-ready day.

I was already gone, moving toward the next performance, the one where I'll never be better, when I'll say, loud enough for anyone within earshot, "My name is Taylor Mason. It's irreversible."

It's a gift, this life. And as with most gifts it's always appropriate to say thank you to the people who gave it to you. So here is the list of people who deserve a sincere thank you. Monique Gomez and everyone at Xlibris. My parents, Bill and Patricia Mason who gave me everything. My brothers Locke and Tony. The many Masons who have supported me, including Art, Matt and Laura, Joe and Jan, Mark, Ike and so many more I can't name them all. My Aunts Ardie, Gloria and Marlene. My Uncles Art, Gene and Phil. The Baroni brothers. Sally Hager. Doug Ingraham, Jim Ellis, Mrs. Randall, Tom Harris, Mike Purcell, Howie Olsen, John Wolfslegel, Donny Sutherland, Paula and Linda and Mr. And Mrs. Mitchell, John Cassidy, Bob McNamara, and a bunch of wonderful high school coaches and teachers: Steinbach, Murphy, Myers, Riley, Sulaski, and Sutherland. A bunch of fraternity brothers including Bosco, Lurch, Pebbles, Mumbles, Artie, Andos, Kirch, Bobby, Wonder, Squeach, Ferd, Kio, Kett, Harlow, Erb, Gawner, Hoff, Mick, Jonesy, Dote, Scott, Ruegs, Rob, Mags, Harvez, Pace, Mike, Preebs, Lance, Donnelly, Fugues, Dets, and a bunch of people I'm forgetting. Thanks to Dean Wessels and daughter Kathy. Dr. Jim Evans, Skip Pickering, Rod Cardinal, Revie Sorey, Mike McCray, Keith Burlingame, Derwin Tucker, Kenny Durrell, Brad Childress, Alan Swain, Loren Tate, Dave Kasey, Jeannie Caggiano, Sara Owens, Paul Wang, Dean Fryburger, Don Schultz, Bert Haas, Ricky Uchwatt, T.P. Mulrooney, Teddy LeRoi, Judy Tenuta, Emo, Brant Harris, Fernando, Joyce Sloane, Paul Sills, Aaron Freeman, Karen McVeigh, Tim Walkoe, Tim Cavanaugh, Mary Wong, Joey Edmonds, John Ferrentino, Rick Rogers, Stan Bernstein, Andrea Levy, Cynthia Coe, Richard of Catch a Rising Star, Bill Schefft, Adrienne Tolsch, Jim David, Cary and Suzanne Hoffman, Ronn Lucas, Jay Johnson, Jeff Dunham, Lynn Traefzger, Dan Horn, David Strassman, Frank Marshall, Mark Wade, Danny de Armas, Ken Davis, Bill and Gloria Gaither,

Reggie and Ladyelove Smith, Derek Shelton and the gang-on-the-bus, Jeff Allen, Tim and Terre Grable, Stephen Dillon, and the millions who have come to see my performances, watched my videos, read my books and followed this wild career!

Finally, sincere and heartfelt thank you to David Nickell, journalist and writer, for the inspiration, the motivation and the artwork.

Made in the USA
Middletown, DE
23 February 2020